W9-AGJ-009

10 Traits of Highly Effective Schools

OTHER BOOKS BY ELAINE K. McEWAN FROM CORWIN PRESS

40 Ways to Support Struggling Readers in Content Classrooms, Grades 6–12 (2007)

Raising Reading Achievement in Middle and High Schools: Five Simple-to-Follow Strategies, Second Edition (2006)

How to Survive and Thrive in the First Three Weeks of School (2006)

How to Deal With Teachers Who Are Angry, Troubled, Exhausted, or Just Plain Confused (2005)

How to Deal With Parents Who Are Angry, Troubled, Afraid, or Just Plain Crazy, Second Edition (2004)

Seven Strategies of Highly Effective Readers: Using Cognitive Research to Boost K–8 Achievement (2004)

Ten Traits of Highly Effective Principals: From Good to Great Performance (2003)

Making Sense of Research: What's Good, What's Not, and How to Tell the Difference (with Patrick J. McEwan) (2003)

7 Steps to Effective Instructional Leadership, Second Edition (2002)

Teach Them ALL to Read: Catching the Kids Who Fall Through the Cracks (2002)

Ten Traits of Highly Effective Teachers: How to Hire, Coach, and Mentor Successful Teachers (2001)

The Principal's Guide to Raising Math Achievement (2000)

Managing Unmanageable Students: Practical Solutions for Administrators (with Mary Damar) (1999)

Counseling Tips for Elementary School Principals (with Jeffrey Kottler) (1998)

The Principal's Guide to Raising Reading Achievement (1998)

The Principal's Guide to Attention Deficit Hyperactivity Disorder (1997)

Leading Your Team to Excellence: How to Make Quality Decisions (1996)

FROM CORWIN PRESS CLASSROOM

The Reading Puzzle: Comprehension, Grades K–3 (2008)

The Reading Puzzle: Fluency, Grades K–3 (2008)

The Reading Puzzle: Phonemic Awareness, Grades K–3 (2008)

The Reading Puzzle: Phonics, Grades K–3 (2008)

The Reading Puzzle: Vocabulary, Grades K–3 (2008)

The Reading Puzzle: Comprehension, Grades 4–8 (2008)

The Reading Puzzle: Fluency, Grades 4–8 (2008)

The Reading Puzzle: Spelling, Grades 4–8 (2008)

The Reading Puzzle: Vocabulary, Grades 4–8 (2008)

The Reading Puzzle: Word Analysis, Grades 4–8 (2008)

10 Traits of Highly Effective Schools

Raising the Achievement Bar for All Students

Elaine K. McEwan

CORWIN PRESS
A SAGE Company

Copyright © 2009 by Corwin Press

All rights reserved. When forms and sample documents are included, their use is authorized only by educators, local school sites, and/or noncommercial or nonprofit entities that have purchased the book. Except for that usage, no part of this book may be reproduced or utilized in any form or by any means, electronic or mechanical, including photocopying, recording, or by any information storage and retrieval system, without permission in writing from the publisher.

For information:

Corwin Press
A SAGE Company
2455 Teller Road
Thousand Oaks, California 91320
www.corwinpress.com

SAGE India Pvt. Ltd.
B 1/I 1 Mohan Cooperative
   Industrial Area
Mathura Road, New Delhi 110 044
India

SAGE Ltd.
1 Oliver's Yard
55 City Road
London EC1Y 1SP
United Kingdom

SAGE Asia-Pacific Pte. Ltd.
33 Pekin Street #02-01
Far East Square
Singapore 048763

Printed in the United States of America

Library of Congress Cataloging-in-Publication Data

McEwan, Elaine K., 1941–
Ten traits of highly effective schools: Raising the achievement bar
for all students/Elaine K. McEwan.
       p. cm.
Includes bibliographical references and index.
ISBN 978-1-4129-0527-5 (cloth)
ISBN 978-1-4129-0528-2 (pbk.)
   1. Effective teaching—United States. 2. Teacher effectiveness—United States.
3. Academic achievement—United States. 4. Educational leadership—United States.
I. Title.

LB1025.3.M3556 2009
371.102—dc22   2008017827

This book is printed on acid-free paper.

08   09   10   11   12   10   9   8   7   6   5   4   3   2   1

Acquisitions Editor:	Robert D. Clouse
Editorial Assistant:	Jessica Bergmann
Production Editor:	Melanie Birdsall
Copy Editor:	Marilyn Power Scott
Typesetter:	C&M Digitals (P) Ltd.
Proofreader:	Cheryl Rivard
Cover Designer:	Lisa Riley

Contents

List of Figures and Forms

FIGURES

FORMS

Preface

Building a new school is a relatively straightforward undertaking. Pass a bond issue, purchase a several-acre site, retain an architect, put out bids, hire a construction superintendent, and hope for good weather. Oh, the process takes time and money, but with enough of each, success is virtually guaranteed. If creating highly effective schools were only that simple. Regrettably, the goal of building highly effective schools still remains an elusive one.

I conducted my first informal research on effective schools in the fall of 1983 when I was hired as the principal of a low-performing school: reading and math achievement on standardized tests in Grades 2–6 hovered at the 20th percentile. To that point in my career as a classroom teacher and media specialist, I had only worked in places similar to Lake Wobegon, that fictitious Minnesota town described by humorist Garrison Keillor (1985). All of the students with whom I'd previously worked were above average. I had never given much thought to what an effective school looked like; I just took for granted that most schools were pretty good. But it was obvious from my first drive-by of Lincoln School that I wasn't in Lake Wobegon anymore.

My initial impression didn't change much when I walked through the grim hallways and worn classrooms. The test scores matched the morale of the teachers and the attitudes of the parents and students: depressed. As I lay awake the night after I signed my contract, I pondered what it would take to create an effective school, one where students were learning, and how long that process would take. I didn't have the luxury of starting from scratch. I was beginning with a tired physical plant, failing students, angry parents, and demoralized teachers. Fortunately, there was some research to guide my staff and me as we set about the goal of creating an effective school (Edmonds, 1979a, 1979b; Purkey & Smith, 1983).

The ten traits of highly effective schools as described in this book are informed by research, both old and new; by my personal experiences as a principal and consultant working with educators around the country; and by interviews with teachers, principals, and central office administrators.

MY GOALS IN WRITING THIS BOOK

I wrote this book with four goals in mind: to inform, affirm, encourage, and motivate. I want to inform every educator that the demographics of a school don't have to determine its academic destiny. I want to affirm those educators who have led and been part of teams who have created effective schools. Their work is difficult and they do not always get the affirmation they deserve, especially from some of their colleagues in nearby schools or districts. I want to encourage those educators who are in the often long and difficult process of improving a low-performing school. The examples from schools around the country will give you renewed hope. And finally, I want to motivate those who are still hesitant about committing to a compelling mission in their own school. You will never regret the adventure. Students will thank you. Parents will honor you. And you will carry the feeling of having made a difference with you for the rest of your life.

WHO THIS BOOK IS FOR

I have written *Ten Traits of Highly Effective Schools* for the following audiences:

- Principals at every level who desire to lead highly effective schools
- Professional learning communities (PLCs), leadership and school improvement teams who are engaged in study and reflection regarding the effectiveness of their schools
- Central office administrators who desire to evaluate the effectiveness of the schools in their districts
- Educators who aspire to become schools leaders and want to know more about how to lead a team in building an effective school
- College and university educators who train educators at every level

WHAT IS A TRAIT?

As in my earlier books on the ten traits of teachers (McEwan, 2001) and principals (McEwan, 2003), I have taken some literary license with the meaning of the term *trait*. *Merriam-Webster* defines it as "a distinguishing quality (as of personal character)" (*Merriam-Webster*, 2003, p. 1326). My goal in writing this book is to identify and describe the critical attributes, distinguishing qualities, and unique characteristics of effective schools—those institutions that enable all students, regardless of their demographics or categorical labels, to attain academic excellence. The traits that are described in the chapters ahead are multidimensional, complex, interactive, and synergistic. They refer to the individuals, behaviors, values, processes, and systems that are found in highly effective schools.

OVERVIEW OF THE CONTENTS

The Introduction briefly summarizes the effective schools research (ESR) beginning with the early studies in the late 1970s and continuing to the present. You will learn how current researchers are substantiating the findings of older studies as well as breaking new ground by identifying the critical variables (traits) that distinguish more effective schools from those that are less effective, both in the United States and across other countries and cultures.

Each of the 10 chapters in the book describes one of the following traits: (1) strong instructional leadership, (2) research-based instruction, (3) a clear academic focus, (4) relational trust, (5) collaboration, (6) high expectations, (7) opportunities to learn, (8) alignment, (9) achievement, and (10) accountability. You will find the following features in each chapter:

- A comprehensive description of the trait
- Research supporting the part that each trait plays in raising the achievement bar
- Snapshots of the trait in schools and districts as well as longer vignettes
- Reflections about the trait in the words of teachers, principals, and central office administrators who are or have been involved in creating effective schools
- Observations and opinions from a wide variety of noted thinkers, theorists, and scholars regarding the trait
- Tools and processes to help facilitate the development of the trait in schools

Finally, a brief conclusion presents a Ten Traits Audit for use in your school or district and suggests how readers can use the ten traits to change and improve their schools.

A MATTER OF DEFINITION

The following terms are used interchangeably throughout the book to refer to highly effective schools: *successful, effective, equitable,* and *excellent.*

The term *challenging* will be used to refer to schools with demographics that far too frequently predict low achievement—high percentages (50% or more) of students in one or more of the following categories: (1) minorities, (2) English-language learners, and (3) students receiving free or reduced-price breakfast and lunch. However, in the context of this book, you will find that the terms *challenging* and *low-performing* are not synonymous.

Challenging schools are singled out to show readers that demographics do not have to determine the educational destiny of students. The educators in these schools are beating the odds and finding solutions rather than focusing on excuses. The terms *failing* and *low-performing* are used in a general sense to refer to schools where overall student achievement is low or where some federal or state sanctions have been applied. In addition to the categories on either end of the school achievement continuum, *highly effective* and *low-performing* or *failing,* there are many thousands of schools that fall into the *good* category. Some of these good schools are on their way to becoming great, and some are stuck at good. An understanding of the ten traits and how they are operationalized in highly effective and improving schools can inform improvement efforts in schools at any place on the effectiveness continuum.

Acknowledgments

I am indebted to the many talented teachers, principals, and central office administrators who shared their opinions, reflections, ideas, and experiences regarding their life's work with me. During the period between June 2006 and January 2008, they kept my inbox filled with e-mail, my post office box filled with snail mail, and my phone messaging system filled with voice mail. Their voices are heard throughout this book. Individuals are quoted by name. However, to save the busy reader time, I have omitted dated citations for these quotations unless they have appeared in a published work. I have included more detailed descriptive information about schools and individuals where appropriate to the context. In all cases, however, I identify the name, position, level, and geographical location of individuals, schools, or districts the first time they are used. In subsequent references, only names are provided.

There is one individual, however, who deserves special recognition: Cathie West, principal of Mountain Way Elementary School in Granite Falls, Washington. This book is dedicated to her. She is always available to bring me the practitioner's point of view in clear and concise ways. She has not only read my work on countless occasions, offering suggestions that never fail to improve what I have written, she has also made contributions to many of my books, including this one. I admire her as a courageous administrator and a tireless advocate for children.

Thank you to my own personal distance learning community, all of the educators who continue to inform and enrich my life and my writing. Thank you for answering my questions, responding to my e-mails and phone calls, inviting me to your schools, sharing your successes, and letting me walk in your shoes as I write. You inspire me.

Once again, I thank my husband and business partner, E. Raymond Adkins, for being there whenever I need him. His patience, kindness, and integrity are models to which I aspire.

PUBLISHER'S ACKNOWLEDGMENTS

Corwin Press gratefully acknowledges the contributions of the following people:

Janet Alleman
Professor of Teacher Education
Michigan State University
East Lansing, MI

John Brummel
Principal
Mililani High School
Mililani, HI

Margarete Couture
Principal
South Seneca Elementary School
Interlaken, NY

Connie L. Fulmer
Associate Professor & Program
    Coordinator
University of Colorado–Denver
Denver, CO

Sara Johnson
Principal
Grandhaven Elementary School
McMinnville, OR

Gina Marx
Assistant Superintendent
USD 262 Valley Center Schools
Valley Center, KS

Debra Morris
Principal
A. L. Brown High School
Kannapolis, NC

Jill Shackelford
Superintendent of Schools
Kansas City, Kansas, Public Schools
Wyandotte County, KS

David E. Whale
Associate Professor
Educational Leadership
    Department
Central Michigan University
Mt. Pleasant, MI

About the Author

 **Elaine K. McEwan** is a partner and educational consultant with The McEwan-Adkins Group, offering workshops in leadership and raising student achievement, K–12. A former teacher, librarian, principal, and assistant superintendent for instruction in a suburban Chicago school district, she is the author of more than 35 books for parents and educators. Her Corwin Press titles include *Leading Your Team to Excellence: How to Make Quality Decisions* (1996), *The Principal's Guide to Attention Deficit Hyperactivity Disorder* (1997), *How to Deal With Parents Who Are Angry, Troubled, Afraid, or Just Plain Crazy* (1998), *The Principal's Guide to Raising Reading Achievement* (1998), *Counseling Tips for Elementary School Principals* (1998) with Jeffrey A. Kottler, *Managing Unmanageable Students: Practical Solutions for Administrators* (2000) with Mary Damer, *The Principal's Guide to Raising Math Achievement* (2000), *Raising Reading Achievement in Middle and High Schools: Five Simple-to-Follow Strategies for Principals* (2001), *Ten Traits of Highly Effective Teachers: How to Hire, Coach, and Mentor Successful Teachers* (2001), *Teach Them ALL to Read: Catching the Kids Who Fall Through the Cracks* (2002), *7 Steps to Effective Instructional Leadership, 2nd Edition* (2002), *Making Sense of Research: What's Good, What's Not, and How to Tell the Difference* (2003) with Patrick J. McEwan, *Ten Traits of Highly Effective Principals: From Good to Great Performance* (2003), *Seven Strategies of Highly Effective Readers: Using Cognitive Research to Boost K–8 Achievement* (2004), *How to Deal With Parents Who Are Angry, Troubled, Afraid or Just Plain Crazy, 2nd Edition* (2004), *How to Deal With Teachers Who Are Angry, Troubled, Exhausted, or Just Plain Confused* (2005), *How to Survive and Thrive in the First Three Weeks of School* (2006), *Raising Reading Achievement in Middle and High Schools, 2nd Edition* (2007), and *40 Ways to Support Struggling Readers in Content Classrooms, Grades 6–12* (2007).

Elaine was honored by the Illinois Principals Association as an outstanding instructional leader, by the Illinois State Board of Education with an Award of Excellence in the Those Who Excel Program, and by the National Association of Elementary School Principals as the National Distinguished Principal from Illinois for 1991. She received her undergraduate degree in education from Wheaton College and advanced degrees in library science (MA) and educational administration (EdD) from Northern Illinois University. She lives with her husband and business partner, E. Raymond Adkins, in Oro Valley, Arizona. Visit Elaine's Web site at www.elainemcewan.com where you can learn more about her writing and workshops, or contact her directly at emcewan@elainemcewan.com.

Introduction

Do Schools Matter?

What effective schools look like is not a mystery. They have a coherent instructional program well aligned with strong standards. They have a community of adults committed to working together to develop the skills and knowledge of all children. They have figured out how to find the time to do this work and are acquiring the skills to do it well.

—Boudett, City, and Murnane (2005, p. 3)

The question of whether schools as institutions have the power to make a positive impact upon the academic achievement and future success of their students, irrespective of their socioeconomic levels, family characteristics, language and culture, or minority status, has been debated for more than 40 years. In one of the first school effects studies, James Coleman and his colleagues (Coleman et al., 1966) concluded that students' demographics largely determine their academic destinies: "The inequalities imposed on children by their home, neighborhood, and peer environment are carried along to become the inequalities with which they confront adult life" (p. 325).

Coleman's (Coleman et al., 1966) conclusions still underpin the beliefs of many practitioners today, although in the 21st century, far more educators are willing to accept the idea that all children can learn, regardless of their demographics. In 1983, however, it was a fairly novel idea. I can still visualize the colorful *All Can Learn* graphic that a talented parent painted on a huge expanse of wall in the front hall of Lincoln School. It captured the mission of our school. It was the first thing everyone saw when they reached the top of the stairs. I hoped that the prominence of the words would serve to remind struggling students, frustrated parents, and especially some cynical teachers of our commitment to equity and excellence. I would like to have painted an accompanying corollary in the teachers' lounge, "All can learn and we are accountable for making it happen," but academic proficiency indices, school report cards, and state assessments had yet to appear on education's radar screen.

Accountability was a difficult concept for some of the Lincoln teachers to support back then. Unfortunately, there are still many educators who deep down are not altogether certain that poor, minority, limited-English-proficient, and special education students *can* achieve academic proficiency. Nevertheless, there is a growing body of quantitative and qualitative evidence published between 1999 and 2007 showing that hundreds of elementary and secondary schools get results no matter what the demographics of their students:

- Carter, S. C. (1999). *No Excuses: Seven Principals of Low-Income Schools Who Set the Standard for High Achievement.* Washington, DC: Heritage Foundation.
- Charles A. Dana Center. (1999). *Hope for Urban Education: A Study of Nine High-Performing High-Poverty Urban Elementary Schools.* Austin, TX: Author.
- Education Trust. (1999). *Dispelling the Myth: High-Poverty Schools Exceeding Expectations.* Washington, DC: Author.
- Manset, G., St. John, A., Simmons, A., & Gordon, G. D. (2000). *Wisconsin's High-Performing, High-Poverty Schools.* Naperville, IL: North Central Regional Educational Laboratory.
- Reeves, D. (2000). *Accountability in Action: A Blueprint for Learning Organizations.* Denver, CO: Advanced Learning Centers.
- Jerald, C. D. (2001). *Dispelling the Myth Revisited: Preliminary Findings from a Nationwide Analysis of High-Flying Schools.* Washington, DC: Education Trust.
- Charles A. Dana Center and the STAR Center. (2002). *Driven to Succeed: High-Performing, High-Poverty, Turnaround Middle Schools.* Austin, TX: Authors.
- McGee, G. W. (2004). Closing the Achievement Gap: Lessons from Illinois' Golden Spike High-Poverty High Performing School. *Journal of Education for Students Placed at Risk, (9)2,* 97–125.
- National Association of Secondary School Principals. (2004). *Breaking Ranks II: Strategies for Leading High School Reform.* Washington, DC: Author.
- Charles A. Dana Center. (2005). *Gaining Traction, Gaining Ground: How Some High Schools Accelerate Learning for Struggling Students.* Austin, TX: Author.

- Education Trust. (2005). *The Power to Change: High Schools That Help All Students Achieve.* Washington, DC: Author.
- Waits, M. J., Campbell, H. E., Gau, R., Jacobs, E., Rex, T., & Hess, R. K. (2006). *Why Some Schools with Latino Children Beat the Odds and Others Don't.* Phoenix, AZ: Center for the Future of Arizona and Morrison Institute for Public Policy.
- Chenoweth, K. (2007). *It's Being Done: Academic Success in Unexpected Schools.* Cambridge, MA: Harvard University Press.

> Only when the school functions to promote the chance of efficient learning being able to take place within the classroom can classroom or teacher-specific interventions have much probability of succeeding.
>
> —*Purkey and Smith*
> *(1983, p. 429)*

THE GENESIS OF THE EFFECTIVE SCHOOLS MOVEMENT

In response to the somewhat pessimistic conclusions of the Coleman study (Coleman et al., 1966), a number of researchers focused their efforts on finding positive answers to the question of whether schools actually make a difference. They designed studies that compared the characteristics of two groups of schools matched for challenging demographic variables—one set of schools getting results with students and a second set positioned on the failing end of the achievement continuum—and identified those characteristics unique to the achieving schools (Brookover, Beady, Flood, Schweitzer, & Weisenbaker, 1979; Brookover & Lezotte, 1979; Edmonds, 1979a, 1979b; Rutter, Maughan, Mortimore, & Ouston, 1979). The research consisted of simple correlation studies based on "frozen in time" snapshots of the schools. There were no longitudinal or qualitative data to illuminate the respective contexts or processes that characterized the effective schools. The research identified five schoolwide correlates that differentiated effective schools from their ineffective counterparts, irrespective of the demographics of the students:

- Strong educational leadership (principal)
- High expectations of student achievement
- An emphasis on basic skills
- A safe and orderly climate
- Frequent evaluation of pupil progress on achievement

This body of research came to be known as Effective Schools Research (ESR). No attempts were made by the researchers to operationally define these five correlates, and practitioners were left on their own to determine the critical attributes and behavioral indicators. An effective school as defined in the first phase of ESR was one in which there was essentially no relationship between family background and student achievement as measured by a norm-referenced standardized test. Purkey and Smith (1983) summarized early ESR in this way:

> We find it is weak in many respects, most notably in its tendency to present narrow, often simplistic, recipes for school improvement derived from non-experimental data. Theory and common sense, however, do support many of the findings of school effectiveness research. (p. 426)

One notable weakness of ESR is that administrators were seen as the main characters in effective schools while teachers were portrayed as targets of effective schools policies enacted by principals (McLaughlin, 1993). In spite of its methodological weaknesses, practitioners who were eager to make a difference in their low-performing schools enthusiastically embraced ESR. The existence of even a few vague variables that were correlated to higher student achievement in challenging schools and neighborhoods offered hope to educators that if they made some strategic changes related to these variables, achievement in their schools might rise.

I was one such individual. When my superintendent handed me the test scores along with my contract, he threw out this remark: "See if you can do something about achievement in this school." His somewhat tentative statement was typical of someone who wanted to believe it could be done but wasn't sure. However, I seized on the mission he articulated, and as a novice principal, I became passionate about raising student achievement. To those of us who worked in low-performing schools in the early 1980s, flaws in research design and lack of generalizability were immaterial. We were inspired and motivated by the existence of even a few schools where students like ours were achieving as well as their more privileged counterparts.

My staff and I conducted action research and tinkered with a variety of alterable variables to determine the qualitative processes that were not particularly well articulated in the original five effective school correlates (Bloom, 1980). I matured as an educator, aspired to become a strong instructional leader, and eagerly digested the second wave of ESR that arrived in the late 1980s and early 1990s (Levine & Lezotte, 1990; Mortimore, Sammons, Stoll, Lewis, & Ecob, 1988; Teddlie & Stringfield, 1993).

Although the second generation of ESR employed improved research designs that collected both qualitative and quantitative information and analyzed the data with more sophisticated techniques, the findings were still only a list of characteristics that were correlated with higher student achievement on standardized tests. Figure I.1 summarizes selected ESR studies.

Despite the flaws in ESR, school improvement models based on the studies enjoyed widespread adoption not only in the United States but also in the United Kingdom, Australia, and the Netherlands. Although ESR stagnated in the mid-1990s, there were some high points (Reynolds, Creemers, Stringfield, Teddlie, & Schaffer, 2002): (1) increased attention to model building and theoretical analysis (Creemers, 1994; Stringfield, 1994), (2) a revival of interest in teacher or instructional effectiveness motivated by reviews showing that classroom influences were much greater than those of the school (Scheerens & Bosker, 1997; Teddlie & Reynolds, 2000), and (3) the merging of the traditions historically associated with school effectiveness together with some of those from the school improvement movement (Reynolds, Hopkins, & Stoll, 1993; Teddlie & Reynolds, 2000).

THE INTERNATIONAL SCHOOL EFFECTIVENESS RESEARCH PROJECT

The most recent ESR, the International School Effectiveness Research Project (ISERP) (Reynolds et al., 2002), remediated several of the weaknesses of earlier studies by asking and answering the following questions:

1. *Which* school and teacher effectiveness factors are associated with schools or teachers being effective in different contexts?

2. How many of these factors are *universal,* and how many are *specific* to certain contexts?

3. What might explain *why* some factors are universal and some specific, and what are the implications of any findings for policy, for practice, and for the school-effectiveness research base?

ISERP involved schools in nine countries (Australia, Canada, Hong Kong, Republic of Ireland, Netherlands, Norway, Taiwan, United Kingdom, and USA)[1]; three levels of effectiveness (more effective schools, typical schools, and less effective schools); and two levels of socioeconomic status (SES) among students (lower SES and middle SES). The study

Figure I.1   Selected Effective Schools Research Studies

Researchers	Description of Study	Factors Found to Differentiate Effective Schools From Ineffective Schools
Brookover, Beady, Flood, Schweitzer, & Wisenbaker (1979) Edmonds (1979a, 1979b) Rutter, Maughan, Mortimore, & Ouston (1979)	These early studies were conducted in response to the dismal conclusions of the Coleman et al. (1996) Report that stated that schools didn't matter. The studies were correlational and focused on poor, urban elementary schools, raising a great deal of criticism as to the quality and the generalizability of the research.	Five correlates of effective schools identified in the early research: (1) strong educational leadership, (2) high expectations of student achievement, (3) emphasis on basic skills, (4) a safe and orderly climate, and (5) frequent monitoring and evaluation of students' academic progress
Mortimore, Sammons, Stoll, Lewis, & Ecob (1988)	Academic and social progress of 2,000 students over four years in England. One of the first longitudinal studies conducted in response to the criticism of the so-called snapshot approach of earlier effective schools studies.	(1) Purposeful leadership of the staff by the head teacher (i.e., principal), (2) the involvement of the deputy head, (3) the involvement of teachers, (4) consistency among teachers, (5) structured classes, (6) intellectually challenging teaching, (7) a work-centered environment, (8) limited focus within a class session, (9) maximum communication between teachers and pupils, (10) record keeping with regard to student progress, (11) parental involvement, and (12) positive climate
Teddlie & Stringfield (1993)	The Louisiana School Effectiveness Study (LSES) was a set of five studies conducted over 12 years at both school and classroom levels in elementary settings. Both quantitative and qualitative methodologies were employed.	Factors that emerged that differentiated effective schools from ineffective schools (outliers in terms of achievement while matched for student demographics and location) in terms of classrooms included: (1) pupil's higher time on task, (2) the presentation of more new material, (3) the encouragement of independent practice, (4) the possession of high expectations, (5) the use of positive reinforcement, (6) the presence of firm discipline, (7) a friendly ambience, (8) the display of student work, and (9) pleasant classroom appearance.

Researchers	Description of Study	Factors Found to Differentiate Effective Schools From Ineffective Schools
Sammons, Thomas, & Mortimore (1997)	Collection and analysis of seven measures of student achievement from 90 secondary schools and nearly 18,000 students in England; in-depth qualitative case studies of six schools and 30 subject departments.	(1) High expectations, (2) strong academic emphasis, (3) shared vision and goals, (4) clear leadership by principals and department chairs, (5) an effective SMT (school management team), (6) consistency in approach, (7) quality of teaching, (8) a student-centered approach, and (9) parental involvement and support

Reproduction of material from this book is authorized only for the local school site or nonprofit organization that has purchased *Ten Traits of Highly Effective Schools: Raising the Achievement Bar for All Students,* by Elaine K. McEwan. Thousand Oaks, CA: Corwin Press, www.corwinpress.com.

employed a longitudinal case study design using mixed methods both in terms of data collection and analysis.

The following 12 dimensions anchored the case studies in each of the 54 schools in the study: (1) general characteristics of the school; (2) a day in the life of a child in the school, in which a typical student was selected and then followed or shadowed by a researcher for an entire school day; (3) the teaching style of teachers; (4) the curriculum; (5) the influence of parents; (6) the principal; (7) school expectations of students; (8) school goals; (9) interstaff relations; (10) school resources; (11) relationships with local authorities; and (12) school image (Reynolds et al., 2002, p. 21).

Mathematics achievement was selected as the overall measure of student achievement in order to eliminate the problems associated with testing both English-speaking and non-English-speaking students. In addition to standardized academic testing, data were also collected on students' attitudes towards school, their teachers, mathematics, and their fellow students.

FINDINGS OF THE INTERNATIONAL SCHOOL EFFECTIVENESS RESEARCH PROJECT

The findings of the ISERP don't provide practitioners with all of the answers to the important questions about improving schools, but they do confirm the findings of prior research as well as providing new insights.

Raising Achievement in
Low-Socioeconomic Schools Is a Challenge

The findings showed that overall, students in low-SES schools scored lower on an initial test of mathematics achievement than did students in middle-SES schools. Students in lower-SES schools need the best of everything that the most effective schools have to offer in order to catch up to their more advantaged peers. But the research demonstrated it can be done.

Effective Schools Can Make a
Difference for Low-SES Students

Students attending schools identified as more effective based on the evidence found in the qualitative case studies attained higher scores on an initial standardized test of math achievement than students attending schools identified as less effective. Furthermore, the more time lower-achieving students spent in a more effective school led by a strong instructional leader and taught by more effective teachers, the less impact the ethnic, educational, and social-class backgrounds of their parents had on their achievement.

Effective Schools Are More Challenging
to Create in the United States

There was much variation between countries regarding the degree to which the social background of students impacted their school achievement. For example, students in Taiwan and Hong Kong showed the least variation in achievement between the two groups identified as lower SES and middle SES. Two possible explanations are offered for this finding: (1) Regardless of social class, students in Taiwan and Hong Kong absorb similar values that arise out of relatively homogeneous cultural and religious traditions, and (2) in the USA, the characteristics of the principal as instructional leader contribute more to the attainment of effectiveness, whereas in places where a centralized system and technology of education are very strong, principals are much less critical in creating and sustaining effective schools.

Less Effective Lower-SES Schools May Require
a Different Approach to School Improvement

The ISERP findings confirmed the findings of earlier studies that described substantial differences between ineffective lower-SES schools and ineffective middle-SES schools. "Staffs at low-SES schools typically have to spend more time creating certain components of school success (e.g., high expectation levels; reward structure for academic success; and safe, orderly climates) than do middle-SES schools where the community has often already generated these components, at least in nascent form" (Reynolds et al., 2002, p. 260). Consequently, staff members in less effective lower-SES schools may have to devote more time and energy to putting baseline systems in place before resources can be fully devoted to bringing about instructional improvement.[2]

There Are Some Universal Traits of Effective Schools

ISERP identified six dimensions (traits) that were rated by observers as being highly descriptive of the differences they noted between less effective and more effective schools. Observers knew immediately whether they were in a less effective or a more effective school when they saw sharp contrasts in the following dimensions: instructional style, expectations for students, principal leadership, school goals, interstaff relations, and the daily experience of a typical student (Brigham & Gamse, 1997).

> The only sure way to transform dysfunctional schools into effective schools is to build capacity in them—to provide smart, strong leadership, a mission clearly and intensely focused on children's learning, highly competent committed teachers, clean lines of responsibility, adequate financial resources, and an environment that fosters collaboration, trust, and continuous learning.
>
> —Wolk (1998, p. 7)

TEN TRAITS OF HIGHLY EFFECTIVE SCHOOLS

The ten traits of highly effective schools as enumerated in this book are synthesized from several sources: (1) the effective schools research, especially the most recent research; (2) reviews of research on specific topics, such as effective instruction and instructional leadership; (3) case studies of highly effective schools that are beating the odds; (4) personal interviews with teachers, principals, central office administrators, and consultants who have been part of creating highly effective districts and schools; and (5) my own experiences as an administrator. The ten traits I have identified are shown in Figure I.2. Think of the traits as the standards that must be mastered by a school in order to achieve effectiveness. Each chapter contains examples of one trait as seen in schools and districts around the country, a comprehensive discussion of the trait from a variety of perspectives, tools you can use to facilitate the development of the trait, and citations to research studies that have examined the trait from a scholarly perspective.

Figure I.2   Ten Traits of Highly Effective Schools

1. The highly effective school is led by a strong *instructional leader* who provides an unequivocal direction through consistent monitoring and supervision of program implementation while simultaneously working collaboratively with teacher leaders on issues of standards, curriculum, instruction, and assessment to raise the achievement bar for all students.

2. *Research-based instruction* that is delivered by highly effective teachers is the core of the highly effective school. Instruction is the channel through which content and skills are recursively transmitted to students. Instructional strategies and lesson designs are constantly being refined through collaborative and embedded professional development.

3. The highly effective school has a *clear academic focus* that encompasses the vision, mission, and goals of administrators and teachers, the dreams of students, and the hopes of parents.

4. *Relational trust* in a highly effective school results in positive personal and professional relationships that are characterized by personal regard, respect, competence, and integrity.

5. *Collaboration* is a hallmark of the highly effective school. The collaboration of teachers and the cooperation of students provide the energy and synergy that power an ongoing increase in the academic, instructional, and leadership capacities of the school.

6. The educators in a highly effective school have *high expectations.* They believe that students can achieve, explicitly teach them how to get smart, and convey a profound and unwavering commitment to their academic success.

7. The highly effective school provides all students with *opportunities to learn* through the provision of highly effective teachers in every classroom combined with differentiated and scaffolded opportunities to learn as needed for all students to achieve academic success.

8. The highly effective school's standards, curriculum, instruction, and assessments are in *alignment* and provide a coherent and consistent educational program for all students.

9. The highly effective school gets *results* as shown by data in two areas: individual growth for all students and overall high achievement in the school as a whole.

10. The highly effective school is characterized by high levels of internal *accountability* that demand continuous improvement and a results-oriented approach to teaching and learning.

Reproduction of material from this book is authorized only for the local school site or nonprofit organization that has purchased *Ten Traits of Highly Effective Schools: Raising the Achievement Bar for All Students,* by Elaine K. McEwan. Thousand Oaks, CA: Corwin Press, www.corwinpress.com.

NOTES

1. ISERP researchers identified both Taiwan and Hong Kong as countries in their final report (Reynolds et al., 2002). At the time ISERP research was conducted, Taiwan was considered a de facto independent country of the world, although the position of mainland China is that Taiwan is part of China. However, Taiwan maintains a strong independent compulsory education system. In 1997, Hong Kong ceased to be a British colony and was reunified with mainland China. However, as in the case of Taiwan, it maintains a separate and independent school system.

2. I can attest to these findings. When I was hired at Lincoln School, student behavior was a problem that needed immediate attention. The topic was brought up at my first meeting with the PTO officers who were concerned with a cafeteria that was out of control and a lunchroom supervisor who routinely "roughed up" students. The problems surfaced again, mentioned by the staff at our first planning meeting. It was also obvious during my early days as multiple students were sent to the office because of classroom infractions that classroom management was a high priority.

1
Strong Instructional Leadership

A leader must be able to create networks, build teams, resolve and creatively use conflicts, foster consensus on the school vision, secure resources, and especially important, focus attention on the goal: student learning.

—Smith and Piele (1997, p. 5)

*I*nstructional leadership is the first of the ten traits of highly effective schools. I have never visited an effective school that did not have a creative and visionary leadership team made up of the principal and a group of strong teacher leaders. No matter how effective the principal might be, the challenges of raising the achievement bar are too complex for a solo act to succeed. On the other hand, without an instructional leader to communicate a compelling vision and articulate a moral imperative for doing the right thing, teachers are not likely to form a committee to improve the school. They undoubtedly recognize

Should we follow our leaders because they know how to meet our needs, and because they are charming and fun to be with? Or should we follow leaders because they have ideas that we find compelling? Leadership based on personal authority places glitz over substance and results in vacuous leadership practice.

—Sergiovanni (1994, p. 224)

the need, but do not have the time, access to resources, or position power to initiate change.

There are no shortcuts to building a highly effective school. I have observed districts trying to bypass ineffective principals in attempts to improve schools by bringing in outside experts to fix things. Any centrally imposed initiative that is research based and meaningful is inevitably successful in those schools led by strong instructional leaders and staffed by a critical mass of teacher leaders. However, without both kinds of leadership, the initiative limps along for a short while and then dies a quiet and unlamented death, often facilitated by the actions of the bypassed principal.

> It should be self-evident that the principal as head of the organization is crucial. As long as we have schools and principals, if the principal does not lead changes in the culture of the school, or if he or she leaves it to others, it normally will not get done. That is, improvement will not happen.
>
> —*Fullan and Stigelbauer (1991, p. 169)*

With strong leadership, improvement initiatives can *begin* without excellence in every classroom, but the ultimate vision will never be realized without an assertive and courageous instructional leader to ensure that the school is becoming more effective on a daily basis through embedded professional development, high expectations, and strategic staffing practices.

The importance of identifying and employing strong instructional leaders with character cannot be overemphasized. Creating an effective school in the United States is almost totally dependent on hiring the right principal and then giving that individual autonomy to improve the school along with strong support from central office for the very difficult job of pruning dead wood and reinvigorating the school culture.

> There may be schools out there that have strong instructional leaders, but are not yet effective; however, we have never yet found an effective school that did not have a strong instructional leader as the principal.
>
> —*Ron Edmonds (as quoted in Lezotte & McKee, 2002, p. 17)*

Principals are arguably the most important factor in terms of moving an ineffective school to effective, or even sustaining a highly effective school. They are responsible for communicating the mission, setting the agenda, determining what gets measured, and then holding teachers and students accountable for accomplishing specific goals. If a school has a very weak or highly aggressive principal, there is little likelihood that its students, whether disadvantaged *or* privileged, are achieving to their highest potential. The effects of even the best teachers are often diminished or even undermined when they are "led" by such individuals.

The principal charts the course for the school. Whether the ship of learning reaches it destination or goes aground to ultimately sink depends largely on the navigational skills of the captain—the principal. A report by the Arthur Andersen (1997) consulting firm made the following recommendation in the late 1990s, and it is even truer today:

> The key factor to the individual school's success is the building principal, who sets the tone as the school's educational leader, enforces the positive, and convinces the students, parents and teachers that all children can learn and improve academically. Our overall assessment is that the school principal has the greatest single impact on student performance. As a result we believe that increased attention and funding needs to be directed towards programs that attract, evaluate, train and retain the best principals. (p. 27)

INSTRUCTIONAL LEADERSHIP RESEARCH

Determining the precise relationship between student achievement and strong instructional leadership is challenging for three reasons: (1) Researchers are unable to design experimental studies to investigate the question and so we must settle for correlational studies, (2) the vast majority of correlational studies are simple doctoral dissertations that do not lend themselves well to sophisticated statistical analyses, and (3) only with the arrival of accountability has instructional leadership been a topic for study in educational leadership programs.

Andrews and Soder (1987) were among the first to publish research describing the relationship between principals' instructional leadership behaviors as perceived by their teachers and student achievement. Although correlational in design, their study motivated educators to expand their understanding of educational leadership to incorporate issues of teaching and learning into principals' job descriptions along with the traditional administrative responsibilities. The study also examined the intensity or amount of instructional leadership exercised by principals, describing a range from strong to weak as indicated by the scores they received from their teachers.

> Schools operated by principals who were perceived by their teachers to be strong instructional leaders exhibited significantly greater gain scores in achievement in reading and mathematics than did schools operated by average and weak instructional leaders.
>
> —*Andrews and Soder (1987, p. 9)*

Hallinger and Heck (1996), in a synthesis of 15 years of research on how principals impact their schools, concluded that principals exercise a *measurable*, although indirect, effect on school effectiveness and student achievement. About the *indirect* aspect, they write, "The fact that leadership effects on school achievement appear to be indirect is neither cause for alarm or dismay. . . . Achieving results through others is the essence of leadership" (p. 39).

A meta-analysis of 70 studies of principal leadership conducted by McREL found a general correlation between effective leadership and student achievement (Waters, Marzano, & McNulty, 2008), but one must exercise caution in concluding that principals directly cause student achievement to rise. A strong instructional leader is a necessary but insufficient part of a highly effective school.

A WORKING DEFINITION OF STRONG INSTRUCTIONAL LEADERSHIP

> All too often, administrators are caught up in school management and end up with very little time to be instructional leaders. If school reform is to happen, school leaders must have clearly designated roles, and the principal must be free to spend the majority of time on instructional issues.
>
> —Beth Madison, Principal, George Middle School (OR)

We can say with a fair degree of certainty based on the research that strong leadership focused on the intersection and interaction of standards, curricula, instruction, and assessment has an impact on the effectiveness of a school and thus has an indirect effect on student achievement. From my perspective, strong instructional leadership has three distinct components: (1) a leadership component—the ability to implement, get the job done, or get results; (2) an instructional component—knowledge and skills related to teaching and learning; and (3) an intensity component—assertiveness—that encompasses personal attributes like self-confidence, self-differentiation, and character.

Leadership

There are dozens of definitions of leadership, most written by organizational behavior theorists with a focus on management tasks and getting things done. The definition I prefer describes leaders as having the following characteristics: "a strong drive for responsibility and task completion, vigor and persistence in pursuit of goals, venturesomeness and originality in problem solving, the drive to exercise initiative in social situations, self-confidence and sense of personal identity, willingness to accept consequences of decisions and action, readiness to absorb interpersonal stress, willingness to tolerate frustration and delay, the ability to influence other persons' behavior, and the capacity to structure social interaction systems to the purpose at hand" (B. Bass as quoted in Stogdill, 1990, p. 81). However, principals need far more than generic leadership skills to be strong instructional leaders.

Knowledge and Skills Related to Teaching and Learning

To be an effective school leader requires not only the abilities to be a "cheerleader, enthusiast, nurturer of champions, hero finder, wanderer, dramatist, coach, facilitator, and builder" (Peters & Austin, 1985, p. 265), but it also demands the ability to be a leader of teachers. This individual must demonstrate a comprehensive "knowing and doing" skill set related to teaching and learning. High school principal Alan Jones put it this way:

> An instructional leader has a passion for great teaching and a vision for what schools should be doing for children. Instructional leaders should have well thought out answers for three fundamental questions about schooling: How do children learn? How should we teach children? And how should we treat subject matter? (McEwan, 2002, p. 7)

To become an instructional leader requires learning how to execute essential management functions through skilled delegation while at the same time focusing intently on teaching and learning. Individuals who enter the principalship on a fast track out of teaching (less than three years of classroom teaching experience) without mastering essential instructional skills are at a huge disadvantage in the current climate of high expectations unless they can soak up these skills along with the teachers they are leading. The leadership paradigm for principals has shifted dramatically in the past 25 years.

When I interviewed principals for an earlier book in 2002, I encountered an experienced principal who made this observation: "Twenty years ago, all I needed to do was keep the parents and the teachers happy. Now I have to get results" (Anonymous). The statement was made with a sense of nostalgia for the "good old days" and a definite tone of resentment for the demands of the new paradigm. Twenty-five years ago, *accountability* referred to keeping the budget balanced and the buses and boilers running. The new paradigm as described by former principal Kathie Dobberteen represents a seismic shift: "I not only feel accountable to the parents and the school board for students' success, but also to society. Instructional leaders must do whatever it takes to help our students become educated citizens who can participate fully in our society." Principals not only need leadership abilities and a solid skill set related to teaching and learning, they also need to be assertive in their approach to leading a school.

Assertiveness

Assertiveness is a mindset that impacts the way principals communicate (words) and behave (deeds) in their everyday (habitual) interactions with teachers, parents, and students. It is a positive, forthright approach to leadership that stands in stark contrast to less effective leadership styles characterized by aggressiveness or hesitancy. Assertiveness is not, as some mistakenly think, a dictatorial attitude or an obnoxious "my way or the highway" approach to leading a school. Assertive principals have the following inner strengths:

- The capacity to view themselves separately from others with a minimum amount of anxiety regarding the opinions and responses of teachers, parents, or students
- The ability to maintain a calm presence when working with and interacting with distressed or dysfunctional teachers, parents, and students
- The maturity to chart their own course through a personal set of values rather than continually trying to figure out what others are thinking before making decisions
- The wisdom to be clear and committed about their personal values and goals
- The willingness to take responsibility for their own emotional well-being and destiny rather than blaming either others or uncontrollable cultural, gender, or environmental variables (Adapted from Friedman, 1991, pp. 134–170)

Form 1.1 contains the Assertive Administrator Self-Assessment, an informal instrument to assist individuals in determining their own level of assertiveness. It assesses the key indicators of assertiveness as adapted for the school setting from the discipline of psychology.

Form 1.1   The Assertive Administrator Self-Assessment

	Never	Seldom	Sometimes	Usually	Always
Indicator 1: I protect and honor my own rights as an individual as well as protecting the rights of others.	1	2	3	4	5
Indicator 2: I recognize the importance of boundaries and am able to stay connected to others while at the same time maintaining a sense of self and individuality.	1	2	3	4	5
Indicator 3: I have positive feelings regarding myself and am thus able to create positive feelings in others.	1	2	3	4	5
Indicator 4: I am willing to take risks but recognize that mistakes and failures are part of the learning process.	1	2	3	4	5
Indicator 5: I am able to acknowledge and learn from my successes as well as my failures.	1	2	3	4	5
Indicator 6: I am able to give and receive both compliments and constructive criticism from others.	1	2	3	4	5
Indicator 7: I make realistic promises and commitments to teachers and am able to keep them.	1	2	3	4	5
Indicator 8: I genuinely respect the ideas and feelings of others.	1	2	3	4	5
Indicator 9: I am willing to compromise and negotiate with others in good faith.	1	2	3	4	5
Indicator 10: I am capable of saying no to others and sticking to a position, but I do not need to have my own way at all costs.	1	2	3	4	5
Indicator 11: I can handle anger, hostility, put-downs and lies from others without undue distress, recognizing that I am defined from within.	1	2	3	4	5
Indicator 12: I can handle anger, hostility, put-downs, and lies from others without responding in kind.	1	2	3	4	5
Indicator 13: I am aware of my personal emotions (e.g., anger, anxiety) and can name them and manage them in both myself and in others.	1	2	3	4	5
Indicator 14: I am prepared for and can cope with the pain that is a normal part of leading a school.	1	2	3	4	5

Copyright © 2005 Corwin Press. All rights reserved. Reprinted from *How to Deal with Teachers Who Are Angry, Troubled, Exhausted, or Just Plain Confused* by E. K. McEwan. Reproduction authorized only for the local school site that has purchased this book.

> It is not the teachers, or the central office people, or the university people who are really causing schools to be the way they are or changing the way they might be. It is whoever lives in the principal's office.
>
> —Barth (1976, p. 10)

Assertiveness is paramount when it comes to making difficult decisions, standing up for what is equitable and excellent, and doing the right thing, even though it may not be popular with everyone. Asking teachers, students, and parents to embrace a bold vision for the future or adopt a paradigm that holds everyone accountable for student learning requires strong instructional leadership—a sense of certainty regarding the worth of the vision and an unshakeable belief in the power of collaboration to achieve it.

INSTRUCTIONAL LEADERSHIP THAT GETS RESULTS

The only way for principals to ensure that things are being implemented according to the plans and that teachers and students are focused on goals is to get out of the office—to spend time in classrooms, closely observing teaching and learning. In reality, the only individuals in the school who can effectively monitor implementation are administrators with e-power, the power to evaluate staff. Coaches can coach. Instructional specialists can provide support and teach sample lessons. Special education teachers have an essential role to play in terms of coteaching, modeling, and coaching. But only principals can monitor implementation. In order for any goal, program, initiative, or curriculum to be faithfully implemented, these conditions must be in place:

1. Principals must have a precise and explicit picture of what a faithful implementation looks like. In some cases, principals are able to model and coach teachers; in other cases, coaches and instructional specialists model and coach. The bottom line is that administrators, trainers, and coaches must be working from the same blueprint.

2. All teachers must have a precise and explicit picture of what a faithful implementation looks like and be progressing toward proficiency in carrying out that implementation in their classrooms. In any school, there will be a continuum of proficiencies. The given is that everyone must be growing and improving.

3. One individual (principal, department chair, assistant principal) with evaluative power must be accountable for monitoring the implementation. In large comprehensive high schools, three individuals should be monitoring and meeting regularly to discuss their findings: the principal; the assistant principal, who may be directly responsible

for evaluating teachers; and the department chairperson who may also have evaluative responsibilities. In a low-achieving school, monitoring cannot be delegated.

4. An implementation monitoring tool designed specifically for the school (or district) must be used to focus observations and classroom walk-throughs.

5. The amount of time that principals spend in monitoring the implementation should be made explicit to both principals and teachers. For example, in the Kennewick District (WA), there is a Two–Ten Goal, meaning principals are expected to spend 2 hours a day or 10 hours a week on instructionally focused activities, 60% of which are to be direct classroom observations.

6. Regular classroom walk-throughs are conducted in which teachers have opportunities to see colleagues teaching commonly planned lessons as well as colleagues teaching different grade levels or content areas and to reflect on what has been observed. The walk-throughs are primarily focused on student engagement and learning.

7. All teachers of a grade level or content area have common planning time to be specifically used for collaborative inquiry, with the specific goal of improving instruction.

8. Implementation monitoring is formative in nature, designed to improve teaching and learning immediately. Data gathered as part of implementation monitoring should not be used for a teacher's summative evaluation unless that individual gives evidence of being unwilling or unable to respond to formative feedback.

SEVEN STEPS TO EFFECTIVE INSTRUCTIONAL LEADERSHIP

What do strong instructional leaders do on a daily basis? What are their habits as they walk the halls, conduct conversations and meetings, and spend time in classrooms? What distinguishes them from average or ineffective principals?

They have high expectations for themselves and inspire the same kind of work ethic from their staff and students. They refuse to blame students for their inability to learn and hold teachers accountable for student achievement. They realize the importance of using every minute of every day and are almost obsessive about protecting classroom time for teaching and learning. Strong instructional leaders always have their doors open, but in reality, they are seldom sitting behind their desks. They seem to be everywhere at once—hallways, auditorium, bus stop, cafeteria—but they spend most of their time in classrooms and meeting with teachers in small groups or individually. They go to bat for their staff at central office, running interference for them so they can concentrate on teaching. They are somehow able to find the money to release teachers for collaborative work or to hire an instructional specialist for a team that needs assistance with developing supplementary materials. Although other schools in town have fewer challenging students with whom to work, the test scores at the schools with strong instructional leaders are comparable and, in some grade levels, higher— a strong indicator that this is a highly effective school led by a strong instructional leader.

The following seven steps to effective instructional leadership are drawn from the research, a qualitative study of strong instructional leaders as identified by their staff members and peers (McEwan, 2002), and my personal experiences in becoming a strong instructional leader over time.

1. Establish, implement, and achieve academic standards.

2. Be instructional resources for staff members.

3. Create school cultures and climates conducive to learning.

4. Communicate the vision and mission of the school.

5. Set high expectations for staff as well as personally.

6. Develop teacher leaders.

7. Develop and maintain positive attitudes with students, staff, and parents.

> Several images comes to mind when thinking about those occasions when the principal is in direct contact with a teacher or teachers with regard to the instructional process: the captain with sword drawn, leading the charge; the coach in the huddle during a timeout diagramming a play; the sales manager giving a pep talk; the orchestra director conducting a rehearsal.
>
> —Acheson (1985, p. 1)

Let's look at these seven steps in the daily practice of a variety of instructional leaders, some just beginning their careers, some still in training as assistant principals, and others with a solid track record of creating highly effective schools and teaching others how to do it as well.

Instructional Leaders Establish, Implement, and Achieve Academic Goals

I first met Dale Skinner when I interviewed him for *Ten Traits of Highly Effective Schools.* He was the exemplar of the Producer trait, leading two Texas elementary schools to Exemplary Status as shown in Figures 1.1 and 1.2. He knows precisely how to establish, implement, and achieve academic goals. He calls it his Formula for Success (FFS). After retiring in 2003, Dale began teaching his formula to California educators. Juan Gonzalez, now principal of Kimball Elementary School in Antioch, CA, was one of Dale's most eager learners.

Figure 1.1   Academic Excellence Indicators, 1994–2000: Loma Terrace Elementary School

Loma Terrace Elementary School

Ysleta Independent School District

El Paso, TX

Implementing Principal: Dale Skinner

First Year of Implementation: 1993–1994

Year	*Rating**
1993–1994	Academically Acceptable
1994–1995	Recognized
1995–1996	Exemplary
1996–1997	Exemplary
1998–1999	Exemplary
1999–2000	Exemplary

SOURCE: Used with permission of Dale Skinner.

NOTE: The Loma Terrace School enrolled between 80% and 90% economically disadvantaged students during this time period. Nearly 100% of the students were Hispanic.

*The Texas Accountability System currently has four tiers: Exemplary, Recognized, Academically Acceptable, and Academically Unacceptable. To receive an Exemplary rating, schools are required to have at least a 90% passing rate on the reading, writing, and math assessments. In addition, 90% of each ethnic group and 90% of economically disadvantaged students must pass the test. To receive a Recognized rating, schools must achieve a passing rate of 80% to 89%. Academically Acceptable schools have a 50% to 79% passing rate. Schools below 50% are considered Academically Unacceptable.

In 2006, the achievement level needed to receive an Academically Acceptable rating increased 10 percentage points to 60% for Reading-English Language Arts (ELA), 40% for Writing and Social Studies, 40% for Mathematics, and 35% for Science. In 2007, the standards increased by five points for all subjects, to 65% for Reading-ELA, Writing, and Social Studies; 45% for Mathematics, and 40% for Science.

In 2008, the Academically Acceptable standards increase by five percentage points for Mathematics and Science. In 2009, the Academically Acceptable standards increase by five percentage points for all subjects (Texas Education Agency, 2007).

Reproduction of material from this book is authorized only for the local school site or nonprofit organization that has purchased *Ten Traits of Highly Effective Schools: Raising the Achievement Bar for All Students*, by Elaine K. McEwan. Thousand Oaks, CA: Corwin Press, www.corwinpress.com.

Figure 1.2   Academic Excellence Indicators, 2000–2003: Villarreal Elementary School

Villarreal Elementary School
Northside Independent School District
San Antonio, TX
Implementing Principal: Dale Skinner
First Year of Implementation: 2000–2001

Year	Rating*
1999–2000	Academically Acceptable
2000–2001	Exemplary
2001–2002	Exemplary
2002–2003	Exemplary

SOURCE: Used with permission of Dale Skinner.

NOTE: The Villarreal School is a Title I school and enrolled between 80% and 90% economically disadvantaged students during this time period. Nearly 100% of the students were Hispanic.

*The Texas Accountability System currently has four tiers: Exemplary, Recognized, Academically Acceptable, and Academically Unacceptable. To receive an Exemplary rating, schools are required to have at least a 90% passing rate on the reading, writing, and math assessments. In addition, 90% of each ethnic group and 90% of economically disadvantaged students must pass the test. To receive a Recognized rating, schools must achieve a passing rate of 80% to 89%. Academically Acceptable schools have a 50% to 79% passing rate. Schools below 50% are considered Academically Unacceptable.

In 2006, the achievement level needed to receive an Academically Acceptable rating increased 10 percentage points to 60% for Reading-ELA, 40% for Writing and Social Studies, 40% for Mathematics, and 35% for Science. In 2007, the standards increased by five points for all subjects, to 65% for Reading-ELA, Writing, and Social Studies; 45% for Mathematics, and 40% for Science.

In 2008, the Academically Acceptable standards increase by five percentage points for Mathematics and Science. In 2009, the Academically Acceptable standards increase by five percentage points for all subjects (Texas Education Agency, 2007).

Reproduction of material from this book is authorized only for the local school site or nonprofit organization that has purchased *Ten Traits of Highly Effective Schools: Raising the Achievement Bar for All Students*, by Elaine K. McEwan. Thousand Oaks, CA: Corwin Press, www.corwinpress.com.

As a brand-new assistant principal at Marsh Elementary School in the Antioch Unified School District, California, Juan was invited to a workshop sponsored by Contra Costa County. He says, "I was amazed by the results Dale and his teachers had achieved at Villarreal, a school with demographics very similar to ours. Hearing them describe what they did gave me a desire to do the same thing at Marsh." During the 2003–2004 school year, Dale provided weekly professional development sessions for Marsh teachers. Juan says, "I wrote down every single word he said. He really coached and mentored me." During that year, Juan, his principal, Veronica Kimble, and the Marsh staff using Dale's FFS achieved a 93-point gain on their Academic Performance Index (API).

Juan says, "For people who don't know about the API, 93 points is an incredible jump. Actually our target goal set by the state was only 10 points." See Figure 1.3 for the first-year test scores at Marsh. Juan says, "What made the difference was focusing teachers' attention on data to help plan instruction. Once teachers began to experience success, everybody started to believe in our students and in their own ability to get results with students. Those beliefs started to become part of the culture. Dale convinced all of us that it could be done."

In April 2005, Juan became the principal of Kimball Elementary, another school in the district. Juan says, "Before I went to the interview, I reviewed all of the data and looked at Kimball's school improvement plan. I said to myself and then to the superintendent, 'I know how to work with this. This is what I would do.' I think my confidence that we could turn this school around helped me to get the position. But when I first arrived, I didn't want to come in and immediately announce all of these changes to the staff. I decided to get to know the staff first. I did take a few teachers to Dale's training so they could get an understanding of the possibilities. Then we read an article by Mike Schmoker (2004) called 'Tipping Point.' It

Figure 1.3   Academic Performance Index, 2002–2004: Marsh Elementary School

Antioch Unified School District

Contra Costa County, CA

Implementing Principal: Veronica Kimble

Assistant Principal: Juan Gonzalez

First Year of Implementation: 2003–2004

Group	Number of Students	2002–2003 API	2003–2004 Growth Target	2003–2004 Actual Growth	2003–2004 API
Total Students Tested	330	595	10	93	688
African American	65	559	8	101	660
Hispanic/Latino	167	583	8	104	687
White	70	626	8	52	678
Economically Disadvantaged	266	588	8	99	667

SOURCE: California Department of Education, Academic Performance Index School Growth Report (2007).

Reproduction of material from this book is authorized only for the local school site or nonprofit organization that has purchased *Ten Traits of Highly Effective Schools: Raising the Achievement Bar for All Students*, by Elaine K. McEwan. Thousand Oaks, CA: Corwin Press, www.corwinpress.com.

emphasized being a results-oriented school, the importance of using data to drive instruction, and having the staff work together as a professional learning community."

Near the end of that year, Juan got his first look at the Kimball test scores. They were disappointing. "Our API was 672, down 13 points from the previous year and one point above the lowest school in the district. The time was right to talk with the staff about plans for the coming year. The numbers were an eye opener for them. They didn't want to be at the bottom of the list and neither did I. They were willing to give my plan a try."

Juan's plan would turn out to be more complicated then he had originally envisioned. During the summer, Kimball was placed under state sanctions and assigned a School Assisted Intervention Team (SAIT). Juan says, "At first, I was discouraged, but then I figured, well, we need help and we're going to get it. This is a great opportunity to make necessary changes. I was very positive and upbeat about it, and this in turn helped the staff to look at the advantages of SAIT. I was able to leverage their help to the specific areas that I thought needed materials and training." With Dale's formula for success fixed firmly in his mind and plenty of resources and expert help in every corner of his school, Juan and his staff were able to pull off a near miracle in school improvement. They achieved a 71-point growth in their API. He describes the feeling: "People were just blown away. We had been under state sanctions the entire time. During 2006–2007, our second year of sanctions, I had 14 or 15 school groups from other districts come to visit the building and see what we were doing. We started off the year with a big celebration for our achievements. We had a medal ceremony for students. Those students who received Advanced ratings in both Math and Language Arts got gold medals. Those who received a combination of one Advanced and one Proficient in Math and Language Arts got silver medals. Students with two Proficient ratings got bronze medals. It was just unbelievable." Juan has always looked for ways to motivate the students to do their best, whether it was by having math competitions, special "Just Prove It" bracelets, Dream Boards to help students visualize their futures, or playing his drums on the school roof. He says, "Student motivation is key."

During the 2006–2007 school year, Kimball added 18 more points to their overall API, made 23 out of 23 subgroups for their Adequate Yearly Progress (AYP), exited from state sanctions, and were invited to apply for the most prestigious award in the state, the honor of being called a California Distinguished School. Kimball's achievement is shown in Figure 1.4.

Figure 1.4 Academic Performance Index, 2004–2007: Kimball Elementary School

Kimball Elementary School
Antioch Unified School District
Contra Costa County, CA
Implementing Principal: Juan Gonzalez
First Year of Implementation: 2005–2006

Group	Number of Students	2004–2005 API	2005–2006 Growth Target	2005–2006 Actual Growth	2005–2006 API
Total Students Tested	367	672	10	71	743
Hispanic/Latino	145	659	8	78	744
White	145	689	8	55	744
Economically Disadvantaged	239	645	8	61	701

Group	Number of Students	2005–2006 API	2006–2007 Growth Target	2006–2007 Actual Growth	2006–2007 API
Total Students Tested	357	743	5	18	762
Hispanic/Latino	158	744	5	20	764
White	119	744	5	20	762
Economically Disadvantaged	255	704	5	25	729

SOURCE: Used with permission of Juan Gonzalez.

Reproduction of material from this book is authorized only for the local school site or nonprofit organization that has purchased *Ten Traits of Highly Effective Schools: Raising the Achievement Bar for All Students*, by Elaine K. McEwan. Thousand Oaks, CA: Corwin Press, www.corwinpress.com.

Instructional Leaders Make Themselves Available to Staff Members

Ileana Fagundo, assistant principal of the Dr. Bowman Foster Ashe Elementary School in Miami, Florida, has eagerly embraced her role as an instructional leader. She aspires to have her own school to lead someday; however, she is currently strengthening her instructional leadership expertise and recognizes the importance of being visible and available to staff members. Bowman Foster Ashe Elementary School, located in southwestern Miami-Dade County, serves a predominantly Hispanic yet nonetheless diverse population. The school has 1,300 students of which

88% are Hispanic, 2% are Black, 6% are White, and 4% are Asian, Indian, or multiracial students. The school has received an A rating for the past six years, no small achievement in a setting where 65% of the students currently receive free or reduced-fee lunch. However, in 2007, their A was precariously close to being a B. Ileana thought about what she could personally do to make herself available to teachers that would renew their focus on effective teaching. She decided to use the CWT (Classroom Walk-Through) method, an adopted practice of the Miami-Dade County Schools. She immediately discovered what other strong instructional leaders who have gone before her know very well. Breaking away from administrivia and keeping to a classroom visitation schedule takes planning, a high energy level, and focus. There are always distractions. For each of the five classrooms she would visit daily, she would later reflect briefly (either in person or via e-mail) with both the teacher and selected students. She says,

> The careful selection of teachers who are or have the potential to be effective teachers may be the principal's most important activity in moving his or her school toward effectiveness.
>
> —*Teddlie and Stringfield (1993, p. 197)*

> I learned that to schedule 25 classroom visits weekly (five per day) in a 1,400-student school with 97 teachers spread out in two buildings two-and-a-half miles apart, 13 portable units, one "concreatable" that houses our 13 third-grade classes, and a Primary Learning Center located two-and-a-half miles away, I had to schedule geographically, or I would need a new pair of shoes very soon.

Ileana's goal was to make herself available to teachers, sharing best practices with them and offering resources and support for those who need help.

Strong Instructional Leaders Create a Climate and Culture Conducive to Learning

The culture that principal Alan Jones created in his diverse suburban Chicago high school is focused on learning for both students *and* teachers.

Every high school possesses a culture—a distinct theme that one feels in the hallways and when talking with teachers. The distinct theme that runs through the hallways of Community High School is its focus on the classroom teacher. Here's how Alan described his focus to me:

While other principals in the area spend time developing different types of schedules, a new mission statement, or the implementation of new programs such as block scheduling or authentic assessment, I have allocated my time and resources to frequent observation in classrooms, coaching of teachers, and the professional development of teachers. Early in my administration, the Board of Education granted my request for monies to support memberships in professional organizations and attendance at professional organizations.

In addition to supporting teacher travel and membership dues, the board also provided more release time for department chairpersons to supervise teachers. Both these board policies have affirmed our belief that what happens in the classroom on a daily basis is the most important dynamic in student learning. After the approval of those policies, I developed systems that would give department chairpersons time and procedures to coach teachers on a regular basis as well as give them the encouragement and resources they needed to pursue topics and interests in their disciplines. Today, every department in our school has staff members who regularly present at conferences. Other teachers have authored textbooks and articles in professional journals, and many have become leaders in various embedded professional development efforts. Most importantly, the culture of our building is focused in the classroom. (McEwan, 2002, pp. 46–47)

Strong Instructional Leaders Communicate the Vision and Mission of Their Schools

Strong instructional leaders communicate the vision and mission of the school by the things they regularly do, day after day. Although they publish weekly bulletins with inspiring messages and quotations, give pep talks and show movie clips to motivate their exhausted teachers, and occasionally sing a solo or read original poetry during the morning announcements, they communicate in very powerful ways by their daily actions. Figure 1.5 is a sample To-Do List for aspiring instructional leaders.

> One thing seems clear to us: the principal must first commit to the goal of instructional effectiveness for every teacher.
>
> —Ackerman, Donaldson, and van der Bogert (1996, p. 44)

Figure 1.5   Instructional Leader's To-Do List

Bonnie Grossen and her staff at the University of Oregon's Center for Applied Research in Education work with teachers in low-performing schools at both the elementary and secondary levels to improve reading achievement. They quickly realized, however, that without the commitment and hands-on involvement from building principals to back up their teaching and coaching efforts, they could well be spinning their wheels. They went to three of their most effective project principals and asked them to list the things they *did* daily so they could begin to coach less effective principals to include more of these behaviors in their daily routines.

❑ Visit every classroom in your school every day. Develop a checklist with all of the teachers' names and check off those you visit. If you can't get there during class time, pop in before or after school. If you don't make it through the entire list in one day, begin where you left off the next.

❑ Focus on each teacher's instructional delivery. Write a comment directly related to some aspect of instruction for at least five teachers. Make *all* of your comments positive and descriptive (Faber & Mazlish, 1990). Work your way through everyone on your staff. Do be sure to personalize your comments as your staff members will no doubt be comparing notes over lunch.

❑ Celebrate the academic success of at least five students today. Make *all* of your comments positive, personalized, and descriptive. You can deliver them orally, put them in writing, or call their parents to deliver the good news. Of course, in order to do this, you will need to visit more classrooms, talk to teachers, look at student work samples, and talk to students.

❑ Learn the names of all of your students and call them by name when you meet them in the hallways, at athletic events or concerts, or in the cafeteria. If you're not there yet, learn five new names per day. Pick a family with several children and learn their names as a family group. Learn their parents' names as well. You cannot track the academic progress of students without knowing who they are, what they look like, in whose classroom they sit, and what their specific needs are.

❑ Help staff members and students to resolve conflicts in an efficient and timely way. Emphasize the need to work together for the overall goal of learning for all students. The place to begin is with your own relationships. If there is someone on the faculty with whom you have had a disagreement or unpleasant conversation lately, tell that person that you miss talking to them and want to repair the rift for the sake of the students. Call a parent with whom you have had a difficult time communicating and share something positive (related to the academic success of one of their children). "What if," you may ask, "their children have not experienced any academic success?" Set about finding how you and the teachers can make this happen—even in the smallest of ways.

❑ Support teachers in their disciplinary actions with students. Affirm teachers who have particularly challenging classes this year. Praise their classroom management skills (be descriptive and specific) and ask if there's anything you can do to help them. Look upon this responsibility as the most basic foundation to academic success for all.

❑ Ensure that teachers have the training, materials, and protected time to do their jobs. Minimize interruptions from the intercom. Ask the teachers with whom you talk today if there's anything you can do to help them be more effective on the job. Follow through in a timely way on these requests.

❑ Plan a coaching session with every teacher. Teach a lesson while a teacher observes you and then schedule a time for you and the teacher to talk about how *you* could improve *your* lesson. It's amazing how much you can accomplish in a coaching session if you take the focus off the teacher and put it on yourself.

Reproduction of material from this book is authorized only for the local school site or nonprofit organization that has purchased *Ten Traits of Highly Effective Schools: Raising the Achievement Bar for All Students,* by Elaine K. McEwan. Thousand Oaks, CA: Corwin Press, www.corwinpress.com.

Strong Instructional Leaders Set High Expectations for Staff and Personally

Beth Madison, principal of George Middle School in Portland, Oregon, raised expectations dramatically for her staff members. She says, "The teachers had been told by other administrators that they were fine and the kids were failing because they were poor and came from difficult homes. While it is inarguable that our kids do come from homes with significant challenges, I knew they could learn and even make up for lost time if we would optimize our strategies. I think the teachers were ready to succeed. They just needed someone to show them how and believe in them."

> Everything that our principal expected of us, he modeled. Everything.
>
> —Becky Guzman, Third Grade, Villarreal School (TX)

Strong Instructional Leaders Develop Teacher Leaders

Principals who work in small districts find that teacher leaders are essential to carrying on the important work of embedded professional development to increase the school's instructional capacity. Cathie West explains: "We have no Curriculum Director, Assessment Specialist, or Subject Area Coaches in our tiny rural district, so this work falls on the principals. How do I cope? I enlist the teachers. My reading specialist has become an expert coach—modeling research-supported techniques, co-teaching, and providing classes after school for teachers wanting to learn more. Other teachers have stepped up by demonstrating teaching strategies in classrooms, observing new teachers and giving feedback, leading book studies and curriculum committees, and sharing instructional materials they have used successfully in their classrooms. We'd be getting nowhere without the help of these superb teacher leaders."

> Before principals envision or mandate changes for others, they benefit from looking at and understanding how their own expectations of themselves as leaders may help or hinder their leadership in action.
>
> —Ackerman et al. (1996, p. 101)

Instructional Leaders Develop and Maintain Positive Attitudes Toward Students, Staff, and Parents

Pam Bradley has been the principal of four different low-performing middle and elementary schools in the state of Oklahoma. Developing positive relationships with students, staff, and parents is a big part of turning around a low-performing school. Here's how she approaches each new situation: "I have found the biggest problem with poor-performing schools is the school climate or culture: an apathetic school community, too much negativity, and very little action (it's easier to sit on the sidelines and complain about why this won't work). My blueprint has always been to determine the sources of the problems (through the input of stakeholders, related data, and some on-site observations), to solicit the assistance of those stakeholders (you'll always have a few 'whiners' that sit back and say it can't be done) and to begin acting as soon as possible.

"The first thing I do in a new school is to seek the input of everyone to determine the source of the challenges. I have found such challenges as negative staff, a poorly aligned curriculum, lazy methods of teaching, poor parental or community involvement or perceptions, lack of support from central office, and student apathy. Once I determine and prioritize the challenges, I set out to solicit the support and expertise of all of the stakeholders. I have learned that it takes the 'whole village' to educate the child: all school staff, parents or guardians, students, and community and business members, to name a few."

Northbrook Middle School (TX) principal Laura Schuhmann specifically concentrates on building trust between teachers and students. "If you want results, building trust between students and teachers is crucial. When I hire teachers, if they don't mention liking or loving or caring about kids, I don't hire them. I look for new, young teachers who have some experience. Initially I made a lot of mistakes by hiring brand-new teachers. I do want enthusiasm, energy, and not someone who watches the clock or is in it for the paycheck, but it helps to have a teacher who isn't brand-new to everything. We do have a strong mentoring system for new teachers. I have a weekly support meeting with all of them. It's their chance to get to know me and to ask questions and talk about any concerns they have. It takes 20 minutes every Friday morning, and I've done it for years. My leadership team and I do a lot of little things to keep teachers' minds free for teaching and building relationships with their students so they will want to come to school. Our goal as a team is to give teachers freedom to teach and students freedom to learn."

George Middle School (Portland, OR) principal Beth Madison finds that maintaining a positive attitude comes naturally for her. Beth admits that she is always looking on the bright side, a trait she has needed in ample amounts since coming to George, where federal sanctions were in place when she arrived. She explains how it works. "One must be a perennial optimist to not fall into despair. I have long been considered a Pollyanna, crashing forward with hope and hype and reaching out far and wide for support from everyone for my schools. To me, every day has to be an excellent day, and I believe this attitude has been helpful in leading teachers to share my strong vision."

Although raising student achievement is the overall mission, Cathie West knows that it happens student by student. She and her staff concentrate on their student heroes and reinforce positive attitudes with lots of praise—for students and each other.

She says, "Raising academic achievement is my school's top priority, and our steady rise in student test scores is a source of staff pride. But it's not test scores we talk about when we get together in hallways, the staff room, or the front office. We tell stories. We talk about the boy who courageously signed up for crossing guard duty despite a neurological disorder that leaves him barely able to walk. We remember how his classmates brought his dream to life by propping him up at his post and carrying his flag for him. We talk about our superb choir—kids barely 10 years old—who brought the house down at a Veterans' Assembly by expertly singing a stirring song of valor—in classical Italian, no less. And we talk about the young desperado whose wild antics had been the source of many a police call. How she graduated from her behavior classroom—after months of arduous training—into a regular classroom, where she has become a shining star. Do we care about our test scores? Of course we do. But it's the accomplishments of individual students that build our memories of school success."

ASSESSING THE PRINCIPAL'S LEADERSHIP CAPACITY

Setting high expectations for teachers while failing to do the same for administrators is an exercise in hypocrisy. How can instructional leaders reasonably expect teachers to set goals, be evaluated regularly, accept feedback on their performance, and continually grow as professionals if they are not willing to do the same? Strong instructional leaders regularly solicit performance feedback from their staff members, use that feedback to set goals, and share those goals with staff members in anticipation of a new cycle of performance evaluation feedback.

In the spring of each year, I asked the Lincoln teachers to complete a short, three-question evaluation related to my job performance:

1. What am I doing as an instructional leader that is contributing to the mission of our school and to your effectiveness as a teacher (office personnel, instructional aide, lunchroom or playground supervisor, etc.)?

2. What am I doing that is standing in the way of your effectiveness?

3. What would you like me to start doing that I am not currently doing that would enable you to be a more effective teacher?

I asked the building leadership team to collate the responses and then select a representative from the group who would be comfortable sharing the results (both the good news and the "bad") with me. I used this feedback to evaluate my own performance and to set goals for the coming year. On one occasion, I used the instrument developed by Richard Andrews as part of the study of strong and weak instructional leaders in Seattle, Washington (Andrews, 1989; Andrews & Soder, 1987). Each staff member completed a questionnaire, and they were collected and mailed to Andrews, who had been hired by the Illinois Principals Association to work with our membership on instructional leadership issues. I later met personally with Andrews to discuss the results of my evaluation. This process illuminated for me how often we principals convince ourselves that we are doing things that we really aren't. Or at least, our teachers perceive that we are not doing them. And teachers' perceptions of their principals' instructional leadership abilities constitutes reality for them. They are unlikely to respect, pay attention to, or consult for help someone they do not believe is a strong instructional leader.

Form 1.2 contains an Instructional Leadership Checklist to assess your own instructional leadership abilities or that of someone with whom you work or supervise. It lists the seven steps as described in this chapter along with a set of behavioral indicators that expand and further explain the step.

SUMMING UP

When you carefully consider the research on effective schools, you will find that principal leadership generally, and instructional leadership specifically, is a key factor in raising the achievement bar for all students. Principals accomplish what they do in an indirect way through teachers— by teaching, encouraging, mentoring, coaching, modeling, supporting, providing, and helping.

WHAT'S AHEAD?

In Chapter 2, we examine the second trait of highly effective schools: research-based instruction. Strong instructional leaders and effective teachers need each other. The better the leader, the more effective even the best teachers will become. The better the teachers, the higher the achievement bar will rise.

Form 1.2 Instructional Leadership Checklist

	Never	Seldom	Sometimes	Usually	Always
Step 1: Establishes, implements, and achieves academic standards					
Indicator 1.1: Incorporates the designated state and district standards into the development and implementation of the local school's instructional programs.	1	2	3	4	5
Indicator 1.2: Ensures that schoolwide and individual classroom instructional activities are consistent with state, district, and school standards and are aligned with one another.	1	2	3	4	5
Indicator 1.3: Uses multiple sources of data, both qualitative and quantitative, to evaluate progress and plan for continuous improvement.	1	2	3	4	5
Indicator 1.4: Instructional leadership efforts on the part of the principal result in meaningful and measurable achievement gains.	1	2	3	4	5
Step 2: Is an instructional resource for staff					
Indicator 2.1: Works with teachers to improve the instructional program in their classrooms consistent with student needs.	1	2	3	4	5
Indicator 2.2: Facilitates instructional program development based on trustworthy research and proven instructional practices.	1	2	3	4	5
Indicator 2.3: Uses appropriate formative assessment procedures and informal data collection methods for evaluating the effectiveness of instructional programs in achieving state, district, and local standards.	1	2	3	4	5
Step 3: Creates a school climate and culture conducive to learning					
Indicator 3.1: Establishes high expectations for student achievement that are directly communicated to students, teachers, and parents.	1	2	3	4	5
Indicator 3.2: Establishes clear standards and communicates high expectations for the use of time allocated to various content areas and monitors the effective use of classroom time.	1	2	3	4	5
Indicator 3.3: With teachers and students (as appropriate), establishes, implements, and evaluates the procedures and codes for handling and correcting behavior problems.	1	2	3	4	5
Step 4: Communicates the vision and mission of the school					
Indicator 4.1: Provides for systematic two-way communication with staff regarding achievement standards and the improvement goals of the school.	1	2	3	4	5
Indicator 4.2: Establishes, supports, and implements activities that communicate the value and meaning of learning to students.	1	2	3	4	5
Indicator 4.3: Develops and uses communication channels with parents to set forth school objectives.	1	2	3	4	5
Step 5: Sets high expectations for staff and self					
Indicator 5.1: Assists teachers yearly in setting and reaching personal and professional goals related to the improvement of instruction, student achievement, and professional development.	1	2	3	4	5

(Continued)

Form 1.2 (Continued)

	Never	Seldom	Sometimes	Usually	Always
Indicator 5.2: Makes regular classroom observations in all classrooms, both informal (drop-in visits of varying length with no written or verbal feedback to teacher) and formal (visits where observation data are recorded and communicated to teacher.)	1	2	3	4	5
Indicator 5.3: Engages in planning with teacher prior to classroom observations.	1	2	3	4	5
Indicator 5.4: Engages in postobservation conferences that focus on the improvement of instruction. (District requirements for procedures and frequency with regard to teacher evaluation may vary and substantially impact the interpretation of this indicator. The scale of descriptors describes a best-case scenario.)	1	2	3	4	5
Indicator 5.5: Provides thorough, defensible, and insightful evaluations, making recommendations for personal- growth and professional-growth goals according to individual needs.	1	2	3	4	5
Indicator 5.6: Engages in direct teaching in the classroom.	1	2	3	4	5
Indicator 5.7: Holds high expectations for personal instructional leadership behavior, regularly solicits feedback (both formal and informal) from staff members regarding instructional leadership abilities, and uses such feedback to set yearly performance goals.	1	2	3	4	5
Step 6: Develops teacher leaders					
Indicator 6.1: Schedules, plans, or facilitates regular meetings of all types (planning, problem solving, decision making, or inservice training) with and among teachers to address instructional issues.	1	2	3	4	5
Indicator 6.2: Provides opportunities for and training in collaboration, shared decision making, coaching, mentoring, curriculum development, and presentations.	1	2	3	4	5
Indicator 6.3: Provides motivation and resources for faculty members to engage in professional-growth activities.	1	2	3	4	5
Step 7: Establishes and maintains positive relationships with students, parents, and teachers					
Indicator 7.1: Serves as an advocate for students and communicates with them regarding their school life.	1	2	3	4	5
Indicator 7.2: Encourages open communication among staff members and maintains respect for differences of opinion.	1	2	3	4	5
Indicator 7.3: Demonstrates concern and openness in the consideration of teacher, parent, and student problems and participates in the resolution of such problems where appropriate.	1	2	3	4	5
Indicator 7.4: Models appropriate human relations skills.	1	2	3	4	5
Indicator 7.5: Develops and maintains high morale.	1	2	3	4	5
Indicator 7.6: Systematically collects and responds to staff, parent, and student concerns.	1	2	3	4	5
Indicator 7.7: Acknowledges appropriately the meaningful accomplishments of others.	1	2	3	4	5

Copyright © 2002 Corwin Press. All rights reserved. Reprinted from *7 Steps to Effective Educational Leadership* (2nd ed.) by E. K. McEwan. Reproduction authorized only for the local school site that has purchased this book.

Research-Based Instruction

We believe teachers and teaching are the heart of the educational enterprise. . . . We further believe that a teacher's skill makes a difference in the performance of students, not only in their achievement scores on tests (as important as that might be), but in their sense of fulfillment in school and their feelings of well-being.

—Saphier and Gower (1997, p. v)

Research-based instruction delivered by highly effective teachers is the second trait of highly effective schools. As noted in Chapter 1, teachers don't have the time or the position power to spontaneously organize themselves to raise the achievement bar for all students. They need a strong instructional leader to provide resources and support. On the other hand, one principal, even with a team of fine assistants, cannot meet the academic needs of hundreds or even thousands of students without a critical mass of effective teachers.

The source of effective instruction is the staff: teachers who consistently teach using methods, models, strategies, and approaches that enable all students to learn. The teachers in a highly effective school are well trained, highly motivated, and masters of content. They favor rigor and standards. They are eager learners themselves, always looking for more effective ways to reach and teach struggling students through collaboration with their colleagues, the investigation of best practices in other successful schools, and observation of their peers. Following are the ten traits of highly effective teachers I described in 2001:

TEN TRAITS OF HIGHLY EFFECTIVE TEACHERS

1. The highly effective teacher is mission driven, feeling a call to teach as well as a passion to help students learn and grow.

2. The highly effective teacher is positive and real, demonstrating the qualities of respect, caring, empathy, and fairness in his or her communications and relationships with students, parents, and colleagues.

3. The highly effective teacher is a teacher leader who positively impacts the lives of students, parents, and colleagues.

4. The highly effective teacher demonstrates "with-it-ness": the state of being on top of, tuned in to, aware of, and in complete control of three critical facets of classroom life: (1) the management and organization of the classroom, (2) the engagement of students, and (3) the management of time.

5. The effective teacher exhibits his or her own unique style, bringing drama, enthusiasm, liveliness, humor, charisma, creativity, and novelty to his or her teaching.

6. The highly effective teacher is a motivator par excellence who believes in his or her own ability to make a difference in the lives of students and relentlessly presses and pursues students to maintain the highest possible behavioral and academic standards.

7. The highly effective teacher is an instructional virtuoso: a skilled communicator with a repertoire of essential abilities, behaviors, models, and principles that lead all students to learning.

8. The highly effective teacher has a sound knowledge of content (the structure of the discipline) and outcomes (what the school, district, or state has determined is essential for students to know).

9. The highly effective teacher has knowledge of the students, the school, and the community in which he or she is teaching and uses this knowledge to solve problems in the instructional setting: street smarts.

> The one thing that keeps me going is student success. I receive so much inner joy as I watch levels of learning increase from the beginning of a school year. I begin with the end in mind, visualizing what it will feel like when the scores come back to us in May. The satisfaction that comes with being successful in a school where students have so many obstacles in their lives is what keeps me going.
>
> —*Louise Sekula,*
> *Language Arts Specialist,*
> *Villarreal School (TX)*

10. The highly effective teacher has a substantive thought life that includes the abilities to be: (1) metacognitive: able to read one's own mental state and then assess how that state will affect one's present and future performance; (2) strategic: able to think aloud and model strategic learning for students; (3) reflective: able to think about personal teaching behaviors for the purposes of self-growth; (4) communicative: able to articulate ideas, issues, beliefs, and values about the act of teaching with colleagues, students, and parents; and (5) responsive: able to adjust to the changing needs and demands of the profession. At the time I developed this list, I did not single out any one of the traits as more important than another, but in the context of creating highly effective schools, instructional effectiveness is a priority. The No Child Left Behind Act (2002) used the term *qualified* to describe the type of teachers required in every classroom. However, to create a highly effective school requires teachers who have more than just a paper trail of certificates, diplomas, and degrees. The highly effective school requires instructional virtuosos.

> As a teacher, there is nothing more thrilling than bearing witness to the "aha" moment of a student! There are always times when one or more students are struggling and I feel that I have exhausted every teaching strategy. These are the low moments when I'm not sure I'm capable of making a difference for that child. But being who I am, I try again. When that "aha" moment arrives, the feeling is indescribable.
>
> —Robyn Loucks, First-Grade Teacher, Mountain Way Elementary School (WA)

AN INSTRUCTIONAL VIRTUOSO: THE RESEARCH

There are a variety of ways to judge teacher quality, but it has become clear over the past decade that a teacher's capacity to improve student achievement cannot be judged by demographic characteristics (Hanushek, 2002). "Measures of teachers (qualifications, experience, and the like) do little or nothing to ensure high-quality teachers" (p. 4). Hanushek argues that we must focus on teacher performance—what teachers are doing in the classroom with students. While effective instruction is the single most important variable responsible for increasing learning (Haycock, 1998; Jordan, Mendro, & Weerasinghe, 1997; Rivkin, Hanushek, & Kain, 2001; Sanders & Horn, 1995), describing and defining precisely what an effective teacher looks like is a complex undertaking.

> The essence of being an effective teacher lies in knowing what to do to foster pupils' learning and being able to do it.
>
> —Kyriacou (1991, p. 1)

The sheer magnitude of what a teacher must know and do to be considered effective is mind-boggling. That is why I followed the lead of

Brophy and Good (1986), who chose the word *virtuoso* to describe the instructionally effective teacher. A virtuoso, according to *Merriam-Webster*, is "a person who has great skill at some endeavor" (*Merriam-Webster*, 2003, p. 1397). As I said in an earlier book, a highly effective teacher is an instructional virtuoso: a skilled communicator with a repertoire of essential abilities, behaviors, models, and principles that lead all students to learning (McEwan, 2002, p. 81).

The virtuoso teacher designs and executes a great lesson much like a virtuoso violinist performs a concerto. "The truly effective teacher knows how to execute individual behaviors with a larger purpose in mind. The larger purpose requires placing behaviors side by side in ways that accumulate to create an effect greater than can be achieved by a single behavior or small set of them. This is why teaching involves a sense of timing, sequencing, and pacing that cannot be conveyed by any list of behaviors" (Borich, 2000, p. 31).

Although we know a great deal more today about effective instruction than we did 30 years ago, many educational researchers are still far more guarded in their statements regarding cause and effect than Madeline Hunter (1984), the grande dame of staff development. She said,

> Teaching seems to be one of the last professions to emerge from the state of "witch doctoring" to become a profession based on a science of human learning. Only recently, however, has long established research in learning been translated into cause-effect relationships of use to teachers. Only recently have teachers acquired the skills of systematically using these relationships to accelerate learning. (p. 169)

> Teaching without learning is like selling without buying.
>
> —Hunter (1989)

Most researchers caution against writing *specific* prescriptions for teaching practices (Brophy & Good, 1986, p. 365), but Borich (2000) cites five behaviors that show promising relationships to desirable student performance, primarily as measured by classroom assessments and standardized tests: (1) designing lessons that are clear and meaningful, (2) providing instructional variety; (3) being oriented to time-on-task and task completion, (4) engaging students in the learning process, and (5) ensuring a high rate of student success (Brophy, 1989; Brophy & Good, 1986; Dunkin & Biddle, 1974; Rosenshine, 1971; Teddlie & Stringfield, 1993; Walberg, 1986).

Brophy and Good (1986), although cautionary in their approach to interpreting any direct cause-and-effect relationships between *isolated* teacher behaviors and student achievement, do conclude that "students learn more efficiently when their teachers first structure new information for them, help them relate it to what they already know, and then monitor their performance and provide corrective feedback during recitation, drill, practice, or application activities" (p. 386). The *direct* role of the teacher in designing lessons and providing clear and unambiguous instruction needs to be reinforced and thoroughly appreciated. Highly effective teachers do not merely facilitate learning. They must also design, direct and orchestrate it, "Effective teachers are clear about what they intend to accomplish through their instruction, and they keep these goals in mind both in designing the instruction and in communicating its purposes to the students" (Porter & Brophy, 1988, pp. 81–82).

> Teachers in effective schools were consistently more successful in keeping students on task, spent more time presenting new material, provided more independent practice, demonstrated higher expectations for students, provided more positive reinforcement, experienced fewer classroom interruptions, had fewer discipline problems, generated more consistent friendly classroom ambiences, and provided more pleasant classrooms than did their peers in matched ineffective schools.
>
> —*Teddlie & Stringfield (1993, p. 193)*

Brophy and Good (1986) remind educators of the dangers of assuming that structured instruction is appropriate only for teaching low-level skills. Many teachers, trained to prefer indirect instructional methods, often fail to recognize that "even for higher level, complex learning objectives, guidance through planned sequences of experience is likely to be more effective than unsystematic trial and error" (p. 366). They further point out that systematic teaching does have an important role to play in the development of learning-to-learn skills, creative writing, and even artistic expression. They suggest that "effective instructors working at higher levels must develop apt analogies or examples that will enable students to relate the new to the familiar or the abstract to the concrete; identify key concepts that help to organize complex bodies of information; model problem-solving processes that involve judgment and decision making under conditions of uncertainty; and diagnose and correct subtle misconceptions" (p. 366).

For those seeking to increase their knowledge and skills with regard to effective instruction, *The Skillful Teacher: Building Your Teaching Skills Classroom* (Saphier & Gower, 1997), *Instruction That Works: Research-Based Strategies for Increasing Student Achievement* (Marzano et al., 2001), and *40 Ways to Support Struggling Readers in Content Classrooms, Grades 6–12* (McEwan, 2007) provide a variety of research-based best practices.

> The major indicator that distinguishes effective from ineffective educational practice is whether students learn that which is purportedly taught.
>
> —*Sanders and Horn (1995, p. 2).*

ESSENTIAL TEACHING SKILLS

The following essential teaching skills are seven areas of expertise in which teachers absolutely must excel in order to be effective (McEwan, 2002). These skills must be learned, practiced, improved, and perfected. Individual teachers may vary somewhat in their abilities to execute these skills, but highly skilled teachers are able to fluently and automatically execute them seamlessly as they teach day by day. These skills are foundational to effective instruction. They are like the operating system on a computer or the electrical system in a car. You don't pay attention to them until something goes wrong—the screen freezes or the car won't start. When lessons start "clunking" for students instead of "clicking," teachers need a tune-up in one or more of these seven essential skills.

Lesson Planning

Highly effective teachers know how to plan and prepare lessons. They are able to articulate the objectives of the lesson, relate it to past and future lessons, and take into account the needs of their students and the nature of what they want to teach. Skillful teachers include components in their lessons that will attract their students' interest and keep them engaged. They are able to mentally walk through their presentations beforehand, anticipating where problems of understanding or organization might occur and making adjustments up until the last minute.

Lesson Presentation

The ability to present lessons that have been planned is the second essential teaching skill. The excellent teacher utilizes good communication skills—giving clear explanation and instructions, asking questions that generate interest and stimulate thinking, and organizing an appropriate number and variety of learning experiences with which to engage students.

Lesson Management

Lesson management is the third essential teaching skill. This skill is different from presentation. Lesson presentation consists of all the things an observer (or student) can see and hear the teacher doing. Management, on the other hand, is about the mental adjustments a teacher makes during instruction—the critical decisions with regard to fine-tuning the content, difficulty, or pace of the lesson. Lesson management is about making midcourse corrections in the flight plan to ensure that students *do* understand and *do* experience success.

Climate Management

The fourth essential teaching skill consists of creating a classroom climate or atmosphere that is positive, supportive, and focused on learning. This skill encompasses the communication of expectations, the encouragement of positive relationships, the motivation of students, and the development of teams in the classroom.

Classroom Management

The next essential teaching skill is the ability to organize and manage the day-to-day operations of the classroom to maximize use of time and minimize off-task behavior. It includes the development of procedures and routines to keep the classroom running smoothly. Classroom management is the oil that lubricates instruction.

Student Management

The ability to deal swiftly and positively (in both proactive and reactive manners) with student behavior (or misbehavior) is essential teaching skill number six. The highly effective teacher is able to handle conflict and confrontation with authority, calmness, and confidence. The highly effective teacher is also able to prevent, forestall, anticipate, and disarm disciplinary problems with students.

Formative Assessment and Diagnostic Teaching

The final essential skill is the ability to assess students' progress with a view to diagnosing, remediating, or enriching. This skill has largely been overlooked in many schools where teachers assess to grade, not to improve instruction. However, teachers in highly effective schools are constantly evaluating their own teaching performance with formative assessments, "a process in which information about learning is evoked and then used to modify the teaching and learning activities" (Black, Harrison, Lee, Marshall, & Wiliam, 2003, p. 111). This cyclical and ongoing process acts as a means of quality control for teachers, enabling them to fine-tune whole-class lessons; plan for additional small-group instruction; or make more major changes to curriculum, learning experiences, or instructional objectives.

DIFFERENTIATED INSTRUCTION

The seven essential teaching skills are generic and essential for teachers at any level and in any content area. Individual teachers may vary widely in exactly how they execute these various styles. But their students learn. However, when faced with particularly challenging students who need differentiated instruction, educators in highly effective schools recommend adding recursive teaching or mastery learning approaches to your repertoire.

Teach for Mastery

If too many students are failing to learn in your school or classroom, consider an alternative instructional mindset—one that can simultaneously meet the needs of both struggling and gifted students. I recommend *mastery learning,* an approach we used in our district with astounding success in the early 1980s, after reading the work of Benjamin Bloom (1971) and working with James Block (1971).

Regrettably, at some point during the past two decades, mastery learning was reconceptualized as a rigid, teacher-directed approach suitable only for dishing up rote skills and trivial information. This may have resulted in some measure from the descriptions given to it in popular educational psychology textbooks: an anticonstructivist, behavioral management technique in which instruction proceeded in a lockstep manner at the pace of the slowest students in the class (R. Gentile, personal conversation, November 17, 2005).

In reality, mastery learning combines the critical attributes of standards-based learning and differentiated instruction in one of the few instructional formats that works at any level or for any content area *and* can truly promise that no student will be left behind (Gentile & Lalley, 2003). Here are the four basic principles around which the reconstituted mastery learning is organized:

1. Explicit instructional objectives, hierarchically sequenced, which all students are expected to attain

2. Criterion-referenced assessments to evaluate and provide feedback on the achievement of those objectives

3. Remedial instruction for students who do not achieve the desired standard of performance

4. Enrichment activities and a corresponding grading scheme to encourage students to go beyond initial mastery of essentials to higher-order thinking that includes a variety of applications of their newly acquired knowledge and skills. (p. 156)

Mastery learning is grounded in a criterion-referenced mindset (i.e., all students can learn) as compared to a norm-referenced or competitive approach to learning (i.e., only some students can learn). James Lalley explains, "Although a norm-referenced mindset may not at first glance appear to be competitive in nature, consider that many teachers typically teach to their best students and move on when those students are able to do well on the test. With this approach, some students achieve less (the losers) than others (the winners) in terms of grading, credit, *and* learning. Unfortunately, if learning new content is contingent upon the mastery of earlier content, a substantial number of students will fall even farther behind" (J. Lalley, personal conversation, November 18, 2005).

Teach Recursively

Recursive teaching occurs when a teacher repeatedly comes back to important concepts, outcomes, or standards. This type of teaching gives students multiple opportunities to master not only the important skills and knowledge that are presently being taught but also those that have been previously taught or are coming up in the very near future. The opposite of recursive instruction is teaching a unit, testing it, considering it taught, and moving on without regard for the students who have not achieved mastery.

A powerful example of recursive teaching is a strategy used in Dale Skinner's Formula for Success (FFS) Schools called *Board Math*. To implement Board Math, teachers divide a full whiteboard into five columns, often using blue tape, and write these headings at the top: Number Sense; Algebra & Functions; Measurement & Geometry; Statistics, Data Analysis, and Probability; and Mathematical Reasoning. (NOTE: These are taken from the California Math Standards.) Based on grade-level content standards, they divide each column into sections. For example, for third grade, under Number Sense, the teacher would have three sections and would label them Place Value, Comparing Numbers; Operations; and Fractions, Decimals. Each day the teacher includes problems for specific standards; for instance, 1.5: Write the expanded notation of 4,208; 1.3: Identify the place value of the underlined digit 12,543 (2 is underlined); 1.4: Round to the hundreds 864. All of the standards of the five strands are spiraled in difficulty. The problems and tasks involve the required standards for that grade level and primarily include skills that are currently being taught, but they also include skills that have been taught in previous units or that will be taught in upcoming units. The inclusion of skills that will be taught in future lessons is a very valuable aspect of Board Math since it helps to build familiarity. When a new skill, based on specific standards, is introduced in a formal lesson or unit, the teacher can make connections with what is being taught to problems the class has worked together during Board Math.

Teachers devote between 20 to 30 minutes daily to Board Math, which includes using problem-solving steps to solve one or two word problems based on the standards for the grade level. Before beginning Board Math, the teacher and students decide how many problems they think they will answer correctly that day—say, 17 out of 20. This becomes their goal for the day. Students sit on the carpet in front of the board. Each student has a mini-whiteboard (9″ × 11″), marker, and eraser, so that all students are engaged in working each problem. After students have been given a few minutes to work a problem, they hold up their mini-boards for the teacher to observe. Then the teacher calls on a student by pulling a tongue depressor from a can containing sticks labeled with each student's name and asks the student to complete one of the tasks on the Math Board. After students answer correctly, their classmates give a silent cheer. If they reach their goal, a paper link is added to the class chain at the front of the room, a visual reminder of their progress toward the prize they are seeking, perhaps free recess with PE equipment or math games choice time (B. Ward, personal communication, October 9, 2007).

Recursive Teaching: Isabel Anaya, Third Grade, Villarreal Elementary School

We use what we call a Reading Toolkit at Villarreal. Each tool corresponds to a different reading benchmark that students are expected to master. Inferring, cause and effect, and summarization are just three of the more difficult tools for students to understand and then begin to regularly use in their independent reading. So I come back to these tools in every single subject I teach all day long and all year long. You can't just teach important reading tools or strategies once or twice and expect that students will get it. The power of recursive teaching is in the repetition and practice students get in different kinds of text day after day.

For example, if I were teaching a lesson about weathering and erosion in science, I would take one of the paragraphs in the textbook and we would talk about what conclusions we could draw from that paragraph. I would of course remind students to look at the chart showing the tools in our toolkit or to look at the chart on their desktop that lists the tools with picture clues. I might ask students why we need to draw conclusions when we read and how drawing conclusions might help them comprehend. Then we might use the conclusions we have drawn to write a short summary of the text.

If it was appropriate to that particular part of the science lesson, we might even create a graphic organizer. I continually talk with my students about the importance of using the tools every time they read, no matter what they are reading.

As I reviewed the science text for the lesson, I might have noticed that it contained five or six words with prefixes and suffixes. One of the skills that my students struggle with sometimes, especially the ELLs (English-language learners), is identifying prefixes and suffixes and using their meanings to figure out what longer words mean. So I might add a little excitement to the lesson by saying, "I have a ticket for every person who can find a prefix or suffix on any of the words in this section of the science book." Of course, I make sure ahead of time that there are plenty of excellent examples before I throw out the challenge. Students can use their tickets to buy things in the school store. Two other skills that I intentionally come back to again and again in every subject are (1) knowing what a detail is and (2) learning multiple meanings of common words. For example, once my students started seeing the word *back* and noting how many different meanings it had (our dictionary showed 11), they were on the lookout for every meaning. It was wonderful to see them so excited about words.

ASSESSING AND BUILDING INSTRUCTIONAL CAPACITY

Instructional capacity is the ability of a given group of teachers in a school to raise the achievement bar for all students. Corcoran and Goertz (1995) enumerate three components of instructional capacity: (1) the intellectual ability, knowledge, and skills of teachers and other staff; (2) the quality and quantity of resources available for teaching, including staffing levels, instructional time, and class sizes; and (3) the social organization of instruction. In a highly effective school, assessing and building instructional capacity are ongoing and almost simultaneous. They are among the chief concerns of a strong instructional leader. However, here we'll consider them one at a time.

Assessing Instructional Capacity

The assessment of instructional capacity simply means figuring out the effectiveness of a given group of teachers. It consists of three components: (1) knowing what a highly effective teacher looks like and in the absence of good models being able to explain and model effective instruction; (2) determining the effectiveness of every teacher (instructional strengths and needs) through drop-in classroom walk-throughs, longer full-lesson observations, and documentation of student learning; and (3) determining the school's level of instructional alignment.

Know What a Good Teacher Looks Like

Strong instructional leaders are students of instruction; they learn from their most effective teachers, they read voraciously; and most important—they continue to teach *and* to solicit feedback from their most effective teachers on best practices. Recall that Indicator 5.6 on the Instructional Leadership Checklist in Chapter 1 states, "Engages in direct teaching in the classroom." This indicator does not include reading stories aloud or assisting teachers with small groups. It includes lesson preparation collaboratively with the teacher, an opportunity for the classroom teacher to engage in an observation of the principal teaching a lesson, and a conference between the teacher and principal to debrief on the lesson.

Determine the Effectiveness of Every Teacher

Strong instructional leaders readily recognize highly effective teachers in action, but reducing the performance of a virtuoso to a simple checklist is unwise. Checklists containing certain key concepts, like those found in the Learning Scan shown in Form 2.1, can be helpful to keep administrators focused on what's important when conducting a classroom walk-through. However, using checklists as an evaluative tool or as the only indicator of effective instruction forces teachers to resort to what I call *rote teaching.*

Earlier in my career, administrators were obsessive about teachers posting their rules and consequences, as if the mere act of stapling a piece of paper to a bulletin board would suddenly transform an out-of-control classroom into a model of decorum. More recently, Word Walls and instructional objectives are two items that have captured the hearts of principals looking for easy answers. The very idea that the act of posting a list of words on poster board or copying an instructional objective out of the standards binder every day will transform an ineffective teacher into a virtuoso is ridiculous. Then administrators march through the building taking names of those who aren't in compliance. If this scenario weren't so common and deeply depressing, it would be funny.

Determine Instructional Alignment

The final step in assessing and improving instructional capacity is the most difficult one to accomplish. Consider this scenario I've observed in many schools: There are many highly effective teachers, but they are all teaching their favorite things—ergo, curricular chaos. To increase capacity requires instructional alignment. Use the following questions to assess instructional alignment across grade levels and then take steps to realign

Form 2.1 Learning Scan

Classroom _____ **Period** _____ **Date** _____

Directions: Please rate the following indicators of the teacher's concern for student learning on a scale of 0 (not evident) to 5 (very evident). Please record evidence to support your rating in terms of one or more of the following: behaviors observed, statements made, or physical evidence seen.

1. Literacy Focus • Students are engaged in reading • Students are engaged in writing • Work displayed shows evidence of reading and writing to learn *Rating:* _____	
2. Relational Teaching • Teachers exhibit positive attitudes with students • Teachers have rapport with students • Teachers are respectful, professional, and polite—even when correcting students *Rating:* _____	
3. Questioning Strategies • The majority of students are called on—not always the same few • Students have time to think before answers are requested or confirmed • Teacher avoids choral responses • Teachers checks for individual student understanding with white boards, exit tickets, work samples *Rating:* _____	
4. Lesson Design • Student-friendly objectives are posted • Activities are aligned with objectives • Students are thinking on higher levels of Bloom's Taxonomy • Students are working bell to bell *Rating:* _____	
5. Student Engagement • Students are actively engaged • Students are able to explain the relevance and purpose of their work • Students are attentive and respectful • Students ask questions of the teacher *Rating:* _____	

SOURCE: Used with permission of Allyson Burnett.

Reproduction of material from this book is authorized only for the local school site or nonprofit organization that has purchased *Ten Traits of Highly Effective Schools: Raising the Achievement Bar for All Students*, by Elaine K. McEwan. Thousand Oaks, CA: Corwin Press, www.corwinpress.com.

using collaborative grade-level teams to reach consensus about decisions not already mandated by the district or state.

- Are all of the teachers at the same grade levels or courses teaching the specified standards?
- Does instruction in all classrooms support the achievement of those specific standards?
- Are all teachers at the same grade levels or courses teaching students the skills, knowledge, and strategies needed to demonstrate mastery of specific standards?
- Are all teachers at the same grade levels or courses teaching at the level of cognition necessary for students to demonstrate mastery of specific standards?
- Do certain classrooms or class periods outperform others? What instructional strategies did the teachers in those classrooms or class periods use?
- Do certain classrooms or class periods do significantly worse than others? What approaches and methods did the teachers in those classrooms or class periods use?
- Are teaching routines, formats, and methods aligned vertically throughout the school (e.g., the use of certain kinds of lesson formats, advance organizers, graphic organizers, cognitive strategies, reading tools, or specialized academic vocabulary)?
- Are students given adequate opportunities in every content area or grade level to read the kinds of text (narrative or expository) as well as the difficulty level of text that they will encounter on summative tests?
- Are students expected to write in response to reading in most classrooms, as appropriate to the grade level?
- What knowledge is needed to achieve specific standards, how is it best taught, and what programs get results?
- Are standards or objectives being taught early and often enough (recursively) for students to attain mastery?
- Are teachers intimately acquainted with the nuances of each standard?
- Have teachers collaboratively unpacked the specific standards that are giving their students difficulty?

Building Instructional Capacity

There are three steps to building instructional capacity: (1) Provide time for collaboration, work groups, study groups, and lesson studies; (2) provide meaningful and differentiated embedded professional development using teacher leaders in the school or district as resources wherever possible; and (3) deal with teachers who can't or won't improve.

Provide Time for Collaboration

Many districts and schools have recognized how essential time for collaboration is. They have a schedule of designated early-release days per week or month. The most distressing conversations I have with many educators involve statements like this: "We're doing PLCs." When I press them for details about exactly what is taking place during the time allotted for PLCs, they cannot articulate precisely what is happening nor can they point to any compelling goals or measurable improvements in student learning that have resulted from their activities. As powerful as building and maintaining a professional teaching–learning community can be, many educators have simply had some training and moved on to the next thing. The mere provision of time is no guarantee that meaningful collaboration and inquiry will take place during that time or that conversations and subsequent teaching will have an impact on student achievement. The implementation of PLCs must be monitored carefully, especially in the beginning. See Chapter 5 for ways to build in accountability.

Provide Meaningful Differentiated Embedded Professional Development

The challenge of raising the achievement bar suggests that huge-group one-day workshops for an entire faculty have outlived their usefulness. I have known this for quite some time, but I often find my resolve to refuse such invitations weakening when a desperate central office administrator twists my arm. However, I recently had an experience that strengthened my resolve. In one of my workshops I use an exercise called Chunking Your Life to help teachers acquire an instructional activity to teach summarizing. I ask teachers to divide their lives to date into several chunks that relate to a specific theme that they select. Examples include places they've lived, cars they have driven, or the men or women in their lives. I also encourage participants to come up with ways that are unique to their experiences and thinking. At a recent workshop, one of the participants was exceptionally creative. He divided up his teaching career according to his changing views of teacher inservice.

- *Beginning of My Career:* I thought inservice days were important and I could use all of the information.
- *Middle of My Career:* I listened with respect but had no courage to read a book or newspaper.
- *Current:* They are a necessary evil of my profession.

In many schools, professional development is still regarded as something that people go to or have done to them rather than a practice that is embedded in the life of the school and answers a felt need in terms of the compelling academic focus of the school. It is often considered to be a one-time event,

> Are the right people on the bus? Are they in the right seats? If not, what is being done about it?
>
> *—Collins (2001)*

rather than a pervasive aspect of the school culture. The recent trend toward creating PLCs in which teachers collaborate around issues of teaching and learning is an exciting one, but only if the teachers and administrators are willing to actually commit to professional development that involves more than "sitting and getting" from "experts."

Deal With Teachers Who Won't or Can't Change

Figuring out how to deal with teachers who are unwilling or unable to become more instructionally effective is psychologically, emotionally, and physically demanding for administrators, department chairpersons, and instructional coaches. I have examined this issue in depth and feel it is one of the most crucial problems facing those who want to improve instruction and raise the achievement bar for all students (McEwan, 2005). Michael Fullan (2003) offers this challenge to principals: "The biggest dilemma facing all leaders with moral purpose is what to do if you don't trust the competence and motivation of the people you are expected to lead. . . . Leaders need to take action to counsel out or otherwise rid the schools of teachers who persistently neglect their own learning" (p. 66). Courageous principals tackle the tough challenges.

SUMMING UP

Research-based instruction delivered by virtuoso teachers is the core of the highly effective school. Saphier and Gower (1997) call effective teachers the heart of the school. Without highly effective teachers, improving schools is impossible. Research-based instruction is the channel through which knowledge and skills are transmitted to students in well-designed lessons that capture students' interest and imagination. Virtuoso teachers are far more than mere teaching machines. They have positive traits that indicate character and intellectual traits that demonstrate knowledge, curiosity, and awareness. These well-rounded individuals not only teach students, they team with the principal to provide instructional leadership.

WHAT'S AHEAD?

In Chapter 3, we consider the need for a compelling academic focus in order for a school to be highly effective. Focus requires the intentional concentration of the leadership capacity (talents and time of the principal) and the instructional capacity (teaching effectiveness of the staff) toward building academic capacity (the motivation, effort, and ability of students to learn and achieve).

Focus

Focus on fundamentals: curriculum, instruction, assessment . . .

—Fullan (1997, p. 28)

In order to raise the achievement bar for all students, those who are in danger of dropping out as well as the best and the brightest ones who find minimal rigor and relevance in their schooling, *a clear academic focus,* the third trait of highly effective schools, is required. The tried-and-true prerequisites for school improvement, an inspiring vision and meaningful mission, are important, to be sure. But only a consistent laserlike academic focus on the part of administrators, teachers, and students actually produces results. Administrators must focus on monitoring, facilitating, and providing resources to improve instruction. Teachers must focus on academic success for every student every day. Students must focus on reaching their daily and weekly academic goals and fulfilling their hopes and dreams. A relentless attention to daily, monthly, and yearly academic goals is the secret to success—whether in districts, schools, or classrooms. Figure 3.1 shows a collection of synonyms for the word *focus.* They illustrate how essential this trait is to raising the achievement bar.

NCLB and strong accountability systems in many states have put the spotlight on low-performing schools. Less likely to be noticed, however, are the instances of students failing to learn in schools that are thought to be excellent. I was shocked not long ago to discover that my granddaughter, who, although she received all A's in third and fourth grade and had been

Figure 3.1 The Meaning of *Focus*

Focus

Noun

- CENTER, focal point, central point, center of attention, hub, pivot, nucleus, heart, cornerstone
- *Learning is the cornerstone of our school.*
- *Instructional effectiveness is a focal point for our faculty.*
- EMPHASIS, accent, priority, attention, concentration
- *Our emphasis is on raising the achievement bar for all students.*
- *Raising the achievement bar is the top priority for our school.*
- SUBJECT, theme, concern, subject matter, topic, issue, thesis, point, thread, substance, essence, gist
- *Student mastery of standards is a thread that runs through the fabric of our school.*
- *Our theme for the next five years is giving every student multiple options for careers or higher education after high school.*

Verb

- CONCENTRATE ON, center on, zero in on, zoom in on; address itself to, pay attention to, pinpoint, revolve around, have as its starting point
- *The teachers zero in on writing in response to reading every day.*
- *The life of our school revolves around students being successful as learners every day.*

Reproduction of material from this book is authorized only for the local school site or nonprofit organization that has purchased *Ten Traits of Highly Effective Schools: Raising the Achievement Bar for All Students,* by Elaine K. McEwan. Thousand Oaks, CA: Corwin Press, www.corwinpress.com.

enrolled in Advanced Language and Arts and Math for the entire school year, could read only at the third-grade level at the end of fifth grade. How could this happen in an award-winning suburban school district? She had managed to slip by multiple teachers and a state assessment with good guessing, highly developed social and verbal skills, and above-average writing skills. The district, while ostensibly one of the best in the state, had allowed my granddaughter to fall through the cracks. An online reading test, given as a pilot in her Language Arts classroom at the end of year, revealed this appalling academic deficiency. The teacher was stunned and also slightly embarrassed but had no suggestions for how to remediate the problem. The school had no programs to help her, during either the summer or the regular school year. Unless her mother enrolled her in a tutoring center (which she did), she would have entered sixth grade three grade levels behind in her decoding, fluency, vocabulary,

> One of the most powerful lessons to be learned [from highly effective schools] is that good things happen when we dog, obsess, and communicate constantly about just a few essential things.
>
> —*Schmoker (2001, p. 21)*

and comprehension skills at just the point in her academic career when textbooks become bigger and the content becomes more difficult.

THE SECRET TO RAISING THE ACHIEVEMENT BAR

I have selected *academic focus* as the third trait of highly effective schools because this attribute is the secret weapon for eliminating low student achievement. Students with attention deficit hyperactivity disorder (ADHD) are common in every classroom in the country. I'm convinced, however, that there are entire schools and districts with ADHD. They jump from one initiative to another, losing sight of the fact that unless each individual student is learning and growing every day, they are spinning their educational wheels. Schools become academically focused in one way: by concentrating on teaching and learning every minute of every school day.

Too often, the measure of success in schools has been the number of activities and innovations going on. Bryk, Sebring, Kerbow, Rollow, and Easton (1998) call schools like these "Christmas tree schools," a phrase they coined to describe schools undergoing school improvement where activity per se had run amok: "There were many new programs—not just a few—and a great deal of activity and hoopla surrounded them. Some of these new initiatives may have some real strength and integrity. But because they do not cohere as a group and may even conflict, their impact is minimal at best, and potentially negative" (p. 123). Without an academic focus, eloquent visions, compelling missions, and yearly improvement goals are meaningless words—a list in the school improvement plan, a poster in the faculty lounge, or a colorful page on the school's Web site. In the absence of a single-minded academic focus, educators are easy targets for the "innovation du jour," seldom finishing anything they start. The dean of American basketball coaches, John Wooden (1997), gave his players this advice, which is admirably suited for educators in Christmas tree schools: "Do not mistake activity for achievement" (p. 20).

Academic focus as a school trait is the collective will and ability of the administration, staff, and students of a school to concentrate without distraction on achieving specific academic goals for every student in every grade level or course. Figure 3.2 illustrates the time frames that circumscribe vision, mission, goals and focus. Success in raising the achievement bar in your schools lies in tackling academic goals, that are based on the vision and

> At Villarreal, instruction is ongoing and there is no stopping. Teachers are engaged with the children all the time. There is no time for grading papers while school is in session. There is absolutely no wasting of precious instructional minutes by the students or the teachers. That is one of the biggies. You can't help but have success when you are engaged at all times.
>
> —*Becky Guzman*

mission with single-mindedness, discipline, and determination. Here are the steps that educators in highly effective schools take to raise the achievement bar for all students: (1) Begin with an academic vision in mind. (2) Articulate a meaningful shared mission statement. (3) Set goals that are measurable and attainable. And finally: (4) Ensure a focus on student learning.

Often a nonexample of a concept is as instructive as good examples. This nonexample of academic focus was featured on the so-called education page of my local weekly newspaper. The article, with an accompanying photo of the students and teachers, described a developmentally appropriate multiage class (Grades 1–3). Their project, the culmination of a seemingly endless interdisciplinary unit, was a life-size dinosaur. The class had spent more than 40 hours constructing it. Based on my background knowledge, I concluded several things about this classroom: (1) The students had been deemed unready for the academic challenges offered in regular classrooms; (2) the students were not reading at grade level, if they were reading at all; and (3) the teachers were proud and delighted at the accomplishments of their students. They didn't realize that they and their administrator were an embarrassment to education. They had completely lost their focus, if they ever had it.

> Developing a collective sense of what the school might become is an essential step on the journey to becoming a learning community, but it is not sufficient. Schools also must be willing to assess their current reality with total candor and honesty, and then describe the specific measurable results they expect to see as a result of achieving their vision.
>
> —*DuFour (2000, p. 71)*

Figure 3.2   The "Do It Now" Framework

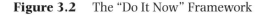

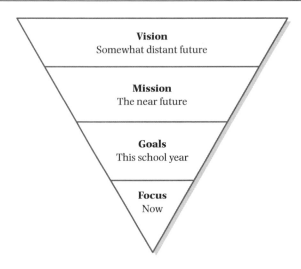

Vision
Somewhat distant future

Mission
The near future

Goals
This school year

Focus
Now

Reproduction of material from this book is authorized only for the local school site or nonprofit organization that has purchased *Ten Traits of Highly Effective Schools: Raising the Achievement Bar for All Students*, by Elaine K. McEwan. Thousand Oaks, CA: Corwin Press, www.corwinpress.com.

Step 1: Begin With a Compelling Academic Vision in Mind

Usually when instructional leaders set out to improve their schools, they are encouraged to visualize where they want to be at some time in the distant future—to conceive of an ideal state that is visionary in nature. Vision is the driving force that communicates an instructional leader's image of the future and is based on personal values, beliefs, and experiences. A vision stretches the imagination and requires the ability to see the future in a way that others may not. That vision, say Pritchett and Pound (1993), should "be like a beacon, a clear beam of light that defines where the culture is headed" (p. 16).

The vision that a strong instructional leader has for a school is often sketched out for stakeholders (teachers, students, and parents) with a broad brush. Few details stand out, and there is often no clear sense of the "who, what, where, and when" that must be nailed down to make the vision a reality. Sometimes leaders take teacher teams to visit schools where a particular vision can be seen in action. Or they might bring in inspirational speakers or show movie clips that motivate stakeholders to commit to working toward the vision.

Although a vision is usually articulated by a strong instructional leader, it must at some point draw on the desires and enlist the support of the faculty, awaken the dreams of students, and whenever possible inspire hope in their parents. Former principal, now consultant, Dale Skinner has been able to communicate his unique vision of a highly effective school to hundreds of teachers and students in two states.

When Dale met the faculty at Villarreal for the first time, he asked them to envision a message on the signboard out in front of their school that read, *Villarreal Is Exemplary,* and then to imagine what it would feel like to go from their current ranking of Acceptable to Exemplary in just one year. At the time, the scores at Villarreal were among the lowest in the Northside Independent School District (San Antonio, TX), and no Title I school in the district had ever achieved an Exemplary status. To some of the teachers, Dale's vision for what could be achieved seemed more like a hallucination than an achievable goal.

Ana Maria Garza was the vice principal at Villarreal when Dale arrived. She describes what the culture was like at that point:

Before Mr. Skinner arrived, we would go through the motions that met the requirements of central office, but it wasn't working. Teachers would sit in the meetings and then go back to their classrooms and do the same old thing. Even though they were intelligent people, what they were doing was not working with kids. The biggest factor in our success was Mr. Skinner giving us the belief that we could actually do it. He inspired us and made it possible for us to believe we could be at the top, that what we did in the classroom was all that mattered. His vision for what our school could become was the key that made it happen.

The intriguing thing about Dale's vision is that it doesn't require teachers to do all of the work. He says, "Fifty percent of our success is motivation for the students. This is one of the most overlooked aspects of education. Most educators spend more energy on gaining parent support. There is no doubt that parents are important, but they are never an excuse for low student performance. Students in an FFS school will be successful almost every time—with or without parent involvement. The outstanding character of the teachers fills the void left by a nonparticipating parent."

Isabel Anaya was a first-year teacher at Villarreal when Dale introduced the FFS concept to both the teachers *and* the students. She describes the experience as life changing:

Our students don't come from families with big dreams about where their children are going to attend college. They don't get a lot of support at home. Mr. Skinner introduced us to the concept of "dream boards," a $12'' \times 18''$ piece of construction paper on which students created a visual of their dreams and hopes—what they wanted to be when they grew up, where they wanted to go to college, what kind of house they wanted to live in, and where they wanted to travel. Teachers also created dream boards illustrating their goals for the future. All of the dream boards were posted in the hallways of the school during the year and became a key part of motivating everyone.

Once the students had envisioned their big dreams, Dale expected them to set individual academic goals based on grade-level standards. To make the process more meaningful, teachers translated the standards into student-friendly language. Students in an FFS school know what they are expected to master during a school year, they keep track of their progress, and they can readily articulate what they need to learn to achieve their next goal. From an inspiring vision flows the compelling mission and ultimately the goals that guide the school's day-to-day behavior. Figure 3.3 is a sample dream board, and Figure 3.4 is a sample goal form. Forms 3.1 and 3.2 are blank templates you can use or adapt for students in your own classroom, school, or district.

According to the teachers at Villarreal for whom Dale ignited a passion to make a difference, his arrival in their school was one of the most exciting days of their teaching careers. They definitely recognized the moral imperative in the vision that Dale articulated for the school.

Figure 3.3   Sample Dream Board

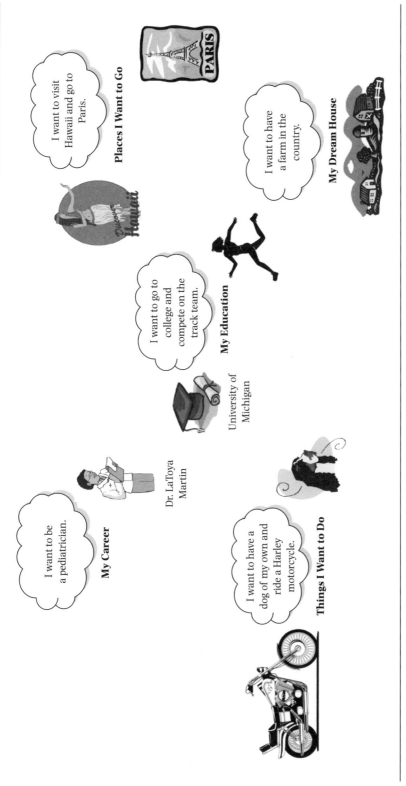

My Career

I want to be a pediatrician.

Dr. LaToya Martin

My Education

I want to go to college and compete on the track team.

University of Michigan

Places I Want to Go

I want to visit Hawaii and go to Paris.

PARIS

My Dream House

I want to have a farm in the country.

Things I Want to Do

I want to have a dog of my own and ride a Harley motorcycle.

SOURCE: Used with permission of Dale Skinner.

Reproduction of material from this book is authorized only for the local school site or nonprofit organization that has purchased *Ten Traits of Highly Effective Schools: Raising the Achievement Bar for All Students*, by Elaine K. McEwan. Thousand Oaks, CA: Corwin Press, www.corwinpress.com.

Figure 3.4   Sample Student Goal-Setting Form

What School-Related Goals Do You Plan to Achieve This Year?

Goal: CST Language Score: Proficient or Higher

Plan: I will pay attention to my teacher, help my classmates learn, do my homework every day, and go to tutoring. I will read one extra story each week. I will look for the main events of the plot and their causes. I will study the characters' personalities and try to figure out why they do the things they do.

Goal: CST Writing Score: at least a 6

Plan: I will listen to my teacher, help my team members, do my homework every day, and go to tutoring. Each week I will write one extra story. Each paragraph will have a topic sentence and supporting sentences. I will always look for good examples of writing when I read stories.

Goal: CST Math Score: Advanced

Plan: I will pay attention in class, help my team members learn, do my homework each day, and go to tutoring. I will create formula math problems, like area/perimeter, and have other team members solve them. I will also give them problems where letters or boxes replace numbers. I will memorize the order of operations and practice.

SOURCE: Used with permission of Dale Skinner.

Reproduction of material from this book is authorized only for the local school site or nonprofit organization that has purchased *Ten Traits of Highly Effective Schools: Raising the Achievement Bar for All Students*, by Elaine K. McEwan. Thousand Oaks, CA: Corwin Press, www.corwinpress.com.

Language Arts specialist Louise Sekula says, "I had been working at our school for many years, and doing a better job for the students was something I really wanted to do. We had been improving and getting better every year. But frankly, we thought we had gone about as far as we could. Hearing Mr. Skinner talk about our becoming an Exemplary school really got my attention. I didn't sleep that night thinking about it."

Step 2: Articulate a Meaningful Shared Mission Statement

After a compelling vision has been conceived and explained, the next step is usually the development of a mission statement that spells out in more specific terms what the vision will actually look like in the school during the first few years of implementation. While the vision may come from the leader, a consultant, or a motivational speaker, the mission should be shared and eventually accepted by the majority of the faculty.

A mission is the overall direction that emerges from the vision, a specific agenda, or to-do list that guides the development of goals that will in turn dictate the day-to-day behavior of the organization. Often the mission represents a paradigm shift or a new way of doing things, some kind of break from the

Form 3.1 Dream Board Form

SOURCE: Used with permission of Dale Skinner.

Reproduction of material from this book is authorized only for the local school site or nonprofit organization that has purchased *Ten Traits of Highly Effective Schools: Raising the Achievement Bar for All Students*, by Elaine K. McEwan. Thousand Oaks, CA: Corwin Press, www.corwinpress.com.

Form 3.2   Student Goal-Setting Form

What School-Related Goals Do You Plan to Achieve This Year?

Goal: **Plan:**
Goal: **Plan:**
Goal: **Plan:**

SOURCE: Used with permission of Dale Skinner.

Reproduction of material from this book is authorized only for the local school site or nonprofit organization that has purchased *Ten Traits of Highly Effective Schools: Raising the Achievement Bar for All Students,* by Elaine K. McEwan. Thousand Oaks, CA: Corwin Press, www.corwinpress.com.

past. But talking about breaking with the past and committing to a new way of doing things do not happen simultaneously. Those of us who have engaged in this process know that talking about it is only the beginning. What is needed is a compelling academic focus, and that takes more than just being able to talk about the change. It means "doing" the change every day.

"Do It Now" Focus: Beth Madison, George Middle School

In July, 2004, when Beth Madison became the principal of George Middle School in Portland, it was one of Oregon's lowest-performing schools and was facing sanctions for not meeting federal requirements for AYP two years in a row. Beth had a clear vision of what the school could become—a place where students, regardless of their demographics, would be successful. She also had some visionary ideas about how technology and community partnerships could provide students, teachers, and parents with the resources and personnel they needed to succeed. However, there wasn't a lot of enthusiasm for a lengthy mission-writing process. She says, "All of the staff members had past experiences where writing a mission had taken a whole day, or even several days or months, and when I suggested a more expedient and direct approach, they were grateful."

The George staff completed their mission statement in a record one-hour staff meeting. Beth simply had small groups post short phrases that described their vision of what the school would look like at its very best. She reports, "As we merged the ideas, we drafted statements that everyone could support, and we were done." Beth believes, along with Pfeffer and Sutton (2000), who explore the knowing–doing gap that keeps many organizations from realizing their potential, that "action counts more than elegant plans" (p. 251).

Here's the first mission statement they wrote together.

George Middle School will provide a rigorous, relevant, and supportive educational experience to ensure that our students become independent, lifelong learners. We will be an excellent, inclusive, research-based school that utilizes technology, inquiry, integrated curriculum, and intensive professional development. We are a results-oriented, adaptable community devoted to increasing achievement and hope for diverse learners by setting high expectations as they discover themselves.

As the staff began to tackle the immediate emergency goal of getting out from under the federal sanctions, Beth sought out a variety of community partnerships to help them. She also fleshed out the details of her vision for using technology at George to engage and motivate low-achieving students, especially those with special needs. Soon the staff approved a revised and more focused mission:

1. To become a model school based on best practices where every child can be successful and safe.

2. To use educational technology to enhance teaching and learning; assist students with special needs; and provide direct instruction, differentiation, and acceleration.

3. To partner with community, education, government, and nonprofit organizations to provide academic and extended-day services to all students.

(Continued)

(Continued)

[NOTE: There are several important key words in this revised mission statement that communicate its academic focus: "every child can be successful," "direct instruction, differentiation, and acceleration." Beth and her faculty realized that it would be hard to measure "students as independent and lifelong learners." They could, however, measure student success quite readily as well as determine through observations whether students were receiving direct, differentiated, and accelerated instruction.]

Beth and her staff have developed and procured programs and opportunities to make her vision a reality. She reports, "We have an extended-day program for students that has won several national and state awards for its effectiveness; outside service providers, like Oregon State University, that bring resources into our school; a federal project health clinic; and a full-time afterschool principal who is supported by all of these organizations. We have well over 35 partnerships contributing money and services to our school."

The role of the principal is to help the staff see a future with hope and possibilities and then to commandeer resources and provide the instructional support to make it happen, as Beth has done. As one principal told me, "As a leader you have to be able to see what your school can become, and the picture has to be a detailed one. The thing that disappoints me about so many of my colleagues is that when you ask them to describe their vision for schools, they describe 'what is,' not 'what could be.' They aren't able to see beyond today" (McEwan, 2002, p. 49).

Figure 3.5   The "Do It Now" Focus at George Middle School

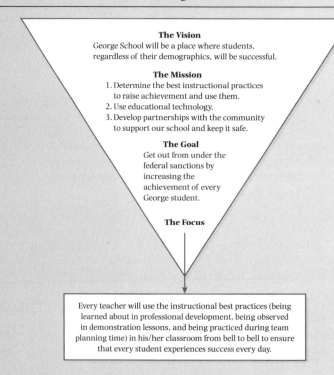

The Vision
George School will be a place where students, regardless of their demographics, will be successful.

The Mission
1. Determine the best instructional practices to raise achievement and use them.
2. Use educational technology.
3. Develop partnerships with the community to support our school and keep it safe.

The Goal
Get out from under the federal sanctions by increasing the achievement of every George student.

The Focus

Every teacher will use the instructional best practices (being learned about in professional development, being observed in demonstration lessons, and being practiced during team planning time) in his/her classroom from bell to bell to ensure that every student experiences success every day.

Reproduction of material from this book is authorized only for the local school site or nonprofit organization that has purchased *Ten Traits of Highly Effective Schools: Raising the Achievement Bar for All Students*, by Elaine K. McEwan. Thousand Oaks, CA: Corwin Press, www.corwinpress.com.

Beth's vision for George Middle School has become a reality in a very short period of time. Over the past three years, eighth-grade reading scores have moved steadily upward. The percentage of eighth-grade students who met or exceeded standards on the state assessment moved from 35% to 53% during the first year of Beth's tenure. In Year 2, 61% of eighth-grade students met or exceeded the standards. In Year 3, 74% of eighth-grade students met or exceeded the standards. Just three years after being placed under federal sanctions, George made the list of top 10 most-improved schools in the Metro Portland area. Figure 3.4 shows how Beth's vision guided the development of a mission and goals that ultimately provided the day-to-day academic focus. Form 3.3 is a template that can be adapted to develop a time line for the vision–mission–goals–academic focus in your classroom, school, or district.

Form 3.3   The "Do It Now" Template

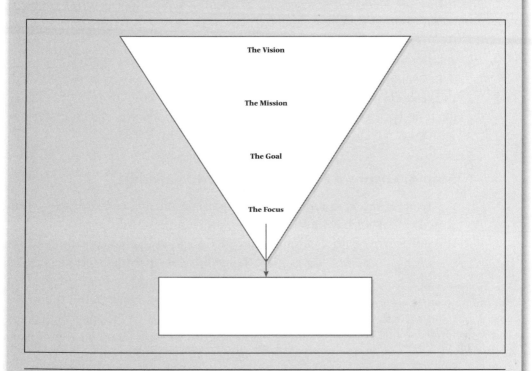

Copyright © 2009 by Corwin Press. All rights reserved. Reprinted from *Ten Traits of Highly Effective Schools: Raising the Achievement Bar for All Students*, by Elaine K. McEwan. Thousand Oaks, CA: Corwin Press, www.corwinpress.com. Reproduction authorized only for the local school site or nonprofit organization that has purchased this book.

Step 3: Set Goals That Are Measurable and Attainable

Goals are specific behavioral objectives that are measurable and attainable. Attainable goals are not slam-dunk easy ones, but neither are they so grandiose that teachers immediately scoff at their impossibility.

They are logical action steps that flow from the mission statement but are smaller and more manageable in scope. In a highly effective school, everyone should be working with a different set of goals related to their specific set of responsibilities, but the thread running through all of them is the academic focus, whether it is increased student learning, more effective teaching, success for all, mastery for all, or some other compelling emphasis. Many goals are a year long in duration, but short-term QuikStart goals that focus on an immediate need can often jump-start a team into taking a new look at their data and agreeing to a brief intervention by way of doing some action research.

An example of one team's 30-Minute/30-Day QuikStart Goal Meeting Agenda is shown in Figure 3.6. The process is designed to focus teacher teams on identifying a specific academic (teaching–learning) problem based on data they have colleted and then setting a 30-day goal to solve that problem. In this example, a ninth-grade math team brainstormed solutions to address the lack of student mastery of basic math skills. Once a goal had been selected and the key tasks to be completed were identified, the recorder filled out the Action Log, as shown in Figure 3.7, to ensure focus on their goal. Forms 3.4 and 3.5 are templates you can adapt for use with your own grade-level or content-area team.

Step 4: Ensure a Focus on Student Learning

Focus is the combination of discipline, intensity, concentration, and commitment with which groups or individuals tackle goals related to student learning. In a commentary in *Education Week* recounting strategies that helped the Cincinnati school system increase their four-year high school graduation rate from 51% in 2000 to 79% in 2007, their success was described in this way: "Having high goals and maintaining an intense focus on them, gave the city's reform efforts coherency and direction" (Nathan, 2008, p. 24). Focus, directed to doing the right things, can help you to raise the achievement bar in your classroom, school, or district.

> Mission starts with determining what you really care about and want to accomplish and committing yourself to it.
>
> —Garfield (1986, p. 96)

The elementary reading scores in the southeastern Washington district of Kennewick are proof of the power of a compelling mission and a sustained focus. In 1995, well in advance of NCLB, central office administrators and school board members envisioned a future in which 90% of their third-grade students (including all ELL and special education students) would read at or above grade level. When they launched their improvement initiative in the fall of 1995, only 58% of Kennewick's third graders were reading at or above grade level.

Figure 3.6   Sample QuikStart Goal-Meeting Agenda

Timekeeper: John   **Recorder:** Stan   **Facilitator:** Mary   **Date:** October 15

Purpose of the meeting: To figure out what the Ninth-Grade Math Team can do about the fact that so many students are failing their course midway through the semester.

Data used to present evidence of problem: First-quarter grades for all ninth-grade students; scores on the end of eighth-grade Math test given to all students.

What problem or problems do the data suggest? (4 minutes)

Students are failing our Math classes because they lack prerequisite skills. Some students had the prerequisite skills as shown on their eighth-grade tests, but they appear to have forgotten everything they learned. Some students never did learn the stuff and clearly aren't ready for ninth grade. Some students are so confused about what's going on that they haven't learned a single thing we've taught so far.

Generate as many probable causes for this problem as you can. (4 minutes)

The eighth-grade teachers didn't do a good job of teaching these kids. These kids just don't seem to have any passion for math at all. The ninth-grade teachers have been going way too fast without considering that without prerequisite skills, students won't get what's going on. The pacing guide is keeping us from achieving mastery.

Brainstorm possible solutions to this problem. (5 minutes)

List the best ideas from the brainstorming session. Describe how they could be measured. Set priorities based on which solutions are perceived to be most effective. (10 minutes)

Write a clear, measurable, attainable, and compelling goal for what your students should be able to do after your selected solution is implemented. (5 minutes)

All ninth-grade students will achieve at least a C grade in ninth-grade Math at the end of the first semester.

Choose Goal Manager, set meeting date, and complete Action Log. (2 minutes)

What Are the Best Ideas?	How Will Results Be Measured?	What Is the Likelihood of Success?
Review the prerequisite math skills on a daily basis while continuing to teach new material using John's Board Math format.	Formative assessment will be used to determine if failing students are improving in their mastery of prerequisite skills. We can borrow whiteboards from some other departments. ESL teachers have lots of extras. Weekly quizzes will demonstrate how well students are mastering new material.	**First Priority** If we can figure out which skills the kids don't know and use problems that relate to only those skills, there is a really good chance this might work. John has been using problems with his students and has a method that is working for him. He will give a demonstration lesson after school for all ninth-grade Math teachers and share his materials.

(Continued)

Figure 3.6 (Continued)

What Are the Best Ideas?	How Will Results Be Measured?	What Is the Likelihood of Success?
Hold afterschool tutoring sessions for the students who got really low scores on the eighth-grade test to catch them up.	Students will improve their scores on weekly class quizzes and demonstrate mastery of prerequisite skills during whiteboard assessments.	**Second Priority** This might not work since we have no way to make kids go to tutoring. Teachers offer help before and after school right now and nobody comes from the ninth-grade classes.
Form Math Teams in each class to compete against each other during review sessions.	Same as above.	**Third Priority** If every Math teacher did this so that when kids compare notes they won't complain, this would be good for a change of pace.

Team members present: John, Stan, Mary, Leslie, Susan, and Sam

Next team meeting: November 17 to share preliminary results and determine if we will continue to use recursive teaching in ninth-grade Math classes for the remainder of the semester.

Reproduction of material from this book is authorized only for the local school site or nonprofit organization that has purchased *Ten Traits of Highly Effective Schools: Raising the Achievement Bar for All Students*, by Elaine K. McEwan. Thousand Oaks, CA: Corwin Press, www.corwinpress.com.

To jump-start the initiative, the Kennewick district did the following: (1) installed data systems to measure student skills and identify targeted remediation, (2) increased expenditures to provide professional development related to reading and instruction, (3) increased direct instructional time based on how far behind students were, and (4) developed three programs targeting family and community engagement (National Children's Reading Foundation, 2007). Their compelling mission has driven continuous improvement for 13 years.

The number of third-grade students reading on or above grade level reached 90% in 2005 and maintained that level through the 2006–2007 school year. During this same period of time, the percentage of students receiving free and reduced-priced lunch or breakfast in the 13 elementary schools increased from 34.6% to 53%, and minority enrollment increased from 16.7% to 29.9%. In the spring of 2006, 8 of 13 elementary schools had 90% or more of their third graders at or above grade level and no school scored below 80% (Fielding, Kerr, & Rosier, 1998, 2004, 2007; N. Kerr, personal communication, July 7, 2007).

Figure 3.7   Sample Action Log

Activity	By Whom	By When	Resources	Completed
Let Clint know what happened at the meeting.	Stan	Call him tonight. 10/15		
John will teach a demonstration lesson on Board Math after school. He'll get some of his students to volunteer to stay.	John	10/16	Bring a video camera to tape the lesson so if people want to watch it again, they can.	
Make copies of the video for ninth-grade teachers who want one.	Stan	Copies will be handed out on Friday, 10/19.	Remember to pick up your video before you go home.	
Get the eighth-grade sample problems book and photocopy it for the team.	Mary	Get the copies made by the end of the week. 10/19	Sam has another resource book. Will give to Mary also.	
Get whiteboards and markers wherever they are.	John	Deliver to every teacher by Friday, 10/19.	Check with the ESL department. They have tons of them.	
Put together the problems for the coming week and get copies to team.	Leslie	Will be in teacher's boxes on Monday AM, 10/22.		
Everybody starts Board Math in all ninth-grade classes this week.	All teachers	10/22	Anybody who wants to watch John's Board Math lessons during the day is welcome to come during their free period. Bring donuts.	
Put together the problems for the second week.	Sam	Will be in mail boxes on Friday, 10/26.		
Problems for weeks 3–4.	Susan	Will be in mail boxes Friday, 11/2.		
Everybody gives quiz on standards kids were low on.	All teachers	Friday of fourth week; grade over weekend 11/9.		
Meeting to discuss results.	All teachers	Monday, 11/12		

Action Plan Manager _____

Reproduction of material from this book is authorized only for the local school site or nonprofit organization that has purchased *Ten Traits of Highly Effective Schools: Raising the Achievement Bar for All Students*, by Elaine K. McEwan. Thousand Oaks, CA: Corwin Press, www.corwinpress.com.

Form 3.4   30-Minute/30-Day QuikStart Goal-Setting Agenda

Timekeeper: _____ Recorder: _____ Facilitator: _____ Date: _____

Purpose of the meeting:

Data used to present evidence of problem:

What problem or problems do the data suggest? (4 minutes)

Generate as many probable causes for this problem as you can. (4 minutes)

Brainstorm possible solutions to this problem. (5 minutes)

List the best ideas from the brainstorming session. Describe how they could be measured. Set priorities based on which solutions are perceived to be most effective. (10 minutes)

Write a clear, measurable, attainable, and compelling goal for what your students should be able to do after your selected solution is implemented. (5 minutes)

Choose Goal Manager, set meeting date, and complete Action Log. (2 minutes)

What Are the Best Ideas?	How Will Results Be Measured?	What Is the Likelihood of Success?

Team members present:

Next team meeting:

Copyright © 2009 by Corwin Press. All rights reserved. Reprinted from *Ten Traits of Highly Effective Schools: Raising the Achievement Bar for All Students*, by Elaine K. McEwan. Thousand Oaks, CA: Corwin Press, www.corwinpress.com. Reproduction authorized only for the local school site or nonprofit organization that has purchased this book.

Form 3.5   Action Log

Activity	By Whom	By When	Resources	Completed

Action Plan Manager _____

Copyright © 2009 by Corwin Press. All rights reserved. Reprinted from *Ten Traits of Highly Effective Schools: Raising the Achievement Bar for All Students*, by Elaine K. McEwan. Thousand Oaks, CA: Corwin Press, www.corwinpress.com. Reproduction authorized only for the local school site or nonprofit organization that has purchased this book.

Greg Fancher, Kennewick's assistant superintendent of elementary education, explains the power of Kennewick's 1995 compelling mission:

> It was simple: 90% of third graders will read at or above grade level. We had a test to measure our achievement and that ensured direct accountability. In some schools or districts, mission statements and goals come and go, but we've had this goal for more than 10 years. Administrators and teachers know this goal is not going to go away. And it wasn't one of those impossible goals that people know will never be reached. Everyone knew that the board and the administration were serious. Now that we've reached the original 90% goal, the challenge is to keep our focus fresh because the demographics and readiness skills of our students are not dramatically improving every year. In essence, we are starting over every year. But we have set a standard and we know how to attain it.

How One Kennewick Principal Maintains an Academic Focus: Dave Montague, Principal, Washington Elementary School

I learned long ago that if I tell teachers that something is nonnegotiable and then fail to follow up and monitor, they will begin to think I didn't really mean what I said. So I am in classrooms every day, making sure our curriculum is being taught, the teachers are providing direct instruction, and appropriate amounts of time are allocated to various subjects. [NOTE: Dave's definition of direct instruction means that during the two-hour reading block, all students are instructed by a teacher during the entire time. Students spend no time during the reading block in centers or completing work independently at their desks. They are always engaged and interacting with a teacher or paraprofessional.] I know most of my teachers are on task but I also know there are a few people, who although excellent teachers overall, are prone to distraction. So I monitor.

I provide each teacher with a list of the things I am looking for when I visit them. This takes the guesswork out of my expectations. A principal cannot just make a pronouncement and then expect it to happen. You have to check and be willing to help teachers if they are having trouble in any area. We all behave a little differently when our supervisors are around (I know I do). Some people always do the right thing—others have to be reminded occasionally. That's my job. It isn't always easy to take the time to get into the classrooms, but it is one of the most important things I do. If I tell teachers that my priority is good instruction, my actions have to back up my words. If I expect my teachers to teach two hours of reading, then I have to make sure this time is sacred. I cannot tell them that this time is important and then schedule other things during reading instruction. It is my responsibility to make sure this two-hour time block is never interrupted. Sometimes I have to stand my ground when central office administrators, parents, or some worthy organization in the community wants part of this time block. My answer is always no! The culture here is that reading instruction is the most important thing we do, and nothing interrupts this time block. [NOTE: See the results of the academic focus Dave and his staff have maintained over the years in Figure 3.8. Also note that finding precisely the right combination of things to do took several years. The Washington staff might well have decided that the district's mission was an impossible one and changed their academic focus. But they persevered, with incredible results.]

Figure 3.8   Reading Achievement at Washington Elementary School, 1995–2007

Washington Elementary School

Kennewick School District

Kennewick, WA

Implementing Principal: David Montague

Third- and Fourth-Grade Reading Achievement

Year	Percentage of Third-Grade Students Reading At or Above Grade Level*	Percentage of Fourth-Grade Students Passing the Reading WASL**
1995–1996	72%	
1996–1997	72%	
1997–1998	68%	66%
1998–1999	78%	60%
1999–2000	94%	78%
2000–2001	96%	76%
2001–2002	99%	80%
2002–2003	94%	84%
2003–2004	98%	91%
2004–2005	99%	92%
2005–2006	98%	94%
2006–2007	95%	98%

SOURCE: Used with permission of David Montague.

NOTE: Between 1995 and 2007, the percentage of students receiving free and reduced-price lunch at Washington School increased from 46% to 57%.

*Third-grade students took the nationally normed MAP (Measurement of Academic Performance) Test. These scores were reported as part of the Board of Education 90% Reading Goal.

**Fourth-grade students began taking the Washington Assessment of Student Learning for the first time in 1997.

Reproduction of material from this book is authorized only for the local school site or nonprofit organization that has purchased *Ten Traits of Highly Effective Schools: Raising the Achievement Bar for All Students*, by Elaine K. McEwan. Thousand Oaks, CA: Corwin Press, www.corwinpress.com.

KNOWING THE RIGHT THINGS TO DO

Most instructional leaders can readily envision where they would like to be and can develop a suitable mission statement. However, knowing the right things to do in order to achieve that mission may not be easy. Sometimes

Knowing the right thing to do is the central problem of school improvement.

—Elmore (2003, p. 9)

educators can be working very hard on all the wrong things. I once was an unwitting participant in doing the wrong thing. I was hired by a grant-driven consortium to provide training for middle school teachers in strategic reading in the content areas. I was intrigued with the compelling vision and mission articulated by the consortium director, and in my naiveté, I neglected to ask some critical questions about the leadership and culture of the school in which I would be working. During my first day there, I sensed problems immediately, not the least of which was the principal.

When I met with the first team of teachers early in the day to talk about strategic reading, the teachers were distracted and some were downright hostile. Based on my marching orders from the director, I had planned to talk about reading, but I soon realized that the consortium's plan wasn't the right thing to do. Instead I decided to use the Force Field Analysis Process to identify the restraining forces that were interfering with teaching and learning. (A sample form from another school is shown at the end of the chapter, in Figure 3.10.)

During the process, individuals complete their own forms and then gather in small groups of three or four to merge their lists. This step ensures that no one individual will be singled out for contributing a particularly controversial item. I discovered that the teachers were overwhelmed with the lack of a coordinated approach to student behavior problems, frustrated by nagging classroom management issues, and demoralized by poor communication and other classroom climate concerns. The two other grade-level teams identified the same issues. The consortium was working on the wrong goal, and so was I. [NOTE: This school is an example of a phenomenon identified by the International School Effectiveness Project and noted in the Introduction: Ineffective lower-SES schools may have to devote more time and energy to putting baseline systems in place before resources can be fully devoted to bringing about instructional improvement.]

The Force Field Analysis Process is an ideal tool for identifying problems that teachers believe are standing in the way of teaching and learning. When teachers feel powerless to deal with issues of culture and climate, they will drop out mentally and even physically, taking mental health days or actually becoming ill. When teachers are distracted by behavioral, organizational, and communication issues, they are often unable to focus on instructional problems. My rule of thumb is to concentrate on changing the things you have the power to change and begin with the biggest roadblock to teaching and learning. All of the problems don't have to be completely resolved to move on, but unless teachers see commitment and progress on critical climate issues, they will be unable to fully focus on teaching and learning. Figure 3.9 shows a sample Force Field Analysis, and Form 3.6 contains a blank Force Field Analysis form.

> To increase student learning, approach it directly, and bring the energy of everyone in the school or district to bear on the effort.
>
> —*Joyce & Showers*
> *(1995, p. 5)*

Northbrook Middle School principal Laura Schuhmann describes the importance of figuring out the right thing to do and then not becoming distracted from focusing on it. Laura has led her school from an Academically Acceptable rating to Recognized over a period of five years. As an assistant principal, she was dropped into the principalship almost overnight after her principal's sudden death. Although she had a vision for what she wanted to see happen, figuring out the right things to do took some time. She says, "As a Title I school, we qualified for every single grant and opportunity in the world. I had to say 'no' to quite a few things so we could stay focused on teaching kids.

"When people ask me how we achieved a Recognized rating, I have to say, 'It's not a simple answer. There are a lot of layers.' But in particular, I have kept people focused on what's important: teaching and learning. If you can do a few things well, you will see improvement in student learning.

Figure 3.9   Sample Force Field Analysis

Mission: To raise the achievement bar at Springwood School	
Facilitating Forces	*Restraining Forces*
Dedicated, caring, hardworking, and knowledgeable faculty	Too many students below grade level when they enroll at our school
Resources to provide staff development	Staff members who are negative and critical
Core group of high-achieving students and parents	Lack of respect for younger teachers
	Low expectations regarding what we can realistically accomplish with low-achieving students
	Discouraged and exhausted teachers
	Lack of affirmation and praise for our hard work
	Too much interference from central office

Reproduction of material from this book is authorized only for the local school site or nonprofit organization that has purchased *Ten Traits of Highly Effective Schools: Raising the Achievement Bar for All Students,* by Elaine K. McEwan. Thousand Oaks, CA: Corwin Press, www.corwinpress.com.

Form 3.6   Force Field Analysis

Copyright © 2009 by Corwin Press. All rights reserved. Reprinted from *Ten Traits of Highly Effective Schools: Raising the Achievement Bar for All Students,* by Elaine K. McEwan. Thousand Oaks, CA: Corwin Press, www.corwinpress.com. Reproduction authorized only for the local school site or nonprofit organization that has purchased this book.

We have a very strong focus on the quality of teaching in the classroom. We have trained all of our teachers in the Madeline Hunter model. Many of our teachers have come to us through alternative certification, and Hunter's work provides a common language and gives teachers tools to plan lessons and manage their classrooms. When I stopped focusing on operational things and we began discussing instruction, things began to change more quickly. Then when we put the data piece in place and began looking at the results of the benchmarks and the TAKS assessment, we began making incredible growth on a yearly basis from about 2001. The only blip on the radar screen of improvement was the year we took in evacuee students from Hurricane Katrina. That was a huge challenge for all of us." Figure 3.10 shows Northbrook's achievement trajectory.

Elementary principal Kathie Dobberteen also spent a fair bit of time early in her first principalship figuring out the right things to do. However, when she finally discovered them, she and her staff became intensely focused. She explains the process they went through: "When I came to my school, it was a typical elementary school staffed by caring teachers who believed that the low socioeconomic status of their students automatically dictated low achievement. Although we knew that change was needed, we grasped at everything new. We focused on multicultural education for a time to build acceptance for our culturally diverse population. Then we emphasized conflict resolution to minimize disciplinary issues in the hope that students would become more self-reliant and take ownership of their learning. None of these programs had any impact on student achievement. Then through several district-level initiatives, we began to look at data and its disaggregation as a means to improve every area of curriculum and instruction. Our program used to be defined by a teacher's favorite theme or area of instructional expertise. Now we are focused on standards combined with effective instruction to ensure that students meet the standards." Kathie's school was the recipient of several awards for their achievement. How did they do it? With a consistent and persistent academic focus.

SUMMING UP

Academic focus is the most underappreciated and overlooked trait of highly effective schools. Focus is difficult to observe behaviorally, but there is a very quick litmus test: Ask the principal, a handful of teachers, and a small group of students to describe their goals for the school year. If all of these individuals aren't working on the same goals (albeit at different levels of responsibility and difficulty), the school lacks focus. Everyone is doing their own thing.

Figure 3.10   Percentage of Students Passing the Texas Assessment of Knowledge and
Skills, Northbrook Middle School

Northbrook Middle School
Spring Branch Independent School District
Spring Branch, TX
Implementing Principal: Laura Schuhmann

Year	*Percentage of Students Passing Reading, Grades 6–8*	*Percentage of Students Passing, Math, Grades 6–8*	*Rating*
2002–2003	60	46	Academically Acceptable
2003–2004	80	67	Academically Acceptable
2004–2005	83	72	Academically Acceptable
2005–2006*	72	63	Academically Acceptable
2006–2007	85	82	Recognized

SOURCE: Used with permission of Laura Schuhmann.

NOTE: Of Northbrook's students, 92% are Hispanic and slightly more than 90% are economically disadvantaged.

The Texas Accountability System currently has four tiers: Exemplary, Recognized, Academically Acceptable, and Academically Unacceptable. To receive an Exemplary rating, schools are required to have at least a 90% passing rate on the reading, writing, and math assessments. In addition, 90% of each ethnic group and 90% of economically disadvantaged students must pass the test. To receive a Recognized rating, schools must achieve a passing rate of 80% to 89%.

Academically Acceptable schools have a 50% to 79% passing rate. Schools below 50% are considered Academically Unacceptable.

The achievement level to receive an Academically Acceptable rating increased 10 percentage points in 2006 to 60% for Reading/ELA, Writing, and Social Studies; 40% for Mathematics; and 35% for Science. For 2007, the standards increase by five points for all subjects to 65% for Reading/ELA, Writing, and Social Studies; to 45% for Mathematics; and to 40% for Science.

In 2008, the Academically Acceptable standards increase by five percentage points for Mathematics and Science. In 2009, the Academically Acceptable standards increase by five percentage points for all subjects (Texas Education Agency, 2007).

*Northbrook enrolled 80 evacuee students from Hurricanes Katrina and Rita. The academic focus was temporarily diverted to dealing with discipline issues.

Reproduction of material from this book is authorized only for the local school site or nonprofit organization that has purchased *Ten Traits of Highly Effective Schools: Raising the Achievement Bar for All Students*, by Elaine K. McEwan. Thousand Oaks, CA: Corwin Press, www.corwinpress.com.

WHAT'S AHEAD?

In the next chapter, we consider the fourth trait of highly effective schools: relational trust. While the four components of relational trust (personal regard, competence, respect, and integrity) cannot compensate for a lack of academic focus, improving schools without high levels of trust between and among administrators, staff, students, and parents is impossible.

Relational Trust

*A broad base of trust across a school community lubricates much of
a school's day-to-day functioning and is a critical resource as local
leaders embark on ambitious improvement plans.*

—Bryk and Schneider (2002, p. 5)

The fourth trait of highly effective schools is *relational trust*, and it is
the basis for positive relationships in the school community. Some
refer to it as the glue that holds a school together; others call it the lubri-
cant that makes everything in the school run smoothly. In order for relational trust to be strong, there must be high levels of respect and regard
between and among four groups of people: administrators, teachers,
parents, and students.

As a teacher, I gave my fifth graders a questionnaire asking them to
name one classmate they would choose to work with in a group and
another classmate they would like to have on their team at recess. I used
that information to develop a sociogram—a graphic organizer with circles
representing the students and arrows showing who picked whom for a
friend or a team member. The information helped me to develop working
groups in the classroom as well as to let me know who needed extra
encouragement and support to become a part of the class. The relationship web in a school community is far more complex than in a class of 25
students, but the underlying principle is the same: When members of a

> The glue that holds all relationships together—including the relationship between the leader and the led—is trust, and trust is based on integrity.
>
> —*Brian Tracy (2007)*

group get along with each other and respect one another, the group achieves more.

The first thing I noticed when I became the principal of Lincoln School was that some of the staff members didn't seem to like me nor did they care what I thought about them. A few didn't even bother to stop in at the office to meet me before school started. It took a little while for me to figure out what was going on, but it soon became apparent: They weren't sure if they could trust me. They were reserving judgment until they had seen me in action and weren't about to give me the benefit of the doubt. I was from out of town, had a brand-new fancy degree, and was a woman. The district had never had a female principal before. My demographics were immediate grounds for distrust.

I also found out that some of the teachers had little personal regard for the competence of either parents or students. They made sure I knew not to expect students to learn or expect their parents to care about their failure. Some teachers had an especially low regard for parents who didn't speak English. The teachers also let me know in a very direct way that the achievement bar was low for a reason, and if I was thinking about raising it, to forget about it. It couldn't be done.

On the flip side, there were quite a few parents who didn't trust some of the teachers—they felt they weren't competent and wanted to make sure that I didn't place their children with those teachers for the school year. They also made sure I realized that some of the staff members had very little respect for either parents or students.

Early in the school year, this mutual lack of respect between teachers and students erupted into a horrifying incident in which three sixth-grade students verbally attacked their teacher by spray-painting obscene statements about her on the red brick walls of the building that faced their classroom windows. It was depressing to see physical evidence of the toxic culture that existed in this school. I was already deeply concerned about this teacher. There had been multiple reports from students about both physical and verbal abuse in her classroom, and during the time I spent in the classroom, there was no evidence of either teaching or learning. At the time, I could not have articulated exactly what was at the heart of the problems in the school, but now I know with certainty: There was a complete absence of relational trust between and among all members of the community. If I had done a sociogram of Lincoln School, there would have been hundreds of circles and very few arrows.

THE ROLE OF RELATIONAL TRUST IN IMPROVING SCHOOLS

The research of Anthony Bryk and Barbara Schneider (2002) confirms the impossibility of improving schools without the presence of relational trust. They concluded, as a result of extensive case studies and survey analyses in 12 Chicago public schools undergoing reform, that trust was a core resource, essential for turning schools around. Although I did not frame the problem at Lincoln School as a lack of trust, I did know that unless we all started working together as a team—principal, teachers, parents, and students—there was little likelihood of turning the school around.

In addition to marked improvements in academic productivity, researchers also cited the following benefits of trust:

- Collective decision making with broad teacher buy-in occurs more readily in schools with strong relational trust.
- When relational trust is strong, change and improvement are likely to be firmly supported by school participants and to be diffused broadly across the school.
- Relational trust generates a moral imperative to take on the hard work of school improvement—doing more and working longer hours without regard for the job description or the contract (Bryk & Schneider, 2002, pp. 122–123).

THE COMPONENTS OF RELATIONAL TRUST

Relational trust, as described and measured by Bryk and Schneider (2002), is a construct composed of four concepts: (1) respect, (2) competence, (3) personal regard, and (4) integrity.

Respect

Respect is the deference someone shows to others without regard for their political position, wealth, job role, or power. For example, when the principal and teachers treat parents, regardless of their social or economic status, the same way they treat school board members or the superintendent, parents are indeed respected at the school. School personnel are willing to listen intently to them and empathize with their problems. They do not insist that parents make appointments days in advance and are willing to interrupt sitting in their closed-door office with paperwork to make time to see parents. Parents are assumed to love their children and to be doing the best they know how to do for them until there is solid evidence to the contrary. Therefore, even when parents do not get what they want (a new teacher for their child, forgiveness of an afterschool detention, or a change of a report card grade), they feel as though their opinions were recognized as valid and that they have been treated with fairness. Parents are highly sensitive to micro-inequities, subtle slights of verbal and nonverbal communication that result from an imbalance of power between two people (e.g., principal and parent or teacher and parent; Rowe, 1990). Examples include fidgeting, not maintaining eye contact, looking right through someone, talking to someone else as though the individual isn't present, interrupting, furrowing one's brow, and ignoring what someone has said.

Competence

Competence is the ability to do something in a superior way, for example, the ability to teach previously low-achieving students and bring them to mastery, the ability to keep the cafeteria running smoothly day after day in a caring and organized way, or the ability to fix a 100-year-old boiler whenever it breaks down. All of the stakeholders in a school community want to be surrounded by competent, intelligent, supportive individuals. Parents want their children to do well in school, and they desire the very best teachers. Teachers want supportive working conditions and value their administrator's allegiance and respect for their craft. The principal wants good community relations that are a natural spin-off of having competent teachers and satisfied parents.

Personal Regard

Personal regard is the presence of positive feelings toward someone. When individuals like each other, they enjoy being together. However, personal regard goes beyond just liking people. It includes a willingness to extend or even inconvenience oneself. For example, in the case of teachers, if they have high regard for parents, they are inclined to stay late for a quick parent conference, tutor children during a free period, or make phone calls to parents from their homes in the evening. Principals may demonstrate their personal regard in other ways—making a trip to the office supply store to buy something that one teacher needs for a project or taking the lunch supervisor's shift so she can go to her child's school to meet with a teacher there.

Integrity

Integrity refers to an individual's adherence to certain moral principles and standards. Integrity also speaks to a level of consistency and reliability in people's behavior. When they promise to do something, it happens. Individuals with integrity are often described as having character.

Consider how trust can be undermined or even destroyed in just one aspect of school life, the chain of events that can rapidly unfold when the members of the school community do not trust each other to do their jobs; they do not trust the competence of other members of the community. If the stakeholders in a school do not trust one another to fulfill their role obligations, there is a strong likelihood that everyone will suffer, but most of all it will be the students. For example, if teachers don't believe that students are competent to achieve the grade-level standards, low expectations create a trust issue that in turn further depresses achievement. Parents who don't feel that the teachers in a school are competent to teach their children become distrustful and in turn communicate this distrust to their offspring who in turn become discipline problems. Educators who believe that parents aren't competent to parent their offspring and communicate this lack of trust in both spoken and unspoken ways create angry and hostile parents. Teachers who don't believe their teammates are competent to teach become demoralized about the extra work they must put forth to take up the slack. Teachers who don't believe their principal is competent to lead are unlikely to expend the extra energy it takes to raise achievement in a low-performing school.

A high level of relational trust between and among students and teachers, teachers and their colleagues, and teachers and administrators is essential to achieving any one of the many compelling missions a school might choose to achieve: creating a school that is equitable and excellent, raising student achievement, reducing the drop-out rate, or becoming a highly rated school by the standards of some external criteria. Relational trust impacts student motivation and engagement that are in turn positively associated with the following: (1) student achievement and behavior in school, regardless of socioeconomic status (Arhar & Kromrey, 1993; Connell & Wellborn, 1991; Finn, 1989, 1993; Mounts & Steinberg, 1995), (2) higher grades and test scores (Goodenow, 1993; Willingham et al., 2002), and (3) lower drop-out rates (Connell, Halpern-Felsher, Clifford, Crichlow, & Usinger, 1995; Croninger & Lee, 2001). The improvement process is interactive, but it can begin only when relational trust levels begin to rise.

Dr. Michelle Gayle, former principal at Griffin Middle School in Tallahassee, Florida, and now Divisional Director of Curriculum and Instruction in the Leon County Schools, reminds us of the critical importance of relationships:

> Relationships can make the difference between a troubled child exceeding expectations or floundering in an abysmal future. Relationships allow faculty and staff to work cooperatively to realize the vision that has been set into place. Relationships encourage parents and other stakeholders to become real contributors to the success of the school. Relationships give students confidence to reach out to each other, to agree to disagree, and to share those prolific ideas that will indeed change the world. Relationships are the adhesive of school improvement.

Improving trust levels in a toxic school culture is a difficult and long-term undertaking, one that may take several years. Only persons of strong moral fiber need apply to lead and teach. When a toxic school culture has taken root in the context of a corrupt and politicized system, improving trust levels may require a complete reorganization of the system as well as the school.

Building Trust and Academic Capacity

From the moment you step into Bowman School, you can sense that everyone knows what they are about and everyone believes they can do it. You don't hear those sidebar conversations blaming the kids and the neighborhood. If someone does or says something inappropriate, it is quickly dealt with by a stern look from a peer. The culture at Bowman is the result of leadership from the principal and teachers, a process of the school coming together.

—Diana Levy, Director of Professional Development,
Hayward Unified School District, CA

Bowman Elementary School in the Hayward Unified School District enrolls between 500 and 600 students. Seventy-five percent receive free and reduced-price lunch, and in addition to Spanish, a variety of other cultures and languages are represented in the student body. Building trust among the various constituencies at Bowman was a high priority at the beginning of Betty Ward's 10-year tenure as the principal of Bowman. Recently retired, Betty credits her 10 Commandments and what she calls the climate meetings, which accompanied serious or chronic behavior problems, with building a high level of relational trust between her, the teachers, the students, and their parents. Bowman's 10 Commandments are not carved in stone like the original version but are written in English and Spanish, one poster for each rule, illustrated with easy-to-understand drawings, and displayed in prominent places around the school.

Betty explains, "These 10 basic rules provide structure and boundaries for student behavior in our Bowman community." Breaking any of the first three rules (involvement with objects used as weapons, hitting and hurting others, or serious defiance) is an automatic *in-school* suspension. The faculty agreed that rather than requiring students to be sent home for serious infractions, they would be collectively responsible for having suspended students from other classrooms sent to their classrooms to serve in-school suspensions. This decision sends a message to students and parents that Bowman teachers believe all of their students should be in school every day, even if they have an occasional bad day. Having an alternative placement allows the student, the classmates, and the teacher a cooling-off period following a serious incident.

At this point in the disciplinary process, Bowman's policies differ from many schools. Suspended students are not permitted to return to their home classroom until they and their parents have attended what is called a *climate meeting*. Climate meetings are held for students who break one of the three aforementioned rules or have received a "red" slip after getting three "pink slips" because of lesser infractions. Bowman's climate meetings are quite different from the typical parent meeting with school officials before a formally suspended student is readmitted.

Here's how a climate meeting works. Based on the belief that parents will respond more favorably to their child's classroom teacher with whom they have developed a positive relationship, this teacher usually contacts the parents to schedule the climate meeting. The meeting is held in the child's classroom. The teacher arranges chairs in a circle ahead of time and is the chairperson of the meeting. If someone other than the classroom teacher issued the red slip, the classroom teacher and this adult confer prior to the meeting so that the adult can brief the classroom teacher regarding the facts and the sequence of events in the situation. This adult, whether another teacher or classified staff member, attends the climate meeting if at all possible and often shares an eyewitness account if the student can't remember or changes the original story.

The meeting begins with the classroom teacher asking the attendees to give their names and describe their roles (e.g., third-grade teacher, parent, P.E. teacher) followed by a description by the teacher of the rule that was broken (pointing to it on the poster that hangs on the wall of every Bowman classroom) and then asking the student to share what he or she did that was unacceptable at Bowman School. The classroom teacher often asks follow-up questions to clarify the student's actions, and then asks the student what he or she could have done differently and what he or she can do next time. At this point, other teachers often ask questions that lead the student to think of more options and offer their support and encouragement. Betty reports, "We don't usually need to raise hands; it just seems to flow."

For example, one of the student's former teachers might say, "When you were a third-grade student in my class, I remember how you demonstrated self-control to avoid fights. Are you still using 'I messages' to let others know how you are feeling?" Another teacher might ask, "If you find that playing basketball leads you to get angry, what other activities could you do at recess? I am on duty this week at the morning

(Continued)

(Continued)

recess. Please come to me if you need any help." Another teacher might say, "It seems like writing a letter of apology might be an important thing to do."

The classroom teacher then summarizes the student's plan for changing his or her behavior, states any consequences (e.g., speaking to a lower-grade class about the importance of never bringing weapons of any kind to school, writing a letter of apology, or signing up to take conflict management training), reminds the student of the support expressed by the adults present, and thanks everyone for coming. As attendees are leaving, the classroom teacher, the parent, and the student often talk informally together.

Betty reports that at climate meetings, students are encouraged and supported, the teacher who hosted the meeting feels supported by the administrator and fellow teachers, and parents report feeling that the whole school community is supporting them and their children. Translators are always available for parents who do not speak English. She says, "Favoritism is deadly. Parents have seen that year after year there is a sense of fairness in climate meetings. Teachers are sincere and dedicated to maintaining a climate of trust based on mutual respect."

Trust levels began to rise soon after the system was put into place. Betty says, "We all committed ourselves, day in and day out, to make this behavior system work, and we began to see the fruit of our labors. The process of successfully working together on student behavior empowered us to take on other challenges and gave us the energy to go 'above and beyond.' Through the years, increasing levels of trust enabled all of us to bring our personal creative ideas, as well as the best practices we had observed or read about, to the staff. As a group we actively listened to the ideas of others, learned more and collectively chose those we would embrace. This led to implementing a variety of research-based best practices in reading and writing. We were all transformed by the students' success that resulted from our efforts."

Betty adds, "When I learned about a Formula for Success (FFS) training at the county office, it was natural to go to a meeting with several staff members to hear the speakers and to see if this would become our next step. When we came back and shared this learning model with the whole staff, they eagerly agreed, 'We've got to participate. Let's apply.'"

As a result of Bowman's participation in the FFS program, Betty and her staff received training and coaching from Dale Skinner. Putting his strategies to work in a school with already high levels of relational trust made for a winning combination. The Bowman teachers under Betty's strong instructional leadership raised the school's Academic Performance Index (API) from 651 in 2003–2004 to 764 in 2005–2006, just before Betty's retirement. [NOTE: The California Accountability System gives schools yearly growth targets for various subgroups of students. After their first year of implementation, Bowman exceeded their growth target of 6 points for Hispanic-Latino Students by 94. The 193 students in this subgroup jumped from 618 in 2003 to 718 in 2004–2005. The following year, the school exceeded their growth target of 2 points for Hispanic-Latino Students by 21, achieving an API rating of 741. The school as a whole moved from an API rating of 651 in 2003–2004 to 764 in 2005–2006, astonishing results when compared to the growth targets.] See Figure 4.1 for Bowman's other ratings.

> The cause of almost all relationship difficulties is rooted in ambiguous, conflicting expectations around roles and goals.
>
> —*Covey (1989, p. 194)*

Figure 4.1   Academic Performance Index, 2003–2007: Bowman Elementary School

Bowman Elementary School

Hayward Unified School District

Alameda County, CA

Implementing Principal: Betty Ward

First Year of FFS: 2004–2005

Group	Number of Students	2003–2004 API	2004–2005 Growth Target	2004–2005 Actual Growth	2004–2005 API
Total Students Tested	320	651	7	85	736
Hispanic-Latino	193	618	6	100	718
Economically Disadvantaged	222	625	6	94	719

Group	Number of Students	2004–2005 API	2004–2005 Growth Target	2006–2006 Actual Growth	2005–2006 API
Total Students Tested	328	736	3	28	764
Hispanic-Latino	212	718	2	23	741
Economically Disadvantaged	242	719	2	28	747

SOURCE: California Department of Education.

Reproduction of material from this book is authorized only for the local school site or nonprofit organization that has purchased *Ten Traits of Highly Effective Schools: Raising the Achievement Bar for All Students*, by Elaine K. McEwan. Thousand Oaks, CA: Corwin Press, www.corwinpress.com.

BUILDING RELATIONAL TRUST

The rules that govern how people behave, treat one another, and solve difficult problems in a school are often unwritten, creating multiple possibilities for misunderstanding, conflict, and distrust. In a toxic school culture, these unwritten or unspoken rules protect the status quo and perpetuate negative attitudes and behaviors. Those of us who have facilitated improvement or been part of a total turnaround in a low-performing school know that eventually things will get better, but that in the beginning, "leaders must settle for far less than universal affection. They must

> Relational trust is not something that can be achieved simply through some workshop, retreat, or form of sensitivity training, although all of these can be helpful. Rather, relational trust is forged in daily social exchanges.
>
> —*Bryk and Schneider*
> *(2002, p. 136)*

accept conflict. They must be able and willing to be unloved" (Burns, 1978, p. 34).

Dale Skinner exemplifies the mindset that Pritchett and Pound (1993) describe in their book *High Velocity Culture Change:* "Attempts at incremental change—'tweaking' the culture—ordinarily die for lack of energy. If you try to go slow, bureaucracy and resistance to change will cancel out your efforts. So get radical" (p. 6). The ability to build relational trust while destabilizing a school culture that is set in its ineffective ways or totally toxic is dependent on several variables: (1) the presence of unqualified support from central office that slightly intimidates the most negative staff members into a certain level of compliance; (2) freedom to make bold moves and do things that have never been done before with only minimal sanctions from supervisors (i.e., the "ask for forgiveness, not permission" approach); (3) a mission that is so compelling that it cannot be ignored, even by a strongly distrustful segment of the faculty; and 4) a passion for students and their success combined with certainty on the part of the leader that the initiative will get results.

Here is how Dale describes his trust-building experience at Villarreal:

> Trust is best earned when teachers can first develop trust in the worth of a vitally important, clearly defined mission. When this occurs, the team can pull together. We are all dependent on each other, and nobody cares who gets the credit when we succeed. I am extremely loyal to dedicated teachers who fight for their kids. I tell them not to be afraid of getting in trouble with a parent, student, or central office. I let them know that I will completely support them if their actions are anywhere in the general ballpark of reasonable. They know they can trust me for all professional matters. I will be there when it counts.

Dale is brutally honest, however, about the challenges of asking people to work harder than they have ever worked in the past:

> During my first year at Villarreal, half of the teachers hated me while the other half loved me. The good teachers worked with enthusiastic passion and delivered a focused effort. The rest did what I asked because they were a little afraid of me. The teachers were told by the superintendent who hired me that at the end of the year that they would be allowed to transfer if they did not like the changes I made. However, two left in October. By the end of the

year, I had to replace 40% of the teachers. Those who left loudly predicted that the Exemplary status we achieved during the first year would collapse.

The school sustained an Exemplary Rating through the spring of 2003 when Dale retired.

The level of trust that a teacher has in a principal depends to a great extent on the principal's competence. Dale's instructional competence helped him to build trust at Villarreal almost immediately. Here's how Louise Sekula describes the process:

> I initially trusted Dale because of his track record. We were aware of the success he had experienced in a school very similar to ours. Personally, it was something I had wanted for our school for a long time, and I felt that he knew how to make it happen. The first time I talked to him, he told me he had a plan to make us successful in just one year, and I believed him from day one. In addition, I saw firsthand Dale's incredible work ethic. It was obvious from the start that he had a specific plan in mind, and he worked every minute of every day putting that plan in place. There are always "brainstormers" around, but unless you put the work in behind all of that brainstorming, there isn't going to be much production. Dale sees his vision so clearly that he doesn't need to spend much time thinking about it. He gets right to doing it.

One way to begin building trust is by establishing a Code of Ethics, a document jointly developed by the teachers and principal that formalizes "the rules or standards governing the conduct of a person or the conduct of the members of a profession"—in this case, teaching. Cathie West has been the new principal in multiple schools during her administrative career. Whenever she takes a new job, she takes along the Code of the Ethics developed by her former staff and uses it in a group process to nurture positive and professional staff behaviors and attitudes that ultimately build trust.

The Code of Ethics from her current school, Mountain Way Elementary School (WA), is shown in Figure 4.2. The process takes between 60 to 90 minutes. The staff is divided into small groups, each group receiving an envelope filled with strips of paper containing the statements from Figure 4.2. Each group is asked to read and discuss the behavioral expectations on the paper strips and decide if they want the statement to be part of their Code of Ethics. They can accept it as written, edit it to change the meaning, or eliminate the statement completely. Each group submits its work, and the principal collates it and brings it back to the faculty for final approval.

Figure 4.2   Sample Staff Code of Ethics

Mountain Way Elementary School

STAFF CODE OF ETHICS

Cathie West, Principal

The Mountain Way Elementary School Staff will build and maintain respectful, cooperative, and professional relationships by exhibiting the following attitudes and behaviors.

Interpersonal Relations

Speaking positively about each other and remaining loyal to our school family

Trusting and respecting each other and accommodating diverse personalities, teaching styles, and opinions

Recognizing that each staff member brings an educational background, professional experience, and compilation of life skills that are unique and valuable to our school

Modeling forgiveness by letting go of past hurts and working actively to build and maintain healthy relationships

Practicing positive decision making through nondivisive strategies, compromise, and respect for different points of view

Climate

Demonstrating that every job is important and that every person deserves recognition and respect

Looking for humor and laughing a lot

Professional Growth

Supporting each other's professional growth through such means as mentoring, peer coaching, and collaborative planning

Improving instruction throughout the school by sharing innovative instructional activities, strategies, and materials

Communications

Increasing communication between individuals and groups of staff members through professional and social activities

Respecting confidentiality in our communications as they pertain to students, parents, and staff

Using face-to-face communication and conflict resolution strategies, such as giving "I" messages, when concerns arise

Agreeing to disagree when there are differences that can't be resolved

Using conflict mediation strategies—including the option of using facilitators—to clear up misunderstandings and resolve conflicts

Keeping open lines of communication between individuals and groups of staff members

Being professional in dress, demeanor, actions, and verbal and written communications

Decision Making

Seeking input from pertinent staff members regarding decisions that affect those members or the faculty as a whole (e.g., major curriculum changes)

Using nondivisive strategies to enhance positive decision making (e.g., decision by consensus, surveys, troubleshooting committees)

Making every effort to reach acceptable compromises and avoiding decisions that divide the staff by giving ample time for discussion so that consensus can be reached

School Operations

Observing schedules and giving advance notice of schedule changes (e.g., arriving on time for events, vacating shared spaces punctually)

Respecting staff members' property (e.g., asking before borrowing; leaving a note when taking items from the office, library, or staff rooms; returning borrowed items in good condition)

Showing consideration for classroom space and noise levels (e.g., keeping music volume down, refraining from interrupting each other's class time, moving students through halls and shared areas quietly, and keeping family members, especially young children, from invading another's work spaces)

SOURCE: Reprinted by permission of Cathie West.

Reproduction of material from this book is authorized only for the local school site or nonprofit organization that has purchased *Ten Traits of Highly Effective Schools: Raising the Achievement Bar for All Students,* by Elaine K. McEwan. Thousand Oaks, CA: Corwin Press, www.corwinpress.com.

Any group process that enables teachers to talk about sensitive issues in a structured setting is beneficial to building trust. During the process of rebuilding and renewing the culture of Lincoln School during the early 1980s, the staff and I developed a set of standards or expectations for teachers. We had previously developed academic and behavioral standards for students that we planned to publish for parents. However, the teachers were eager to also include a set of standards for parents and I agreed, but only if they would also develop a set of behavioral standards for themselves. The process was a lengthy and sometimes contentious one, but it was essential to talk about, write down, reach consensus, and then individually sign off on the document. The teachers took the process very seriously and realized that by giving a copy of these expectations to parents, they were in essence agreeing to be held responsible for them. They wanted to make certain that every word was parsed to its precise meaning. The following list of expectations represented a quantum leap in our school's culture (McEwan, 2002, p. 96):

- State clear expectations and desired outcomes for students.
- Communicate classroom and school rules to students and parents.
- Hold students accountable for following school rules and completing assignments.
- Provide quality instruction for students.
- Maintain discipline and control in the classroom.
- Provide a classroom environment conducive to learning.
- Evaluate and communicate student progress to parents and students.
- Present a positive role model to students and have neat personal habits.

As I review this list, now nearly 25 years old, I remember exactly why certain issues were spelled out so explicitly. There were some faculty members who failed to hold students accountable, one faculty member who wasn't always a positive role model, and a few whose classrooms were focused on activity rather than achievement. This document didn't turn around our school on its own, but its development served as a crucial tipping point in sending the message that expectations for teachers had just been notched up by the entire faculty. My role as the school leader was to deal positively and forthrightly with the inevitable conflict that came from confronting those individuals who were not willing or able to rise to these shared expectations. Bryk and Schneider (2002) point out, "Principals must be prepared to engage conflict in order to advance reform. Yet they also need social support and trust from a solid core of the faculty if reform is to have a chance of succeeding" (p. 73).

The process of developing a set of teacher standards gave me the leverage and trust I needed to engage conflict, knowing I had a leadership team that realized our achievement goal would never be fully realized until the professionalism of their colleagues rose to a higher level.

While trust-building processes and long-term initiatives to build relational trust are often needed, the majority of trust-building activities take only minutes. In a school where relational trust has all but disappeared, there is only one individual who can lead the way to rebuilding it—an instructional leader. Trust cannot be mandated by a memo. Trust is built only through dozens of positive daily interactions: accepting, listening, empathizing, smiling, nodding, touching, praising, forgiving, apologizing, helping, and giving are the building blocks of relational trust. Figure 4.3 contains a set of 16 indicators of relational trust in a school.

My fellow Corwin Press author, Robert Ramsey (2003), includes the following Seven Step Code of Communication in his book *School Leadership From A to Z*. It could also be called the Seven Steps to Building Relational Trust.

1. Say only what's true.

2. Say what needs to be said.

3. Say what you mean.

4. Say it to the right people.

5. Say it as soon as possible.

6. Say it as simply as possible.

7. Keep on saying it. (p. 128)

SUMMING UP

The highly effective school has high levels of relational trust. Researchers call relational trust a core resource for improving schools. It is also a prerequisite for creating a collaborative and cooperative school. You can almost feel relational trust in a school when you walk through the front door for the first time. People are polite and respectful of each other and you, the visitor. There is a feeling that people know what they are doing and are eager to

Figure 4.3   Relational Trust Indicators

All staff members feel positively and act respectfully toward all students, even those who are challenging. When difficulties arise, they handle them through appropriate channels (e.g., climate meetings, teacher assistance teams, referral, consultation with principal).

Principal and staff believe that by working together, the home and school can have a profound influence on student achievement. Teachers are held responsible not only for all students mastering certain basic skills at their grade levels but for the stimulation, enrichment, and acceleration of the students who are able to learn more quickly and the provision of extended learning opportunities for students who may need more time for mastery.

Principal and staff members serve as advocates of students and communicate with them regarding aspects of their school life. Behaviors might include lunch with individual students or groups; frequent appearances on the playground, in the lunchroom, and in the hallways; sponsorship of clubs, availability to students who wish to discuss instructional or disciplinary concerns; knowledge of students' names (other than just their own classes) and family relationships, addressing the majority of students by name; and willingness to listen to the students' side in faculty–student problems.

Principal encourages open communication among staff members and parents and maintains respect for differences of opinion. Examples of open communication might include an open-door policy in the principal's office, acceptance of unpopular ideas and negative feedback from staff and parents, provision of channels for staff and parents to voice grievances or discuss problems, and provision of channels for staff members and parents to interact with each other.

Principal demonstrates concern and openness in the consideration of teacher, parent, or student problems, participates in the resolution of such problems where appropriate, and has established procedures jointly with the faculty and parents for the resolution of problems.

Principal models appropriate human relations skills. Behaviors must include but not necessarily be limited to (a) establishing a climate of trust and security for students and staff; (b) respecting the rights of students, parents, and staff; (c) handling individual relationships tactfully and with understanding; and (d) accepting the dignity and worth of individuals without regard to appearance, race, creed, sex, disability, ability, or social status.

Morale in the school is outstanding. Morale-building behaviors by the principal result in teachers working together in a highly effective way while gaining personal satisfaction from their work. Principal has identified specific activities that build morale and systematically engages in these activities. These might include but are not necessarily limited to involvement of staff in planning, encouragement of planned social events, openness in the dissemination of information, equity in the division of responsibility and allocation of resources, opportunities for achievement, recognition for achievements, involvement of the staff in problem solving, and assistance and support with personal and professional problems.

Principal systematically collects and responds in a timely way to staff, parent, and student concerns. Examples of vehicles used to collect information might include but are not necessarily limited to one-on-one conferences, parent or faculty advisory committees, student council, suggestion boxes, or quality circles.

Principal appropriately acknowledges the earned achievements of others. Activities might include but are not necessarily limited to staff recognition programs, student award assemblies, certificates, congratulatory notes, phone calls, recognition luncheons, and newspaper articles.

All staff members, classified and certified, are able to communicate openly with one another and say what they feel. Discussion is always freewheeling and frank. There is no hesitation on the part of all staff members to "tell it like it is," even in high-risk discussions and decision making. Staff members feel free to express their feelings as well as their ideas.

The individual abilities, knowledge, and experience of all staff members are fully used. All staff members are recognized as having gifts and talents that are fully used in accomplishing building goals, and roles are shared and exchanged.

Conflict between various individuals (teachers, parents, students) is resolved openly and effectively, and there is a genuine feeling of respect for one another among these groups. People are skilled at recognizing conflict and have a variety of conflict resolution strategies in their repertoire that they use with great success.

The entire school community can articulate and is committed to the vision and mission of the school. People have worked through their differences, and they can honestly say they are committed to achieving the mission of the school.

Staff members can express their views openly without fear of ridicule or retaliation and let others do the same. Constructive feedback is frequent, frank, and two-way; staff members accept and encourage it. Group processes are used that intentionally monitor and encourage the free flow of opinions, ideas, and suggestions for improvement.

Staff members can get help from one another and give help without being concerned about hidden agendas. Staff members have no reluctance in asking for help from others or in offering help to fellow staff members. There is transparency and trust among staff members. Processes are used regularly to examine how well the staff is working together and what may be interfering with its cooperation.

The school climate is one of openness and respect for individual differences. Parents and staff respect and affirm the unique gifts and talents of each individual, with appreciation for the variety of learning styles, personalities, and intelligences.

Reproduction of material from this book is authorized only for the local school site or nonprofit organization that has purchased *Ten Traits of Highly Effective Schools: Raising the Achievement Bar for All Students*, by Elaine K. McEwan. Thousand Oaks, CA: Corwin Press, www.corwinpress.com.

answer questions and talk about their school. Relational trust is not only the glue that holds a school together and the oil that keeps everything running smoothly, it is also the only antidote to hostility, anger, and distrust.

WHAT'S AHEAD?

In a school with high levels of relational trust, collaboration and cooperation are embedded in the culture. In Chapter 5, we examine how teacher collaboration and student cooperation can increase the instructional, academic, and leadership capacities of a school.

Collaboration

When groups, rather than individuals, are seen as the main units for implementing curriculum, instruction, and assessment, they facilitate development of shared purpose for student learning and collective responsibility to achieve it.

—Newmann and Wehlage (1995, pp. 37–38)

I've taught in several schools where my colleagues were very social. They bowled together on Monday nights, went out for dinner once or twice a month, and annually had a fabulous Christmas party where everybody brought their favorite appetizers. The social committee made sure that when faculty members were sick, they got flowers, cards, and even hot dinners on occasion. They had wonderful traditions and celebrations. However, their focus was not on teaching and learning. I call schools like this "country club" schools.

I remember the routine. When the bell rang, everyone hurried to their individual classrooms and closed their doors. They didn't talk to each other about teaching and learning. In fact, most of the faculty members had never even observed their grade-level or departmental colleagues teaching a lesson. Teachers in these schools were like independent contractors, not interdependent members of the same organization with a common goal—finding ways to ensure the success of all

> The traditional pattern that "teachers teach, students learn, and administrators manage" is completely altered. . . [There is] no longer a hierarchy of who knows more than someone else, but rather the need for everyone to contribute.
>
> —Kleine-Kracht (1993, p. 393)

students. Occasionally a school committee would be formed for the purpose of choosing a new spelling series or writing a technology plan, but discussions about common standards, exemplary lessons, or best practices for figuring out how to help struggling students were nonexistent. In contrast, the highly effective school is a professional community that coalesces around teaching and learning.

COLLABORATION AND COOPERATION

Collaboration, the fifth trait, is one of the hallmarks of highly effective schools. Collaboration is working with others to achieve a shared goal. Collaboration is powerful when the goal is a challenging one, calling for a variety of talents, essential when different points of view and thinking styles are needed to accomplish a task, and empowering when all group members can do their best work without fear of failure. However, the trump card of collaboration is that it is the only way a diverse faculty with diverse students can hope to achieve the alignment of content standards, curriculum, instruction, and assessment that are needed to raise the achievement bar for all students.

Collaborative groups of teachers who have a grade level, content area, or group of students in common have come to be known as *professional learning communities* (PLCs). Collaboration around and for increased student achievement through the improvement of instruction is the critical attribute of PLCs that distinguishes them from committees, task forces, or grade-level teams working on more mundane issues. Teachers aren't the only members of the school community that benefit from working together. Students who work in cooperative groups where there is individual and group accountability also achieve more. Ongoing and highly focused collaboration among groups of students who are in the same grade level or content area is called *cooperative learning*.

In a highly effective school, all members of the community are responsible for teaching others and for learning themselves. No one is exempt. The head teacher–learner is the principal. In schools where the principal only leads, teachers only teach, and students only learn (or try to learn), the capacity of the school to improve is diminished.

Oh, improvement may occur but at a much slower pace. If teachers are only teaching and not learning from their administrators, fellow teachers, and students, their professional and intellectual growth will be stunted as will the growth of their students. The equation is a simple one:

Teaching by All and Learning by All =
Improved Instruction and Achievement for All

Although *collaboration* and *cooperation* have identical dictionary meanings, educators usually speak of teachers collaborating to improve instruction and students learning cooperatively (and teaching recipro-cally) to improve their understanding and mastery. Whatever term is used to refer to the processes employed for learning and working in groups, both students and teachers need to be intentionally taught the expecta-tions and processes that are essential to working together.

My faculty and I were able to fully realize the many benefits that result from collaboration and cooperation only after we had participated together in a week of cooperative learning training in preparation for shifting all of our reading and writing instruction to a cooperative student team structure (Cooperative Integrated Reading and Composition [CIRC]). We learned that cooperative student teams and collaborative teacher teams do not spring to life by fiat. To build productive teams, teachers need training in how to build consensus, deal with con-flict, and establish positive group norms. Students require intensive training in the routines, rubrics, and rules of cooperative learning. Training is a prerequisite to realizing the extensive research-based benefits of cooperative learning for students (Johnson & Johnson, 1989; Johnson, Johnson, & Stanne, 2000; Slavin, 1978) and collaborative inquiry in professional learning communities for teachers (Hord, 1997).

> [The phrase] instructional leader suggests that others have got to be followers. The legitimate instructional leaders, if we have to have them, ought to be teachers. And principals ought to be leaders of leaders, people who develop instructional leadership in their teachers.
>
> —Sergiovanni (1992, p. 48)

PROFESSIONAL LEARNING COMMUNITIES

A PLC can refer to an entire school (usually a smaller one) in which "interac-tion among teachers is frequent and teachers' actions are governed by shared norms focused on the practice and improvement of teaching and learning" (Bryk, Camburn, & Louis, 1999, p. 753). More commonly, however, PLCs are smaller groups of teachers in a content department, grade level, or interdisci-plinary team responsible for one group of students. Whether in the school as a whole or in smaller units, three behaviors characterize a true PLC:

A school that experiences consistently high student achievement scores is not necessarily a school that exemplifies a professional learning community. Frequently, such a school is one in which student demographics or needs have not changed significantly over time and school staff have found a comfortable place in their teaching of the basics assessed by achievement tests. If, however, this school staff is expected to address higher curriculum standards, if they are required to provide higher-quality intellectual learning tasks for their students, or if their community experiences a significant change in student population or demographics (not uncommon in our ever-changing society), they are often ill-prepared to address their students' academic needs.

—*Morrissey (2000, p. 19–20)*

(1) reflective dialogue and problem solving among teachers about instructional practices and student learning; (2) peer observations of one another's teaching; and (3) peer collaboration to create products to be used in the classroom—for example, lessons, rubrics, or common assessments.

Although the term *professional learning community* had not yet become a buzzword in the early 1980s, the teacher leaders at Lincoln School independently recognized the benefits of "deprivatizing" the act of teaching. They developed a plan to open up their classrooms to peer observations and then did a marvelous marketing job to convince several of our more senior teachers that they had everything to gain and nothing to lose from such a venture. Although all of the teachers had been trained in clinical supervision (i.e., a process of observation and conferencing), we used a modified version of the model developed by Goldsberry (1986) in which colleagues observed each other and then attempted to identify patterns of teacher or learner behavior. Teachers were initially reluctant to engage in this activity, but we emphasized a data-based approach where the observer records information about either the teacher (e.g., how many positive vs. negative comments were made, how many and what kind of attention-getting moves were used, or the differences in teachers' interactions with high-achieving vs. low-achieving students). This approach removed the possibility of subjective judgments that can be threatening to a teacher and focused on "just the facts." The program notched up expectations for everyone and set a new standard of professionalism.

THE BENEFITS OF COLLABORATION

There is an extensive body of research substantiating the benefits for both teachers and students when teachers collaborate in PLCs (Hord, 1997). For teachers, the following results have been documented:

- Reduction of isolation of teachers
- Increased commitment to the mission and goals of the school and increased vigor in working to strengthen the mission

- Shared responsibility for the total development of students and collective responsibility for students' success
- Powerful learning that defines good teaching and classroom practice and creates new knowledge and beliefs about teaching and learners
- Increased meaning and understanding of the content that teachers teach and the roles they play in helping all students achieve expectations
- Higher likelihood that teachers will be well informed, professionally renewed, and inspired to inspire students
- More satisfaction, higher morale, and lower rates of absenteeism
- Significant advances in adapting teaching to the students, accomplished more quickly that in traditional schools
- Commitment to making significant and lasting changes
- Higher likelihood of understanding fundamental systemic change (p. 27)

> All of the talk of reforming schooling must never lose sight of the ultimate goal: to create institutions where students can learn through interaction with teachers who are themselves always learning. The effective school must become an educative setting for its teachers if it aspires to become an educational environment for its students.
>
> —*Shulman (1989, p. 186)*

The documented benefits to students when their teachers collaborate in PLCs include the following:

- Decreased dropout rate and fewer classes skipped
- Lower rates of absenteeism
- Increased learning distributed more equitably in the smaller high schools
- Greater academic gains in Math, Science, History, and Reading than in traditional schools
- Smaller achievement gaps between students from different backgrounds (Hord, 1997, p. 28)

> Collaboration and the ability to engage in collaborative action are becoming increasingly important to the survival of public schools. Indeed without the ability to collaborate with others, the prospect of truly repositioning schools in the constellation of community forces is not likely.
>
> —*Schlechty (2005, p. 22)*

The documented benefits to students when teachers collaborate to improve instruction are more modest but undeniable. However, the research demonstrating the impact of cooperative learning methods and models on student achievement is impressive.

Raising the Achievement Bar in a Professional Learning Community: Teri Fleming, Biology Teacher, Alief Hastings High School, Houston (TX)

Alief Hastings High School (AHHS) in Houston, TX, part of the Alief Independent School District, is a comprehensive high school of more than 3,500 students. The demographics at AHHS are undeniably challenging: (a) a student population with a 20% mobility rate, (b) a high percentage of students who are economically disadvantaged (54%) or are designated at-risk (66%), and (c) a veritable United Nations of languages (more than 50) and ethnic groups (more than 60). In spite of these obstacles to student achievement, AHHS's scores on the Exit Level Texas Assessment of Knowledge and Skills (TAKS), given during the junior year, are among the highest in the district in all four content areas: English-Language Arts, Science, Social Studies, and Math.

The faculty at AHHS has a long history of working in teams, so the concept of PLCs was an intriguing one. Biology teacher Teri Fleming and more than 60 other teachers and administrators from the district were introduced to the concept of PLCs during a three-day training with the DuFours and Robert Eaker (Du Four, DuFour, Eaker, & Many, 2006). Teri says, "I bought into the concept hook, line, and sinker." As a 34-year veteran in the district, Teri was tapped to work with Assistant Principal Raymond Lowery to create consensus among her 200-plus colleagues at AHHS. Part of what made their job easier was a pledge by the central office administration to end a history of what Teri calls "the flavor of the month" approach to improvement. The board and superintendent promised that PLCs would be given both the opportunity and responsibility to improve instruction from within, ending the traditional way of doing business—responding to the next new thing. Teri says, "Teachers agreed that organized teams focused on teaching and learning were just what they needed to notch up expectations for students."

The biology team immediately focused their attention on the improvement of instruction. Teri says, "Leaders like Andi Malin, now an instructional specialist for science, and Mary Beth Davis led our team in notching up our quality of instruction for every student. There is definitely greater equity. Students are getting similar lessons of similar difficulty with the same high level of expectations. We constantly challenge ourselves to get rid of the language of low expectations in our classrooms. That language is subtle, and we are all guilty of letting it creep into our interactions with students."

As the current PLC leader, Teri feels accountable for eliminating low expectations among the biology teachers. She reports, "I was walking down the hall, and I heard a teacher collecting homework from students. Some students were apparently not finished, and the teacher made the statement: 'Anything is better than nothing.' It was a low-expectations statement. So at our next meeting, I put the statement on the table. I said, 'I'm not quoting anybody, but here's a statement I heard this week in one of our classrooms.' What was interesting is that everybody at the table looked a little guilty. The person who said it recognized the statement immediately. But several others may have said something similar during the week."

The biology PLC has very explicit norms, shown in Figure 5.1, that govern their interactions with each other. Team members are encouraged to periodically reflect about their success at upholding the norms.

The work of the biology PLC is structured around the units they teach. After each unit, teachers give a common assessment, and once the tests are scored, data is disaggregated by item, teacher, and student subgroups. PLC members then complete a data analysis sheet, as shown in Figure 5.2. The program developed by AHHS teacher Jeff Hunter is now used almost districtwide by other PLCs.

Teri leads the biology PLC by example. She says, "None of us is exempt from the spotlight. As the team leader, I have to model the attitudes and behaviors I expect from my team. I remember, we had a section on mutations in the unit. There were three questions, and my students did poorly on that section compared to the results in the other sections of biology. I had to humble myself and admit that my lesson on that topic wasn't up to par. Even though I was using a lesson plan that we had developed collaboratively, I think I changed some of the wording and ending up confusing my students rather than helping them to master the concept."

The biggest roadblock to collaboration in schools is the lack of time. And indeed, fitting collaborative meetings into a schedule already packed with lesson planning, grading, parent communication, recommendation letters for students applying to colleges, special education reports, and other committee meetings requires prioritizing, careful planning, and a nearly obsessive concern, for time on-task can be a huge challenge. AHHS teachers do, however, have more time than many of their counterparts in other schools. Figure 5.3 shows the total monthly time available to teachers for planning and PLC meetings (1,440 minutes) as well as the time that the biology team has chosen to allocate from that time available to do collaborative work (840 minutes).

Teri believes that the successful implementation of PLCs is dependent on two variables: (1) the quality of teacher leadership within the group and (2) the quality of monitoring and supervision provided by the principal and assistant principals. "Leadership matters," says Teri.

Figure 5.1   Alief Hastings High School Biology PLC Norms, 2007–2008

Biology PLC Norms

Directions: The checklist in italics is for personal reflection about our commitments.

1. We will be restricted to a two-minute "quacking" period [NOTE: a time to talk about topics other than teaching and learning] prior to the start of the meeting. Civility will be extended to all members. _____

   Have I limited "quacking" and greeted all members? _____

2. We will attend every meeting. If members of the team cannot attend, they will contact the team leader ahead of time, read the minutes, and complete assigned tasks. _____

   Have I attended every meeting or notified the team leader? _____

(Continued)

(Continued)

3. We will participate fully in the meetings and carry out our assigned tasks between meetings. _____

   Have I participated fully in the meetings? _____ Carried out my tasks? _____

4. We will start on time and plan to stay the full time. Our maximum meeting time will be 45 minutes of any 50-minute period and team time on Wednesdays. _____

   Have I been on time and stayed to finish the work? _____

5. We will listen to all members' ideas and opinions respectfully. _____

   Have I listened respectfully to all members? _____

6. We will support team decisions (reached by consensus) both inside and outside of team meetings. _____

   Have I supported team decisions? _____

7. We will deal with conflicts directly, respectfully, and in a timely manner. _____

   Have I dealt with conflicts expediently and directly? _____

8. We will have and commit to an agenda, and it will be sent out at least two days prior to the meeting. _____

   Have we had an agenda and adhered to it? _____

9. We will keep meeting records and send them out within three days. _____

   Have we kept meeting records and sent them out within three days? _____

10. We will work to improve instruction daily and follow the curriculum. _____

    Have I worked to improve instruction daily and follow the curriculum? _____

11. I will not carry on sidebar conversations during meetings. _____

    Have I refrained from sidebar conversations? _____

SOURCE: Used with permission of Teri Fleming.

Reproduction of material from this book is authorized only for the local school site or nonprofit organization that has purchased *Ten Traits of Highly Effective Schools: Raising the Achievement Bar for All Students,* by Elaine K. McEwan. Thousand Oaks, CA: Corwin Press, www.corwin press.com.

Figure 5.2   Alief Hastings High School Biology PLC Data Analysis Form

From the Grades Screen in the Apperson Scanner:

1. What was the team's percentage of students passing at 65%? ___ At 70%? ___

2. Record your percentage of each class that mastered 65% and 70% of the test, separating classes.

	Regular On-Level Classes		Cotaught Classes: Regular Education Teacher and SPED Teacher With 1/3 of Class SPED Students		Support-Facilitated Classes: Some SPED Students (seven or less) and a Noncertified Aide		Accelerated Classes		ESL: Non-English Speakers With Teacher Certified in Science and ESL	
Period	65%	70%	65%	70%	65%	70%	65%	70%	65%	70%
1										
2										
3										
4										
5										
6										
7										

Note the number of students "on the Bubble."* How many? _____

3. Rate the performance of your classes by period.

Ranking	Period Number
First Place	
Second Place	
Third Place	
Fourth Place	
Fifth Place	
Sixth Place	

(Continued)

(Continued)

From the Item Analysis Screen in the Apperson Scanner:

4. Look at your summary sheet and identify any question where more than 45% of *your* students missed the right answer. List the question number; find the topic and the major distracter by looking at the test.

Question Number	Topic–Objective	Major Distracter

5. How many students were absent from each class period for the test?

Period	Number of Students Absent
First Period	
Second Period	
Third Period	
Fourth Period	
Fifth Period	
Sixth Period	

6. Note the total number of questions in each color category for your six classes.**

Color Category	Total # Questions
Green	
White	
Yellow	
Red	

7. What two things could I have done to improve my instruction and increase the success of my students?

1.	
2.	

8. What two things could the team do to improve instruction?

1.	
2.	

9. Were there any extenuating circumstances that may have affected the success of our students in this unit? Was sufficient time allotted? Did we teach only the required standards? Was instruction interrupted, therefore disjointed? Explain.

10. Were there any extenuating circumstances that may have affected the success of our students in this unit? Was sufficient time allotted? Did we teach only the required standards? Was instruction interrupted, therefore disjointed? Explain.

Check Below if Sufficient	Strategies and Activities
	Labs. Did they work for the intended purpose?
	Literacy strategies
	Engagement sctivities
	Writing activities (prewriting, exit cards, vocabulary activities)
	Feedback to students so they can improve

11. What feedback from the students will we take into the next unit to improve instruction? (Students answered three questions: What was most difficult in this unit? What was most helpful in this unit? What was least helpful in the unit?)

Category	Student Feedback
Most Difficult	
Most Helpful	
Least Helpful	

(Continued)

(Continued)

12. Are there personal factors that you as a teacher could have changed to improve your instruction? (For example, better lesson plans, increased class attendance, more and better modifications for students, more drill, more reading)

| |
| |
| |

13. What do students need to do to succeed in your class?

| |
| |
| |

Name: _____ Assessment: _____ Date: _____

SOURCE: Used with permission of Teri Fleming.

*Students "on the bubble" are those that scored between 65% and 70% and with just a little more effort can be bumped over the threshold (70% passing).

**In the data analysis program, each question is highlighted by color for each teacher. Questions highlighted in green scored significantly above the group average. Questions highlighted in white scored marginally above the average. Questions highlighted in yellow scored marginally below the group average, and questions highlighted in red scored significantly below the group average. For example, if a teacher had 20 questions highlighted in green and 4 questions highlighted in white, there would be a total of 24 questions in the plus (+) column. If that same teacher had 13 questions highlighted in yellow and 3 highlighted in red, they would have a total of 16 questions in the minus (–) column. That teacher's overall score would be 8. The team then adds up all of the teachers' scores to get an overall rating for the team.

Reproduction of material from this book is authorized only for the local school site or nonprofit organization that has purchased *Ten Traits of Highly Effective Schools: Raising the Achievement Bar for All Students*, by Elaine K. McEwan. Thousand Oaks, CA: Corwin Press, www.corwinpress.com.

Figure 5.3   Available and Allocated Time for Biology PLC at Alief Hastings High School

Part I: Total Monthly Time Available to AHHS Teachers for Planning and PLCs

	Monday	Tuesday	Wednesday	Thursday	Friday
Conference Period*	50 min.	50 min.	40 min.**	50 min.	50 min.
Early Release Period			160 min. ***		
Daily Time Available	50 × 4 = 200	50 × 4 = 200	160 × 3 = 480**** 40 × 4 = 160	50 × 4 = 200	50 × 4 = 200
Total Monthly Time Available = 1440 minutes					

Part II: Total Monthly Time Allocated by Biology PLC to Collaborative Work

	Monday	Tuesday	Wednesday	Thursday	Friday
Conference Period*	30 min.	30 min.			
Early Release Period			160 min.		
Daily Time Available	30 × 4 = 120	30 × 4 = 120	160 × 3 = 480****	30 min × 4 = 120	
Total Monthly Time Allocated = 840 minutes					

SOURCE: Used with permission of Teri Fleming.

*The conference period is used for individual teacher tasks, including lesson planning, grading, and communication with parents.

**The conference period on Wednesday is shortened by 10 minutes because of the compressed schedule to accommodate the early release of students.

***The early release period after students leave the building runs from 1:40 pm to 4:00 pm.

****Three of the early release days are allocated to PLC Meetings. The fourth day is used for meetings and training by the administration.

Reproduction of material from this book is authorized only for the local school site or nonprofit organization that has purchased *Ten Traits of Highly Effective Schools: Raising the Achievement Bar for All Students,* by Elaine K. McEwan. Thousand Oaks, CA: Corwin Press, www.corwinpress.com.

BENEFITS OF COOPERATIVE LEARNING

...ative learning is currently used in one form or another at every level of education, and more than 900 research studies validate the effectiveness of cooperative classrooms when comparisons are made to classrooms where students compete with one another or work as individuals (Johnson et al., 2000). There are few instructional methods that have such a wide and deep theoretical base (e.g., anthropology, sociology, economics, political science, psychology) and so many well-researched models (e.g., Jigsaw Procedure, Team Accelerated Instruction, and CIRC). Newcomers to cooperative learning can find highly scripted instructional activities that are easy to use, while experienced teachers can adapt the method to their own content and teaching style, as Jay Pilkington demonstrates in the case study to follow.

Cooperative learning as a classroom methodology works best in schools where collaboration is embedded into the culture. Johnson and Johnson's (1989) whole-school model, known as the Cooperative School, expects teachers to teach in teams, engage in collaborative faculty study groups, and to make use of cooperative processes in professional development and regular faculty meetings. In the highly effective school, teachers collaborate and students cooperate daily.

Cooperative Learning for Student Mastery: Jay Pilkington, Social Studies, Peter Kiewit Middle School, Omaha (NE)

Jay Pilkington teaches middle school social studies in a suburb of Omaha, NE. As a new teacher, he used the lecture approach almost exclusively in his classroom. He did a lot of talking and telling but with very discouraging results. His students weren't mastering the content, and he was exhausted. Jay wisely decided to try a new teaching approach, a research-based one that provided opportunities for students to cognitively process the course content with classmates: cooperative learning (Johnson, Johnson, & Holubec, 1994).

Jay quickly realized, however, that to use this popular model effectively, he would have to explain, demonstrate, and facilitate his students' mastery of the routines of cooperative learning—*before* he could begin teaching the content. He also discovered that he needed some motivating instructional activities that fit his content, standards, time frame, schoolwide expectations, *and* his students. Hoping to engage his students' interest, he came up with three content-based cooperative games. Jay no longer stands in front of his podium talking and telling.

Row Feud is a note-taking and discussion activity formatted like the television game show *Family Feud*. Jay's version is a combination of note taking, a pop quiz (everyone is required to answer one question), and spirited competition. Here's how he describes the activity:

"I prepare a set of questions (five, to go with the number of rows I have in my seating plan) and notes (answers and additional material I want to make sure the students have mastered) for the part of the chapter that has been assigned as homework reading. First, students write the five questions into their social studies notebooks. Then each team (row) is randomly assigned one of the five questions, and away we go."

Read, Revel, and Reveal is a cooperative learning activity in which small groups prepare oral presentations on different parts of a chapter—a jigsaw. Each group does the following:

a. Reads their assigned part of the chapter

b. Revels in the information by discussing the main points of their section and identifying the critical information that needs to be presented to the rest of the class

c. Prepares an "infoposter" that presents that information in any style they choose: outline, time line, bullet list, chart, web, Venn diagram, or acrostic poem

d. Reveals the important information by presenting their infoposter to the rest of the class and leading a brief discussion

Share 'n' Compare is a partner note-taking and group discussion activity. Two students put their desks in "pods" facing each other. Jay describes the activity this way:

"I prepare a set of 10 questions and answers that relate to the chosen section or chapter in the textbook. The questions can be from any level of Bloom's Taxonomy, depending on the lesson objectives for the day. Students have either read the chapter in class the day before or it has been assigned as homework for the prior evening. Students enter the 10 questions I dictate into their social studies notebooks. [NOTE: Jay's district limits the amount of paper that teachers can use, necessitating teacher dictation to students.] These notebooks are collected for a grade after each chapter. Our school uses the two-column note-taking strategy, so I've set up the questions in that fashion. The Partner Pods then work together to identify, analyze, discuss, and record the answers to the questions into their notes.

"Once students have completed this part of the process, I give them the 'Lights out and Listen' signal (I flick the lights as a signal that students should immediately stop talking and listen to me). I give the instruction to 'Depod and head back to camp.' We then begin to Share 'n' Compare. This is a large-group discussion of the answers students have written. I ask students to share the information their pod discovered and then I compare that with the information I found. This gives students an opportunity to check the accuracy of their notes and for me to elaborate on what I have written in my notes."

Jay arranges his classroom in five rows of four to six desks, an ostensibly old-fashioned seating plan. But Jay's utilization of this plan is flexible and functional. Each row has a designated leader (the student in the first seat) and a caboose (the student in the last seat) who perform certain duties. He uses the five-row format (with an even number of students in each row) to support a variety of unique instructional activities, all designed to ensure that his students are actively involved and processing the content and "big ideas" of his subject.

Sometimes the rows break up into pairs. At other times, the rows become cooperative learning teams that compete against other rows. On still another day, each row becomes a piece of a cooperative "jigsaw" as students prepare group presentations on an assigned section of a textbook unit. Using these three cooperative activities, Jay is now facilitating, affirming, motivating, and coaching, rather than lecturing. Meanwhile, his students are mastering the content as never before (McEwan, 2006, 2007).

THE CHARACTERISTICS OF AN EFFECTIVE PROFESSIONAL LEARNING COMMUNITY

PLCs do not magically morph into successful collaborative work groups. The team-building process takes leadership, time, training, and the willingness to persevere through episodes of conflict and periods when productivity might temporarily slump. However, over time, here are the characteristics that emerge:

> If schools want to enhance their organizational capacity to boost student learning, they should work on building a professional community that is characterized by shared purpose, collaborative activity, and collective responsibility among staff.
>
> —Newmann and Wehlage (1995, p. 37)

- *Trust:* People can state their views and differences openly without fear of ridicule or retaliation and let others do the same.
- *Self-Reflection:* People are able to step back and view their own teaching with objectivity and consider other possibilities and options.
- *Support:* People can get help from others on the team and give help without being concerned about hidden agendas.
- *Communication:* Because of mutual trust, people can say what they feel.
- *Shared Mission:* With each new goal or problem that confronts the group, people work through their differences until they can honestly say they are committed to achieving the goal or solving the problem.
- *Conflict Resolution Skills:* People do not suppress conflicts or pretend they do not exist but work through them openly. (McEwan, 1996)

> Five years ago, staff meetings were conducted each week to disseminate information and discuss some schoolwide issues. In the past five years, an evolution has taken place until now teachers meet in grade-level teams at least twice per month. They work on long- and short-term plans, analyze student work, discuss methods for reaching standards, and so forth. The teaching staff has developed a strong spirit of collegiality and is committed to bringing its best to students. Over time, the unifying focus of leaving no child behind has created an underlying desire to constantly refine and improve our instructional delivery.
>
> —Dobberteen (2001)

Collaborative work groups need yearly checkups to assess their effectiveness. Teams often develop their own checklists like the one used by the biology PLC. Form 5.1, PLC Behavior Checklist, can also be used to assess the collaborative behaviors of a PLC. Forms 5.2 and 5.3 can be used to record responses and interpret the scores.

Form 5.1   PLC Behavior Checklist

For each indicator, select the descriptor that best describes PLC members' behavior. Then record the descriptor's number on the line beside the indicator on the PLC Collaborative Behavior Checklist Scoring Form 5.2.

Indicator 1: PLC members are able to communicate openly with one another and say what they feel.

Scale of Descriptors:

1. Discussion is inhibited and stilted. PLC members hesitate to lay their true feelings on the table and are afraid of criticism, put-downs, and reprisals.

2. A few self-confident or politically connected PLC members speak openly, but most members are reluctant.

3. Many PLC members speak openly, but usually only after a communication trend has been established.

4. Although most communication is open, there are some topics that are taboo or select individuals who inhibit open communication with what they say or do.

5. Discussion is always freewheeling and frank. There is no hesitation on the part of all PLC members to "tell it like it is" even in high-risk discussions and decision making. PLC members feel free to express their feelings as well as their ideas.

Indicator 2: The individual abilities, knowledge, and experience of all PLC members are fully utilized.

Scale of Descriptors:

1. The PLC is controlled by one individual who runs the show.

2. A select and chosen few do all the work.

3. At least half of the members do something, but the same people are always in charge.

4. A majority of the members participate, but no effort is made to share or exchange roles.

5. All PLC members are recognized as having gifts and talents that are fully utilized in accomplishing PLC goals, and roles are shared and exchanged. The chairperson (whoever is in that role) does not dominate.

Indicator 3: Conflict is resolved openly and effectively.

Scale of Descriptors:

1. PLC members suppress conflict and pretend it does not exist.

2. PLC members recognize conflict but do not approach its solution directly and positively.

3. PLC members recognize conflict and attempt to resolve it with some success, but they are sometimes clumsy and unskilled in their methodology, resulting in frequent misunderstandings.

4. PLC members recognize conflict and can frequently resolve it through appropriate methods, but there are no standardized methodologies for handling conflict.

5. PLC members are skilled at recognizing conflict and have a variety of conflict resolution strategies in their repertoire that they use with great success.

Indicator 4: PLC members are committed to improving instruction and raising the achievement bar.

Scale of Descriptors:

1. PLC members are openly committed to their own agendas and are unwilling to set aside personal goals for the PLC objective.

2. PLC members pretend to be committed to improving instruction and raising the achievement bar but frequently work at cross-purposes.

3. A core of PLC members is committed, but a few naysayers and bystanders work to undermine the PLC's objectives when it serves their purposes.

4. The majority of PLC members are committed, but no intentional efforts have been made to work through any existing group differences.

5. PLC members have worked through their differences, and they can honestly say they are committed to improving instruction and raising the achievement bar. PLC processes are in place to assist members in accomplishing this goal.

(Continued)

Form 5.1 (Continued)

Indicator 5: PLC members can state their views openly, without fear of ridicule or retaliation, and let others do the same.

Scale of Descriptors:

1. PLC members never express views openly.
2. PLC members sometimes express views openly, but it is usually done with hesitancy and reluctance.
3. Some PLC members feel free to express views openly, but many members are reluctant to express their true feelings.
4. Constructive criticism is accepted, but there are no mechanisms for ensuring that it is a regular aspect of PLC meetings.
5. Constructive criticism is frequent and frank; PLC members accept and encourage it. Group processes are used that intentionally monitor and encourage the free flow of opinions, ideas, and suggestions for improvement.

Indicator 6: Everyone accepts responsibility for keeping communication relevant and the PLC operation on track.

Scale of Descriptors:

1. Meetings are usually disorganized and frequently off-task. Agendas are poorly constructed or exist only in the mind of a single individual.
2. One or two individuals consistently undermine the effectiveness of PLC meetings with "birdwalks," sidebars comments, and inappropriate nonverbal language.
3. Meetings are run with an agenda and structure, but time limits are not monitored and little of worth is accomplished.
4. Most PLC members accept accountability for the group's behavior, but the accomplishment of tasks is inconsistent.
5. PLC members monitor one another's behavior and all members take responsibility for the effectiveness of PLC meetings. Agenda items are routinely cared for, and PLC business is accomplished effectively.

Indicator 7: PLC members can get help from others on the PLC and give help without being concerned about hidden agendas.

Scale of Descriptors:

1. PLC members are reluctant to admit ignorance or the need for assistance. People are in the independent rather than interdependent mode.
2. Some PLC members will admit to the need for assistance, but many are territorial and competitive.
3. PLC members want to be collaborative but lack the necessary skills.
4. PLC members assist each other, but there is no systematic plan for evaluating the effectiveness of the collaborative atmosphere.
5. PLC members have no reluctance in asking for help from others or in offering help to fellow members. There is transparency and trust between PLC members. Processes are used regularly to examine how well the PLC is working together and what may be interfering with collaboration.

Indicator 8: The PLC climate is one of openness and respect for individual differences.

Scale of Descriptors:

1. PLC members are suspicious, competitive, and disrespectful.
2. A few PLC members are trying to improve the climate but are having a difficult time bringing about change.
3. The majority of PLC members work well together, but there are some who attempt to undermine a healthy climate.
4. The PLC works well together, but little is done to encourage, develop, and affirm this sense of sharing and collaboration.
5. PLC members respect and affirm the unique gifts and talents of each member with appreciation for the variety of approaches to problem solving. The PLC takes time for morale-building exercises that improve the climate.

Copyright © 2005 Corwin Press. All rights reserved. Reprinted from *How to Deal With Teachers Who Are Angry, Troubled, Exhausted, or Just Plain Confused* by E. K. McEwan. Reproduction authorized only for the local school site that has purchased this book.

Form 5.2   PLC Behavior Checklist Scoring Form

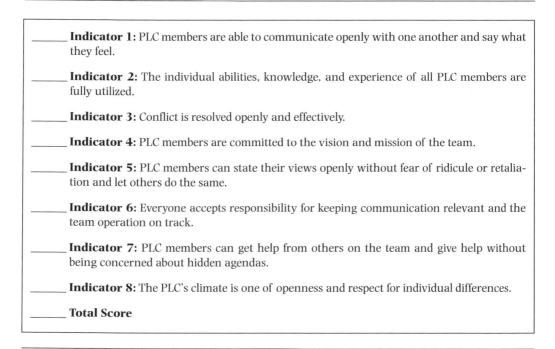

_____ **Indicator 1:** PLC members are able to communicate openly with one another and say what they feel.

_____ **Indicator 2:** The individual abilities, knowledge, and experience of all PLC members are fully utilized.

_____ **Indicator 3:** Conflict is resolved openly and effectively.

_____ **Indicator 4:** PLC members are committed to the vision and mission of the team.

_____ **Indicator 5:** PLC members can state their views openly without fear of ridicule or retaliation and let others do the same.

_____ **Indicator 6:** Everyone accepts responsibility for keeping communication relevant and the team operation on track.

_____ **Indicator 7:** PLC members can get help from others on the team and give help without being concerned about hidden agendas.

_____ **Indicator 8:** The PLC's climate is one of openness and respect for individual differences.

_____ **Total Score**

Copyright © 2005 Corwin Press. All rights reserved. Reprinted from *How to Deal With Teachers Who Are Angry, Troubled, Exhausted, or Just Plain Confused* by E. K. McEwan. Reproduction authorized only for the local school site that has purchased this book.

Form 5.3   PLC Behavior Rating Scale

Score	Rating
31–40	Mature, effective PLC. Continue to do all of the positive and productive things you are doing, and regularly monitor your team skills.
20–30	Good PLC. Even though your team gets the job done, there are some problem relationships that if confronted, could notch up your performance to the next level.
10–19	Borderline PLC. Your team is ignoring the "elephants" that are standing in the way of productivity. Tell it like it is!
Under 10	Dysfunctional PLC. One more crisis and your team will self-destruct. Do some team-building exercises and put your problems on the table.

Copyright © 2005 Corwin Press. All rights reserved. Reprinted from *How to Deal With Teachers Who Are Angry, Troubled, Exhausted, or Just Plain Confused* by E. K. McEwan. Reproduction authorized only for the local school site that has purchased this book.

COLLABORATION BUILDS CAPACITY

School capacity has been defined as "the collective power of the full staff to improve student achievement" (Newmann, King, & Youngs, 2000, p. 261). However, limiting the definition of school capacity to only the abilities and energies of the teaching staff presumes that principals and students are not part of the package. In reality, schools have three types of capacity: instructional, academic, and leadership. These terms are defined in Figure 5.4.

When we speak of the *capacity* of a disk drive or a storage rental unit, it refers to the number of files that can be saved on the drive or the amount of stuff that can be crammed into the rented space. Eventually, physical or digital capacity reaches its limit. However, the capacity that refers to the output or productivity of a given individual or organization is expandable and unlimited. This kind of capacity is almost always far greater than anyone might have imagined, especially in schools.

How much can a given group of students learn? Taught by an ineffective teacher with low expectations, it may learn very little. Taught by a caring teacher with exceptional instructional skills and high expectations, the group's capacity is limited only by the amount of effort the students are willing to invest. With hard work and superior instruction, the academic capacity of students is unlimited.

Figure 5.4   Components of School Capacity

Term	Definition
Instructional Capacity	The collective capacity of the teachers in a given school to teach and get results. When a staff, department, or team is engaged in collaborative, content-specific learning, the instructional capacity increases and the achievement bar is raised (Knapp, Copland, & Talbert, 2003; Senge, 1990).
Academic Capacity	The collective abilities of students to learn and demonstrate their learning in relevant and rigorous work products (daily assignments, writing projects, problem-solving tasks, and group projects) as well as in the results of formative and summative assessments.
Leadership Capacity	The collective leadership abilities of the administrators and teacher-leaders in a school to build and maintain a professional learning community and solve problems of teaching and learning toward the goal of success for all students.

Reproduction of material from this book is authorized only for the local school site or nonprofit organization that has purchased *Ten Traits of Highly Effective Schools: Raising the Achievement Bar for All Students*, by Elaine K. McEwan. Thousand Oaks, CA: Corwin Press, www.corwinpress.com.

The capacity of a school is like a sum of money in an interest-bearing account. With minimal deposits of academic, instructional, and leadership abilities, the total capacity remains quite small, like a tiny bank account earning a very low interest rate. However, as the deposits or capacity of the school grow through the employment of strong instructional leaders and highly effective teachers, embedded professional development that takes place in collaborative communities that are committed and focused on student engagement and learning, the compounding effect will result in astonishing growth.

> To build a professional learning community, meaningful collaboration must be systematically embedded into the daily life of the school.
>
> —DuFour and Eaker (1998, p. 118)

Building Instructional Capacity in a Formula for Success School: Dale Skinner

Villarreal School was a laboratory for teaching and learning under the leadership of Dale Skinner from 2000 to 2003. The faculty as a whole functioned as a professional learning community, although that terminology was not used. In the beginning, Dale was the leader of the collaborative team, but before long, teachers and instructional specialists discovered new roles as collaborators with their fellow teachers. Isabel Anaya describes how her first year as a teacher unfolded:

The support I received from Mr. Skinner, my third-grade team, and the instructional specialists was unbelievable. Every Monday after school, he provided professional development sessions geared specifically to what students needed to learn. Teachers were introduced to specific reading tools or strategies and ways to make learning more relevant for the students. For example, he might take a passage or a story, and we would read part of the story together, then talk about how to teach students how to draw conclusion or use context clues. He would model for us just how the lesson should look. He always taught us something that we could take back and teach to our students that week.

> Some schools would rather get experts in. Our philosophy is, just because somebody else hasn't been able to figure out how to do this doesn't mean that we can't. I have no illusions about being smart enough to do everything by myself. But we have the collective knowledge of 25 people, and if we want to do something, we will figure out how.
>
> —Dave Montague, Principal

(Continued)

(Continued)

Louise Sekula describes a typical professional development session:

In our weekly professional development meetings, Mr. Skinner would teach a lesson focused on a particular standard. We would then discuss it and suggest how to adjust his lesson for our specific grade level. During the week, he would be in our classrooms helping us do the things we had learned at the Monday meeting. If needed, he would model for us with our students. Then once again, we would create lessons to teach that kind of writing, thinking, or problem solving to our students. We were expected to constantly reflect on the effectiveness of our lessons and talk with each other almost daily about what was working best in our classroom. It was an entirely different approach to teaching than any of us had ever experienced.

SUMMING UP

Working together is essential to raising the achievement bar for all students. Scholar Philip Schlechty (2005) suggests that without it, schools may not survive the competition from education entrepreneurs and online learning options that they will face in the 21st century. In the opinion of Principal Dave Montague, the power of collective knowledge can solve any problem his school might face. Researchers have weighed in with evidence regarding the power of collaboration and cooperation to build instructional, academic, and leadership capacities in schools. Collaboration is a hallmark of highly effective schools.

WHAT'S AHEAD?

In Chapter 6, we explore the role of high expectations in raising the achievement bar. Teri Fleming spoke of eliminating the language of low expectations from biology classrooms. Educators with high expectations not only believe their students are able to master the standards, they are confident of their own abilities to teach them.

High Expectations

6

Never have we seen a banner on the wall of an entry hall that reads "We Have Low Expectations for Our Students Here!" or a sign in a classroom reading "We Treat Our Students with Disrespect and Disdain Here."

—Scheurich and Skrla (2003, p. 47)

The educators in a highly effective school have *high* expectations, the sixth trait of highly effective schools. They believe in their students' ability to achieve, explicitly teach them how to do that, and convey a profound and unwavering commitment to their academic success. As powerful as a widely held set of high expectations for students has proven to be in creating schools of equity and excellence, the attitudes and behaviors that convey these expectations are not easily fostered in some educators. Although many individuals are willing to pay lip service to the idea of high expectations, a fair number quietly resist feeling accountable for their students' learning. I believe, however, that their biggest problem is a lack of efficacy. Underneath what appears to be a lack of cooperation is often a lack confidence both in their abilities to teach and in their students' abilities to master the standards.

> Classrooms are dynamic and complex societies that are rife with expectations: expectations that teachers have for students, and that students have for teachers and for each other. These expectations explain a good deal of what we see when we visit a classroom—both the good and the bad, the productive and the wasteful. But the expectations themselves can't be seen. They hang in the air almost like an atmosphere; they exist only between people and comprise a part of their relationship.
>
> —*Saphier and Gower (1997, p. 47)*

HIGH EXPECTATIONS AND EFFICACY

To have faith in one's ability to raise achievement in a school where students have previously never been engaged and motivated requires a strong sense of personal efficacy. Ensuring academic success for very-low-performing students also requires collective efficacy, a belief in the abilities of one's colleagues to come alongside and do their share. However, some educators simply do not believe that raising the achievement of low-performing students is possible. They have closed their minds to the confirming data and impressive results from other schools. These individuals fall into a category of educators that Jeff Howard (2003) of the Efficacy Institute describes this way: "There is a widespread culture of disbelief in the learning capacities of many of our children, especially children of color and the economically disadvantaged. Most educators, along with other Americans, have been socialized to believe that intelligence is innate, fixed at birth, and unequally distributed: 'Some have it and some don't'" (p. 83). In addition to the disbelievers, there are many educators who are worried that they may not be capable of motivating and engaging disengaged students. Both the disbelievers and those who feel powerless to make a difference need embedded professional development, high expectations, encouragement, and multiple opportunities for scaffolded learning from a strong instructional leader and their colleagues.

Some teachers pose this question when they overhear gossip in the teachers' lounge about a former student who has failed another course or been suspended one more time. "What did you expect?" they say, throwing up their hands. "I could have told you so."

Here's my answer to the question, "What did you expect?"

"Well, actually I expected a whole lot more. I expected the student would be able to make the grade and stay in school. I expected that working as a team, this staff could make a difference in this student's life."

Success for students, whether low achieving or honor roll, is about expectations. Students who don't arrive at school with a built-in set of expectations need highly effective teachers to give them theirs.

Psychologist Albert Bandura defined self-efficacy as the "belief in one's capacity to organize and execute the courses of action required to produce given attainments" (Bandura, 1997, p. 3). There have been many studies showing a strong relationship between teachers' perceived self-efficacy and their students' achievement (Ashton & Webb, 1986; Tschannen-Moran, Hoy, & Hoy, 1998). Perceived *collective* efficacy refers to "the judgment of teachers in a school that the faculty as a whole can organize and execute the courses of action required to have a positive effect on students" (Goddard, Hoy, & Hoy, 2004, p. 4).

The experience that is most predictive of future success is a previous mastery experience. For example, a group of teachers or a team of athletes that has achieved success at least once automatically increases their likelihood of doing it again.

Sportscasters often pontificate about the chances of one team v
another during the playoffs or World Series. One variable that is tho
to impact a team's ability to advance to the next level is whether they
done it before as a team or even whether a number of new players on the
team have done it before with other teams. The theory is that if you've
done it once, you have some extra measure of knowledge and confidence
that those who have never done it at all don't possess. The educators at
Villarreal, Washington, and Kimball are examples of how powerful a successful experience can be in leading to a repeat.

However, the faculty of a low-performing school that is trapped in a
vicious cycle of low expectations cannot conceive of how their students
could possibly become high performers, particularly if they have not experienced strong instructional leadership and relevant embedded professional
development. They have zero perceived collective efficacy and cannot imagine what they would do differently than what they have already done to
bring about change. They believe that the problem
lies with their students, not with them.

Even if there is a critical mass of teachers who
believe that their students are incapable of high
achievement and there is no one on the staff or
administration who has ever been part of turning
around a low-performing school, there *are* other
ways to build collective efficacy: (1) Site-visits to see
firsthand how other schools have achieved results
with students similar to those in their school can
begin to build collective efficacy; (2) informal conversations with teachers and administrators who have
actually done it can enable skeptical teachers to ask
tough questions and get honest answers; (3) efficacy
training conducted by a skilled facilitator who can
structure difficult conversations can bring educators
face-to-face with their fears, failings, and often inac-
curate preconceived beliefs (Howard, 1995); and
(4) embedded professional development in which
teachers are coached on the job in the needed strategies can turn around a low-performing school.

> Our team held high expectations for our students—too high, many people said. Don't ask for too much, they warned. Passing grades and graduation would be good enough. But we wanted more. We asked our students to come to school every single day, to stay away from drugs and alcohol, to change their bad habits, to complete every classroom and homework assignment, to resist the pressure to join gangs, to give up their bad attitudes and clean up their language. We asked for everything we could think of, and they gave us everything they had.
>
> —*Johnson (1995, pp. ix–x)*

PROGRAMS AND PRACTICES THAT CONVEY HIGH EXPECTATIONS

The following programs and instructional practices are just a few
examples of how highly effective schools communicate high expectations
to students and parents:

Include All Students

The tracking of students of varying ability levels or the segregation of students with any types of special needs sends a message to these students, their parents, and teachers that they don't have what it takes to make it in regular classrooms or that they are just too different to be taught by anyone other than specialist teachers. In highly effective schools, all or nearly all students with special needs are included in regular classrooms. The achievement of these students invariably goes up when they are both included and given the opportunities they need to learn. The No Child Left Behind Act (NCLB), for all of its flaws, has helped many districts realize that their expectations for special education (SPED) students have been entirely too low for too long.

Administrators and teachers of the North East Independent School District in San Antonio, Texas, were somewhat embarrassed in 2005 when 10 of their 61 schools failed to make Adequate Yearly Progress (AYP) under NCLB. It wasn't that they didn't have high expectations for their students. In fact, their high expectations for SPED students were partially to blame for the problem they faced. Administrators had decided to test all SPED students using on-grade-level tests, even though such a move far exceeded the requirements of NCLB. But high expectations without opportunities to learn rarely produce the desired results.

SPED students were not experiencing the same opportunities to learn that their regular education peers enjoyed. Most of the special needs students were in self-contained classrooms. To their credit, central office administrators quickly mobilized their resources to train principals and teachers in data analysis, provide embedded professional development to help SPED and regular education teachers begin to collaboratively plan and coteach, and offer ongoing support from content and technology specialists (Samuels, 2007).

Alicia Thomas, associate superintendent and chief instructional officer, spearheaded the initiative. In addition to a full menu of how-to sessions, implementation also focused on raising educators' expectations for what SPED students were capable of doing. She says, "We had the idea in our district that special education was something separate. But we immediately realized that these are all our kids, and they are deserving of the content taught in the general education classroom. Our SPED students needed to participate in that content to the maximum extent possible."

Implementing a program to include nearly 90% of their SPED students at every level in regular

> Schools need to shift from an ability-based model to an effort-based model. Or, in plain language, it is not how smart the child is, but how hard he or she works that determines success.
>
> —Bottoms (2003, p. 1)

classrooms required the adoption of a new set of beliefs for some of the teachers and administrators, but the district could not afford to wait for everyone to get completely onboard philosophically. Thomas says, "We believed our way into new ways of acting. Teachers made moves with kids because we told them they had to. But when they obtained results from their students, using the strategies and approaches learned during our embedded professional development sessions, they became believers."

Teach Kids How to Get Smart

The explicit teaching of an effort-based concept of intelligence and learning ability (Resnick, 1995, 1999) is a powerful way to operationalize high expectations. However, the idea that students can get smarter by working harder is not widely accepted, either by students or their teachers. In 1990, the Office of Educational Research and Improvement convened a national conference on student motivation with one goal in mind: activating the untapped power of student effort and engagement (Office of Educational Research and Improvement, 1992, p. iii). Those who pondered this problem nearly 20 years ago summarized their findings with these statements:

- Most students believe their ability and effort are the main reasons for school achievement. By the same token, if asked whether they would prefer to be called smart or hard-working, they will choose smart almost every time. Why? Because they believe that hard-working students risk being considered either excessively ambitious or of limited ability, both of which they would find embarrassing.
- To avoid unpopular labels, students—especially the brightest—believe they must strike a balance between the extremes of achievement, not too high and not too low. Many students adopt an attitude of indifference to hard work, a stance that implies confidence in their own ability and a casual regard for academic success.
- At the extreme, many low-achieving students deny the importance of learning and withhold the effort it requires in order to

> If a school is inviting, welcoming, and safe, if the curriculum is relevant and exciting, if staff works to connect with students and build good relationships, students will want to be in school and involved in learning activities. In my experience, a positive school climate has a huge influence on student attendance, behavior, and achievement. I've always hated the adage about leading a horse to water, so I have rewritten and paraphrased it to read: "You can get students to school—and, if you make it engaging and enticing enough, those students will learn."
>
> —Pamela Bradley

avoid the stigma of having tried and failed. (Office of Educational Research and Improvement, 1992, p. 1)

Contemporary educators would likely agree that little has changed in the nearly 20 years since the conference was convened. In schools where students have little or no faith in their own ability to succeed, educators need to provide both explicit instruction regarding the power of effort to help students get smarter and multiple opportunities to learn.

Students are like chameleons in the sense that they take on the coloration of their surroundings—the culture and the climate of the school. If teachers believe in them, students will begin to believe in themselves, to develop a sense of efficacy. If effective effort is the prevailing value, students will put out more effort. Students acquire efficacy in the same way that teachers do: through mastery experiences. Once students have experienced even a small measure of personal success, they can envision it happening again and will put forth even more effort to realize their dreams.

However, where do teachers begin when faced with classrooms full of perennial low achievers? There are answers from research and from the practical experiences of two teachers who do it regularly. Both the research and teacher testimonies illustrate the importance of helping students to set personal goals and to develop an implementation mindset to achieve those goals.

In a simple experiment, Oettingen, Honig, and Gollwitzer (2000) showed the power of envisioning and planning to get students moving in the right direction. After the teacher of the experimental class gave an assignment, the students were asked to envision a game plan for completing it. They had to specifically think through when and where they could complete the assignment. This request on the part of the teacher was sufficient to motivate the majority of students to develop a specific plan. In the control classroom, the same assignment was given without additional comment or instruction. The brief visualization of a game plan in the experimental class resulted in a significant increase in the number of students who actually completed their homework assignments as compared to the control classroom.

The researchers hypothesize that helping students to mentally represent their game plan gave them a structure within which to operate. Middle school teacher Kathy Hoedeman, described in the case study, Teaching One Student to Be Successful, has operationalized and fine-tuned the central concept of this research in her classroom. She summarizes her approach to teaching math and science this way: "Rather than rewarding those students who are responsible and organized with praise, good grades, and success, I do everything I can to teach every student to be successful." Hoedeman has developed procedures and routines to teach her students a game plan that rarely fails (McEwan, 2005, pp. 191–192).

Teaching One Student to Be Successful:
Kathy Hoedeman, Boyce Middle School, Upper St. Clair (PA)

When asked to choose one student who personified disengagement and lack of motivation, middle school math and science teacher Kathy Hoedeman selected Mark (a pseudonym), a sixth grader who had been labeled a lost cause by his previous teachers. "The teachers didn't like him, the kids followed their lead, and consequently he spent a good bit of the year in the office for behavioral problems," Kathy says. "Mark was a learning support student who was very bright, a bit quirky, and the most disorganized student I had ever met. But his learning support teacher, my partner who teaches language arts and social studies, and I made Mark our personal project for the year. We would not give up on that kid. Everybody stayed on him, but in a very positive and caring way. We locked arms and would not let him get through our blockade of care, support, and instruction. When one of us got frustrated, one of the others would read a poem aloud that Mark had written on the back of a math assignment he didn't turn in. When somebody else got discouraged, I would tell them something amazing that Mark had just done.

"By the end of the year we all loved that kid," Kathy said. "The world has to have people who think outside the box. Mark lived outside the box. But he was always interesting and thought provoking. Both my partner and I appreciated his intelligence and gave him a forum where he could speak out in class. Interestingly enough, by the end of the year, not only was he getting all of his homework and assignments turned in, but the kids in the class respected him."

Corno (2004) concludes, "What good students do to guide their academic endeavors—their good work habits and work styles—comes about through exposure to particular experiences and remains open to ongoing contextual influences. In fact work habits and work styles develop through participation in different educational environments, so they are sensitive to instruction" (Corno, 2004, p. 3). In an upcoming case study, Gloria Rodriguez explains her approach to envisioning and implementing plans with students who have grown accustomed to failure. Researcher Corno and educators Hoedeman and Rodriguez are in agreement: Work habits and work styles are highly amenable to excellent instruction.

Teaching a Class How to Achieve:
Gloria Rodriguez, ESL–Bilingual Teacher,
Cy-Fair Independent School District, Houston (TX)

I began teaching Math and Science in the Cy-Fair Independent School District (Houston, TX) in the middle of a school year. It was a combined Structured English Immersion class of fourth and fifth graders. To that point, the class had been taught by a series of substitutes. The students had very low self-esteem and even lower test scores. After I looked at their files and studied their test data, I sat down with the students individually and explained to each one where they were strong and where they needed to catch up. I told them, "Here is what you know. This is what you need to know how to do by the time we take the test. Let's make a plan. My expectations are very high." I said, "Eighty to ninety percent of you are going to pass the tests by the end of the year."

The students were excited. "How are we going to get there?"

I told them, "In order to get there you will have to study, review, do your homework every night, and do everything I'm going to ask you to do in class. I will teach you what you need to know." In addition to teaching kids what they need to know, I motivate them with music, movie clips, and inspiring stories. Our theme song for the semester was "I Believe I Can Fly." I brought in the CD, put the words on a transparency, and we sang it once or twice a week. I showed them clips from inspiring movies, like *Rudy* and *Facing the Giants*. Every week I told them a story about a real person, someone famous who had overcome obstacles.

I talked to them about my own experiences. My native language is Spanish. I told them, "I was just like you. My family was just like yours. We are successful because of these things that we did, and you can do them too."

Gloria was disappointed in the students' end-of-year state test results: 90% of her students scored Proficient in Math, but only 70% scored Proficient in Science. Gloria explains why: "Science was a brand-new subject for me, but a level of only 70% Proficient was unacceptable for me. That summer I took all of the professional development I could find in science. Prior to that time, math had been my passion. Then science became my passion also."

You can have the perfect curriculum, but if you do not motivate kids and your expectations are not high, they will not learn. The following year, a student was assigned to my fifth-grade math–science classroom who had failed all of the state assessments at every grade level to that point. Before the year began, I went to one of her former teachers to ask about what was going on with this child. The teacher looked at me, pointed to her head, and said, "Gloria, this student has nothing up here." After a year in my classroom, that student received Academic Recognition in both science and math. During the summer, I got an e-mail from the student that said, "Ms. Rodriguez, you built my confidence and now I know I can do anything." At the end of her first full year of teaching math and science to fifth graders, 90% of Gloria's students scored Proficient.

Eliminate Low Expectations

I was once hired by a central office administrator to work with the principal of a low-achieving school. Achievement in the building was actually much lower than one would predict given the demographics of the neighborhood. Central office was trying to figure out why achievement wasn't higher and looking for ways to boost the far-lower-than-expected test scores.

> Once you convey to children—whether consciously or not—that they are too "dumb" to learn, they will almost always prove you right.
>
> —Howard (as quoted in Feinberg, 2004, p. 1)

The principal was a charming person, and when I spoke with her by phone, she suggested I visit as many classes as possible during the morning reading block. When I arrived for my visit, I checked in at the office. It was beautifully decorated. I was sure that far more time had been spent choosing furniture and accessories than in reviewing test scores. The school looked like a wonderful place to learn. But it was obviously missing one or more of the ten traits. The problem jumped out at me in the first classroom I visited. Low expectations! My visit bottomed out in a primary classroom where the teacher wrote four sentences on the board and then in a demeaning tone of voice taunted her students, "I don't suppose there's anybody here who could read this." And there wasn't. She confided to me seconds after I entered the classroom that she was planning to retire next year, an obvious ploy to get me to lower my expectations. Later, when I addressed the teacher's dreadful treatment of her students, the principal reassured me with these words: "She's planning to retire next year."

"But what about the poor students who have to endure the next eight months of low expectations and disrespect from their teacher?" I asked. The principal's reply sealed their fate: "Well, what can I do?"

> Getting a slow start increases a student's odds of failure. In RTI [Response to Intervention] schools, it is viewed as too risky to conclude that a below-benchmark student is simply experiencing a developmental lag that he or she will outgrow.
>
> —Hall (2008, p. 1)

Intervene Before They Fail

Response to Intervention (RTI) is a data-based model that is designed to help all students achieve academic success. It was originally developed as an early reading intervention model, but it is now being implemented in other content areas and upper grade levels as well. Teachers refer students to special education only after multiple tiers of intensive help are provided and the student's response to the intervention hasn't been a successful one. The special education professionals define RTI as "a practice of providing high-quality instruction and interventions matched to student need, monitoring progress frequently to make decisions about changes in instruction or goals and applying child response data to important educational decisions" (National Association of State Directors of Special Education, 2006, p. 3).

RTI implementation in Grades K–3 provides multiple opportunities for struggling primary students to learn how to read without enduring endless years of waiting for a special education placement. Many teachers and principals are reluctant to take on what they perceive to be the extra work involved, but for educators committed to high expectations, there is no better way to turn around a low-performing elementary school from the bottom up (Bursuck & Damer, 2007; Hall, 2008).

Teena Linch and the faculty at Evergreen Elementary School (AZ) began using data-based instruction and tiered interventions during her first year as a principal. It was what she had done as a teacher, and since it had worked in her classroom, she introduced the concept to her teachers. "I didn't know I was implementing RTI," explains Teena. "But when I read a book that described it (Hall, 2008), I recognized the model immediately.

"My vision was to have a school in which each teacher had an accurate picture of what students knew, where they needed more intensive teaching, and how to plan interventions that got results. This model provides so many opportunities for students to learn because the intensive instruction is always targeted at their weakest areas. There are two big challenges to implementing RTI: figuring out how to collect and use the assessment data and keeping up with the pace of instruction. All of Evergreen's K–3 teachers are engaged in direct instruction during the 120-minute reading block. I tell new teachers that I'll be happy to provide them with a desk, but they won't have time to sit at it. I had one new teacher who lasted for only a year. She was a good teacher, but she was a slow starter in the morning. She just couldn't keep up with the pace.

"We are committed to delivering the highest-quality instruction during the 120-minute language arts block schoolwide, along with proactive early intervention in Grades K–3. Although it's a lot of work, it's far easier than remediating in fourth grade and up."

The teachers at Evergreen also use data to motivate students. At least once during every month, the teachers do what are called "test talks," in which they share with each child what their score was on a specific benchmark during the prior month and remind the child what work needs to be done to meet that benchmark. If students make their goals, there's a little celebration. If they don't, teachers help them understand how practice at home can help.

Build In Rigor and Relevance

In a qualitative study designed to investigate the reasons that many young people drop out of high school, nearly half of the dropouts interviewed said that their classes were not interesting and that they were bored and disengaged from high school (Bridgeland, Dilulio, & Morison, 2006, p. iii). The Rigor/Relevance Framework is a tool developed by the staff of the International Center for Leadership in Education (2007) to help educators pay more attention to the rigor (level of difficulty) and relevance (connection to students' real-world experiences) of their lessons and assignments. Rigor and relevance in classroom activities and student work products communicate to students the belief that they are not only capable of doing meaningful work but that the work their teachers are asking them to do and the knowledge they are expected to assimilate and apply is important for their success in the real world. In many highly effective schools, rigor and relevance levels are routinely monitored by administrators during classroom walk-throughs.

More than a decade ago, the concepts of rigor and relevance were called *authentic pedagogy* (Newmann & Associates, 1996; Newmann, Marks, & Gamora, 1996), meaning that students are given school experiences that are connected with their real lives. Authentic learning tasks required students to integrate various skills and strategies to organize, synthesize, interpret, evaluate, and create. Newmann and Wehlage (1995) analyzed the achievement results of 800 high schools in the United States. They then developed a rating system that determined the degree to which students received authentic instruction and were expected to produce work products in which they applied their skills and knowledge to relevant experiences in their lives. The findings are impressive:

An average student who attended a "high authentic instruction school" would learn about 78% more mathematics between Grades 8 and 10 than comparable students in a "low authentic instruction school. (p. 25)

Rigor and Relevance at Kerr High School: Raymond Lowery

When Raymond Lowery became the principal of the 800-student Kerr HS in the fall of 2007, one of the first things that he and a small faculty committee did was introduce the staff to the Rigor/Relevance matrix. [NOTE: The Alief Independent School District

(Continued)

(Continued)

(AISD), Houston, TX, enrolls about 12,000 high school students, making the student population at Kerr HS about 7% of the total population.]

Students are admitted to Kerr through an application process, but any interested students from AISD may apply. Students are generally selected based on statements from both their middle school counselor and teachers that they are able to work independently. Although the screening process chooses students with fairly clean discipline records and no significant attendance problems, students are not necessarily selected on the basis of their high grades. Many of the accepted students received B's and C's in middle school. However, most have passed the required state tests.

Raymond explains why rigor and relevance are crucial at Kerr. "We end up with a lot of really good kids here, and it's very easy to just pile on the work and think that doing more problems or answering more questions is a measure of rigor." At Kerr, students do not attend formal classes nor do teachers routinely lecture or lead whole-class discussions in traditional classroom settings. Learning activities, assignments, and final projects are structured by a semester-long curriculum found in what is known as a course PAK (Personal Activity Kit). Students work independently, in small cooperative groups and in ad hoc seminar groups that are pulled together as teachers discover a need for more in-depth explanations or question-and-answer sessions. Once a course PAK has been completed, students turn in their work and are given a test ticket to take the final exam. Tests are administered after nearly every PAK. Every student works diligently at meeting the course requirements, but the question that was foremost on Raymond's mind as he began his tenure was this: How rigorous and relevant is the work we are expecting students to do?

The rigor and relevance of the course PAKs was to be the focus of Raymond's first year on the job. Each department had chosen one PAK to thoroughly analyze and improve using collaborative inquiry in their PLCs. [Kerr has a PLC structure similar to that at Alief Hastings High School, described in Chapter 5.] Midway through the school year, the faculty convenes to showcase their model products and reach consensus on what the next step should be in their goal to make students' work more rigorous and relevant.

With input from faculty members, Raymond has developed an observation tool that incorporates the Rigor/Relevance framework. He questions students using the probes on the form and after the observation submits it to the teachers in that department with a reflection question he has posed. He later meets with the teachers as a group to hear them reflect on the question. Test scores at Kerr are routinely excellent, but Lowery has a more expansive vision of effectiveness for the school than merely checking off another year of higher test scores.

SUMMING UP

High expectations are tricky. Teachers can say they have high expectations because they expect their students to do tons of work and pass very difficult tests. However, tons of work and difficult tests do not necessarily mean high expectations. In order to qualify for membership in the high-expectations club, teachers have to believe that their students can achieve, explicitly teach them how to get smart, and convey a profound and unwavering commitment to their academic success.

High expectations can be communicated in dozens of ways: the daily interactions of student and teachers, programs that raise expectations while offering scaffolded learning opportunities, the rigor and relevance of the work that students are expected to do, and the dogged determination of the dedicated teachers who refuse to let their students fall through the cracks. Wherever the expectations come from, the results will be the same: Students will rise to those expectations, particularly if they are accompanied by opportunities to learn.

WHAT'S AHEAD?

Some would ask the question, Doesn't every child who attends a school have opportunities to learn? Unfortunately, the answer to that question is "no" in some communities across our country. Even students who attend excellent schools in upscale communities may not be afforded the same opportunities to learn if they are assigned to one of the few ineffective teachers in an otherwise good school or are segregated from the mainstream because they are different in some way from their classmates. Every child is guaranteed a free public education (if you don't count the school fees), but not every child is guaranteed excellent teaching or the kind of opportunities to learn that may be needed to achieve success. Chapter 7 explores the importance of opportunities to learn in highly effective schools.

Opportunities to Learn

7

The variations we observed across classrooms were striking—even in the same school, at the same grade level, and using the same curriculum, students had very different opportunities to learn based on the abilities of their teachers.

—Pianta, Belsky, Houts, and Morrison (2007)

When I became the principal of Lincoln School, I discovered two tracks: one in which poor white and Hispanic students were assigned to the most dysfunctional and ineffective teachers beginning in first grade and continuing through sixth grade and a second track in which the middle-class students or those whose parents were more educated were assigned to the most effective teachers. These tracking practices had a deleterious effect on all students. [NOTE: The school had only one kindergarten teacher, but because certain students were bused and others walked to school, she was able to track her classes quite neatly.]

Opportunities for all students to learn are available in highly effective schools. These opportunities are provided regardless of where students may be on the achievement continuum. Enhanced and accelerated classes, AP classes, opportunities to take classes for college credit and high school credit simultaneously at a local community college, and independent study modules are provided for the students who need them. Scaffolded opportunities to learn are provided during additional periods of time in which the students who have not acquired mastery have the opportunities they need to achieve. These opportunities may come in the form of in-class booster sessions provided by the teacher; double or triple class periods; tutorials before, during, and after school; study halls; lunch hours; Saturday or vacation sessions; or summer school.

A MENU OF OPPORTUNITIES TO LEARN

To focus on raising the achievement bar without also discussing the provision of opportunities to learn is meaningless. High expectations and opportunities to learn are the opposite sides of a coin—the currency of students' achievement. On one side of the coin are the words *I expect you to do it.* On the other side are the words *I won't let you fail.* Here are three categories of ways to provide opportunities to learn for all students: (1) Give them highly effective teachers every year and in every content area, (2) maximize the use of their allocated learning time, and (3) provide extended learning opportunities during and outside of the school day.

> No amount of good feeling is adequate without that pedagogical dimension, without students actually knowing more and being able to do more at the end of a school year than they could at the beginning.
>
> —*Kohl (1998, p. 27)*

Provide Highly Effective Classroom Teachers

There are some students who are able to learn in spite of ineffective teachers. They are self-motivated, able to make sense of garbled lectures, and work hard no matter how confusing, impersonal, or disinterested the teacher may be. Unfortunately, there are very few of these types of students, especially in challenging schools. Most students need the very best teachers from their first day in kindergarten until they graduate from high school.

When I originally considered the parameters of opportunities to learn, I thought solely in terms of the extra time and interventions that many students need in order to be remediated or caught up. However, highly effective schools actually provide an up-front opportunity to learn that is missing for many children, especially those who are poor, come to school with fewer readiness skills, or reside in urban areas—a highly effective teacher every day and every year of their K–12 experience. I have seen firsthand what happens in a school where the "haves," students whose parents have more resources and education, are assigned to the best teachers year after year and the "have-nots," those students whose parents are not educated and do not have resources, get the ineffective teachers.

Sanders and Horn (1995) found that groups of students with comparable levels of achievement in second grade had widely divergent scores by the time they were in fifth grade. The scores were strongly correlated with the quality of the teachers in whose classrooms the students spent the intervening three years. Fifth graders who had had three years of ineffective teaching averaged 54 to 60 percentile points lower on standardized tests than students who had had three years of effective teaching.

Opportunities for poor and minority students to learn are held hostage by vast numbers of underqualified and unqualified teachers in high-poverty and high-minority communities. This practice has been substantiated by a variety of studies (Education Trust, 2006; Haycock, 1998; Peske & Haycock, 2006), but the lack of opportunities for students to have highly qualified teachers is not just a problem in urban areas. *Opportunities to Learn in America's Elementary Classrooms* (Pianta et al., 2007) points out that even in better schools where most of the students are middle class, much of the instruction is mediocre.

> Quantity of instructional time can be doubled or tripled in a semester. Quality of instructional time cannot. Filling an enlarged instructional window with quality instruction does not happen without excellent curriculum, rigorous training, and diagnostic assessments. Improving quality occurs over extended periods of time, at different rates among teachers in the same school, and as a constant process of arduous, intelligent labor. That is why the primary and immediate strategy for catch-up growth is proportional increases in direct instruction time.
>
> —*Fielding et al. (2004, pp. 52–53)*

Maximize Time for Learning

Educators frequently blame a lack of time on their inability to teach the standards. Remarkably, effective schools with high-achieving students have the same number of school days as low-performing schools. Both kinds of schools also have roughly the same number of hours in a school day—allocated learning time. What, then, do highly effective schools do differently that gives their students more opportunities to learn?

Protect Teaching Time

They do not waste instructional time. Administrators in highly effective schools protect teaching time. They do not interrupt teaching and learning in cavalier ways by making announcements, scheduling frivolous assemblies, and permitting staff members to interrupt one another while they are scheduled to be teaching. They do not permit teachers to go off on tangents that are not related to the mission or to the selected curriculum. They realize that "the lesson is sacred," as they say in Japan.

Maximize Academic and Interactive Learning Time

Teachers in highly effective schools excel at maximizing academic learning time, the amount of time students are successfully engaged in academic tasks and moving toward specified goals at appropriate levels of difficulty. They minimize or eliminate the amount of time that beginning readers, for example, are engaged in tasks that have no relationship to mastering reading skills: cutting, pasting, and coloring. These teachers are also very adept at providing interactive learning time, the time in which instruction is specifically tailored to students' specific needs. They intimately know the strengths and weaknesses of the targeted students in their classrooms, and once directions and explanations are completed, they monitor those students to make sure they have understood what is required and have immediately begun to work. They teach the target students routines for what to do when they don't understand and where to go for help when the teacher is not immediately available.

Teach the 3Rs

In highly effective schools, the majority of teachers use short blocks of instructional time at the beginning of the school year, 1–3 weeks depending on the grade, to teach their students "the 3Rs (routines, rubrics, and rules)" of their classroom and school (McEwan, 2006). Once taught and mastered by students, the 3Rs ensure that the time that is wasted in many schools is reclaimed for learning.

For example, at Northbrook Middle School (Spring Branch, TX), teachers use a schoolwide camping theme to teach scripted lessons about their behavioral expectations for students while in the auditorium, at lockers and in the hallway, in the cafeteria, and on the bus. Teachers are free to add their own creative touches to the scripts, which are tweaked periodically to reflect changes in the rules. Principal Laura Schuhmann says, "Four to six weeks into the year, we take a day to review the rules, quizzing the students and leading discussions about problems that may have arisen."

At Joliet Central High School (IL), teachers subscribe to the 3 + 3 = 33 concept: The more consistently they teach their students the routines, rubrics, and rules (3Rs) at the beginning of the school year (3 weeks), the more productive the rest of the year (33 weeks) will be. Teachers who begin their school year in this way can anticipate the following rewards:

- Increased time for teaching
- Increased time on task for students
- More academically successful students
- More positive attitudes from students
- Fewer discipline problems and referrals

- Higher student achievement
- A high degree of parental support
- Increased levels of job satisfaction

Model and Monitor Effective Instructional Practices

Educational research doesn't give us all the answers to raising the achievement bar, but it gives us enough to fill a full year of embedded professional development. There are dozens of instructional practices that are strongly associated with increased student achievement, as shown by comprehensive reviews of the literature. In highly effective schools, these instructional practices are discussed by teachers in grade-level teams; modeled by administrators, coaches, and teacher-leaders; and monitored by strong instructional leaders. Figure 7.1 summarizes three reviews of research on effective teaching.

Learning Opportunities During and Outside of the School Day

Educators who are committed to the belief that all children can achieve the established state or district standards quickly realize the impossibility of attaining these goals if extended learning opportunities are not offered to struggling students. The critical issue for educators should be not *when* a student learns something but *whether* a student learns something. Spady (1992) likens this commonsense principle to the Scout merit badge system, an apprenticeship program, or simply receiving a license to drive a car or fly a plane. Educators must find ways to break through the time barrier that keeps large numbers of students from achieving academic success.

Ideally, students would not fall behind but would be caught before they fell through the cracks, preferably early in kindergarten. Unfortunately, in schools where achievement is lowest, kindergarten students arrive already two to three years behind the grade-level expectations for kindergarten, so catching up is the first order of business, not something to undertake in later grades—by then, it's too late. Students who are seriously behind in key content areas like Mathematics and Reading need booster sessions (more intensive small-group instruction on prerequisite skills at the elementary level) or double and triple periods of instruction in key content areas at the secondary level. The older the students, the more time is required to catch up.

At Washington Elementary School in Kennewick, Washington, there is scarcely a second wasted. Every child in Grades K–3 receives 120 minutes of continuous instruction in reading. Saphier and Gower (1997) call this interactive instruction and define it as "time with a teacher actively

Figure 7.1   Research Reviews of Instructional Best Practices

Reseachers-Authors	Topic	Instructional Practices That Are Associated With Increased Student Achievement
Brophy (1999)	Synthesis of the principles of effective teaching	1. A supportive classroom climate 2. Curricular alignment 3. Thoughtful discourse (questions and discussion about "big ideas") 4. Scaffolding (the provision of help for struggling students) 5. Goal-oriented assessment 6. High and consistent expectations for achievement
Marzano, Gaddy, and Dean (2000)	Instructional approaches that improve student achievement	1. A supportive classroom climate 2. Curricular alignment 3. Thoughtful discourse (questions and discussion about "big ideas") 4. Scaffolding (the provision of help for struggling students) 5. Goal-oriented assessment 6. High and consistent expectations for achievement
Walberg and Paik (2000)	Nine instructional practices that work in K–12 settings	1. Giving students feedback on homework 2. Focusing instruction on specific learning goals 3. Providing direct instruction to include sequencing of lessons, guided practice, and immediate feedback 4. Making connections between past and present learning and alerting students to the main ideas 5. Teaching learning strategies 6. Tutoring students one to one 7. Insisting that students master foundational concepts and skills before moving on to new learning 8. Teaching cooperative learning techniques and expecting students to work in cooperative learning groups 9. Combining approaches like tutoring, mastery learning, cooperative learning, and strategic instruction

Reproduction of material from this book is authorized only for the local school site or nonprofit organization that has purchased *Ten Traits of Highly Effective Schools: Raising the Achievement Bar for All Students,* by Elaine K. McEwan. Thousand Oaks, CA: Corwin Press, www.corwinpress.com.

working on material as opposed to seatwork, written assignments, or silent reading" (p. 68). Every group of students is receiving continuous instruction (interactive instruction) from a teacher or a paraprofessional during the entire 120 minutes. Continuous instruction is an art form at Washington, and one can see from the evidence (recall Figure 3.4) that teachers have become more skilled at delivering it each year. According to Dave Montague, 120 minutes creates only annual growth (i.e., one year of growth) for students. Students who are behind need more time to catch up. Some need 30 minutes in addition to the 120, some need an hour, and some need even more. He says, "We give them whatever time they need to reach the goal. Time is allocated proportional to their deficiency. The greater the deficiency, the more direct instructional time they receive."

At Northbrook Middle School, students who have failed to master required outcomes in the prior school year are required to attend a mandatory six-week after-school tutorial in the beginning of the new school year. During one-and-a-half-hour sessions, two times weekly, students are provided with tutorials focused on their specific academic deficiencies. The students receive incentive rewards, snacks are always served, and teachers are given discretionary funds to purchase small items they feel will motivate their students. At the end of the six-week session, students are treated to a special fine arts performance. Principal Laura Schuhmann reports that she and her staff experienced a great deal of resistance from both parents and students during the first year of mandatory afterschool tutoring. Since their test scores have risen and success has become part of the school's culture, everyone is now onboard. "Compared to three years ago, there's been an amazing shift of attitude."

At Kamiakin High School in Kennewick, Washington, ninth graders who are entering high school below grade level are given increased opportunities to become more successful students. Four English teachers are assigned a ninth-grade reading class as part of their schedule. Each of these teachers also has at least two and sometimes three sections of ninth-grade English. The reading classes are limited to 15 students. A student who comes to Kamiakin High School with pre-ninth-grade reading skills is assigned a reading teacher and has English with that same teacher later in the day. Each English teacher is teamed with a ninth-grade Social Studies teacher and a ninth-grade Science teacher. All students assigned to that English teacher also have the same teacher for Science (although not all in the same class period) and for Social Studies (although not all in the same period). The reading teacher coordinates with these two other content-area teachers. The reading teacher then assists the students with their reading challenges in English, Social Studies, and Science (D. Bond, personal conversation, October 3, 2007).

Opportunities to Learn at the Secondary Level: Central Valley School District (WA)

The Central Valley School District (CVSD) located in suburban Spokane Valley has very high expectations for all students. The community demands it. For example, although only 19 credits are required for high school graduation in Washington State, CVSD mandates 23 credits. In addition to passing the tenth-grade Washington Assessment of Student Learning (WASL) in Reading Literacy, Writing, and Mathematics (a state requirement), CVSD expects students to produce a lengthy culminating project on a topic of their choosing—researching, writing, and orally presenting their results to classmates and faculty (a district requirement). See Figure 7.2 for a demographic snapshot of CVSD.

Students who fail the tenth-grade test or even one of the required classes are at risk for dropping out. Repeating a class during the regular school day while keeping up with the usual class load is almost impossible for most struggling students. Failing two classes requires summer school attendance, a costly option in terms of time and money for students and parents. The combination of one or more failed courses coupled with failure on the WASL is often the tipping point for students who may already be disengaged from the traditional ways of doing high school.

High expectations aren't unusual in suburban bedroom communities. What is unusual about CVSD is its commitment to scaffolding success for struggling students, those students who are often overlooked in favor of more privileged students. Effective schools, however, provide enhanced opportunities to learn for all students. Jana McKnight, head teacher at Barker, the district's alternative high school serving 125 students, says, "There's a tendency in some places to look at the standards, select a packaged curriculum or textbook, put it out there, and then expect all of the kids to learn. But CVSD recognizes that all kids don't learn the same way. It would be nice if they did, but that's not the way it is. That's the beauty of our district. There are options."

Providing enhanced opportunities to learn requires smaller class sizes, more teachers, and looking for solutions outside the typical secondary school "box." Jean Marczynski, Executive Director for Learning and Teaching in CVSD, says, "Our district philosophy is to allocate our resources for teaching staff. For example, we have the fewest central office administrators compared to other districts our size in the state." She credits the creativity and commitment of secondary teachers at the district's three high schools who have developed "outside the box" options for students. These individuals include people like Jana McKnight, head teacher at Barker Center; Cheryl Regnier, counselor at Central Valley High School (CVHS), who coordinates its extended-day program; CVHS English teachers Elaine Fotland and Deb Albert, who have developed a unique extended-day program for helping students retrieve lost English credits; and Scott Sutherland, teacher of the school-within-a-school at University High School. Elaine also teaches the CVHS Collection of Evidence class, so named by the Washington Department of Education as an alternative way to satisfy the requirements of the Reading and Writing portion of the WASL. These educators exemplify the commitment in CVSD to the philosophy that all students can learn, given additional time and well-designed opportunities.

Figure 7.2   Demographics of the Central Valley School District (Spokane Valley, WA)

District enrollment	12,033
Central Valley High School enrollment	1,862
University High School enrollment	1,774
Barker Alternative HS enrollment	125
District on-time graduation rate	96%
Free and reduced-price lunch*	30.7%
Caucasian	92%
Hispanic	3%
African American	2%
Asian	2%
American Indian	1.5%
Transitional bilingual	2%

SOURCE: Used with permission of Jean Marczynski.

NOTE: "The Valley," as the area is known, is somewhat of a bedroom community for the city of Spokane, Washington. CVSD has been stable with little mobility until the last few years. The growth rate has gone from a steady 1+% to closer to 3%. Spokane Valley is for the most part a traditional, hardworking middle-class and upper-middle-class community.

*CVSD has pockets of both extreme wealth and extreme poverty. According to Jean Marczynski, Executive Director for Learning and Teaching in CVSD, "The pockets of poverty are particularly difficult because they are not highly visible. However, the students living within them have as many challenges as inner-city poor students where more resources and services are available because of the density of the low socioeconomic population." The percentage of low-SES students in CVSD has increased yearly for the past several years by about 2%.

Reproduction of material from this book is authorized only for the local school site or nonprofit organization that has purchased *Ten Traits of Highly Effective Schools: Raising the Achievement Bar for All Students*, by Elaine K. McEwan. Thousand Oaks, CA: Corwin Press, www.corwinpress.com.

The Central Valley High School Extended-Day Program

Counselor Cheryl Regnier coordinates three extended-day programs at CVHS as described in Figure 7.3. Cheryl says, "The purpose of the labs is to meet the academic needs of students who are having difficulty succeeding in regular classrooms or have failed one or more courses." She keeps the extended-day program running smoothly by selecting students, contacting their parents, and then placing them in the right program to achieve academic success. She takes care of the administrative details, leaving teachers free to teach their students.

(Continued)

(Continued)

Figure 7.3   Central Valley High School Extended-Day Skill Development and Credit Retrieval Labs

Course	Language Arts Lab	Learning Assistance Program	History-Science-Math-Health Electives
Curriculum	CVHS ninth-, tenth-, and eleventh-grade Language Arts (LA) curriculum developed by Elaine Fotland and Deb Albert and delivered via Blackboard (2007), the online course management system	Language Arts curriculum based on WASL skills and standards developed by Learning Assistance Program teacher, Chrisy Riddle	Courses developed by Marcie James integrating the online lessons and resources of both PLATO (2007) and DigitalCurriculum (2007) and managed via Blackboard
Space	Computer Lab	Classroom	Computer Lab
Students	Tenth and eleventh graders and second-semester ninth graders who have failed a LA class and need the credit to graduate	Ninth, tenth, eleventh, and twelfth graders who do not qualify for Special Education but still struggle with decoding, comprehension, and writing skills as identified by the teacher	Eleventh and twelfth graders (first semester); ninth, tenth, eleventh, and twelfth graders (second semester) who have failed a History, Science, Math, or Health class or are in need of elective credits for graduation
Time	After school three days per week, one to one and a half hours per day	After school three days per week, one and a half hours per day	After school four days per week for one and a half hours per day
Seats	15	12	20
Staff	Elaine Fotland and Deb Albert	Chrisy Riddle	Marcie James
2004–2007 Student Retention	38 of 39 students enrolled in the course completed and received credit	55 of 57 students enrolled completed course and received credit	97 of 100 students enrolled and completed one or more courses and received credit
Funding	State of Washington		
Transportation	Students either provide their own transportation or take the late-activity bus		
Credit	Students earn .5 credit toward graduation upon satisfactorily completing the course work and taking the final examinations		

SOURCE: Used with permission of Cheryl Regnier, CVHS Counselor and Coordinator of the Extended-Day Program.

Reproduction of material from this book is authorized only for the local school site or nonprofit organization that has purchased *Ten Traits of Highly Effective Schools: Raising the Achievement Bar for All Students*, by Elaine K. McEwan. Thousand Oaks, CA: Corwin Press, www.corwinpress.com.

Retrieving Language Arts Credit at Central Valley High School

Deb Albert and Elaine Fotland are the designers and teachers of the credit retrieval programs for language arts at CVHS. Although PLATO Learning Environment™ (2007) online courses were available, Deb and Elaine weren't satisfied that they met the needs of their students.

Deb explains: "PLATO's Language Arts courses didn't match our curriculum or the state's learning targets. Since our students must pass the WASL, whether they take it as sophomores or later on in high school, we needed a course that hit our learning targets and replicated what we do in the classroom as closely as possible." Elaine and Deb decided to design one.

CVHS was able to partner with Eastern Washington University to access Blackboard (2007), an online learning platform. It was there that Deb and Elaine constructed three credit retrieval courses to replicate to the greatest extent possible the freshman, sophomore, and junior language arts classes at CVHS. Chunking the adopted literature texts, the teachers embedded questions that require thoughtful written responses. Before students begin reading a selection, they are given background knowledge, key vocabulary meanings, and an anticipatory set to motivate and engage them in the text. Elaine and Deb provide one-on-one assistance, grade work online, and give students immediate feedback on their progress. Because students work at their own pace, some finish the courses very quickly.

Elaine and Deb's energy and creativity have flourished in the teaching–learning community at CVHS. Although grant monies fund course development and pay an hourly rate for the three to four nights they spend with students after school, it can't begin to compensate them for the emotional investment and sense of accountability these gifted teachers bring to their work. Deb says, "When we piloted the first course, we mistakenly thought that since students were doing this on their own time, all we had to do was meet with them intermittently to monitor progress. That did not work. We discovered structure was essential. So we mandated attendance for three after-school sessions of one and a half hours each. Students had to have an ongoing accountability relationship with a teacher to succeed."

Not every student sails through the online course. Elaine says, "Sometimes we literally hound the kids to get them into the computer lab and working. We follow them in the halls. We call them and their parents at home. We do everything we possibly can to assure their success."

Deb and Elaine have discovered that some students who fail to thrive in the regular classroom do very well in the credit retrieval course. "Even though they have the ability and the skill levels to be successful in the regular classroom," Elaine says, "learning is not a social activity for them. They just want to do the work and be left alone. This online program meets their needs."

The Collection of Evidence Course at CVHS

The online credit retrieval option in language arts is perfect for students who have basic literacy skills and are able to handle the rigor of reading grade-level text and responding in writing to higher-level questions, but there is another group of students whose literacy skills are too low to meet WASL standards. That's where Elaine

(Continued)

(Continued)

Fotland's course known as The Collection of Evidence Class (a name given to the class by the state) fills the gap. The two-period-block class is required for students who have failed the tenth-grade WASL. The course is literature based and designed to bring students to mastery of reading skills and the writing standards for expository and persuasive writing. Elaine works with just two learning targets at a time for her class of under 20 students. For example, if she is teaching drawing conclusions and evaluating the author's point of view, she will teach these skills using many different strategies and multiple literature selections until students achieve mastery. She says, "I've never worked so hard to design instruction in all of my years of teaching. Because there are no programs or textbooks for this class, I need to find skill-level-appropriate examples of literature to teach the WASL skills. To meet these standards, students must be able to independently read a selection, write responses to WASL questions, and provide text evidence for each response.

School Within a School: University Alternative Center

Scott Sutherland is the baseball coach at University High School where he has taught for 18 years, and he is also the sole teacher for the in-house alternative school known as UAC (University Alternative Center). His student body is small, usually 20–22 juniors and seniors who aren't on track to graduate because they have failed one or more courses. Scott began his teaching career as a high school special education teacher, but after eight years of teaching Language Arts and Math (his two minors) in a SPED Resource Room, he found his true calling—working with students who weren't able to succeed in traditional classrooms but wanted to stay on campus for specific extracurricular activities like sports, music, art, or drama.

How does one man teach Geometry, Algebra I, Health, US History II, and Global Studies to 22 students who failed these classes the first time around? Scott meticulously plans and teaches bell to bell, but admits he couldn't do what he does without technology and a cozy environment. All of the students have personal Compaq computers with word processing and presentation software, access to online courses from PLATO (2007) and NovaNET (2007), a big-screen TV, and comfortable couches for viewing Scott's customized PowerPoint presentations. Scott exemplifies thinking outside the box when it comes to personalizing learning opportunities for at-risk students. For example, one of his students had a new baby and no daycare options. He knew she would drop out and probably never get her diploma if she couldn't stay at UAC. So he bought a playpen. "Fortunately," he says, "the baby was pretty good and slept a lot. There were some days, though, that I was up in front talking about U.S. History with that baby on my chest." The young mother graduated from high school and went on to earn her associate degree at the community college.

Barker Center

Barker Center is designed for CVSD students who have tried all of the options at CVHS or University High School and are still struggling to fit in and succeed. Jana McKnight, head teacher in alternative settings for 26 years, knows the needs of the students. "The kids who come to us are discouraged and fearful of taking any risks. They are scared they're going to fail, but at the same time, they're scared that they'll succeed and have to do it again." Students who enroll at Barker attend regularly and hardly ever drop out. In fact, some students spend a fifth or sixth year at Barker in order to obtain their diplomas. Students are initially grouped with one of the school's five teachers according to the styles of both the students and teachers.

Building trust is as important at Barker as academics. Jana explains: "Friday is workshop day, and we run a variety of community-building workshops as well as special activities, like a resident author who does a writer's club, a social worker who runs a teen parent club, and the Kiwanis Key Club, among others. Two activities sum up the culture at Barker: (1) their annual day-before-Thanksgiving dinner cooked by the staff and (2) an outdoor graduation ceremony at which all of the seniors speak.

Thanksgiving 2007 was the first year that Barker alumni were invited to the Thanksgiving dinner, and more than 20 former students came back to celebrate with the faculty and current Barker students. "We have a steady stream of alumni coming back to visit," says Jana. "Young adults in their late 20s still feel connected to what they experienced here. I think it's because we have promoted the idea of a safe environment, where the challenges are academic and intellectual—not emotional and psychological."

The graduation ceremony is a tearjerker according to Jana. She says, "The graduation ceremony is what keeps the teachers coming back year after year. The kids aren't just doing school here. They're doing long-term self-improvement. They have made the connection between what they're doing now and the future. Their outlook has become, 'If I could do this, what else could I do?' When they stand at the podium and talk about the goals they have accomplished and what Barker has meant to them, we all shed a few tears.'"

The secondary educators in the Central Valley School District epitomize the big idea of this chapter: On the one hand, they expect all of their students to graduate from high school. On the other, they give them multiple opportunities to be successful, communicating in dozens of different ways, whether by chasing them down in the halls, fixing Thanksgiving dinner, or buying a playpen, that they aren't about to let them fail. Jean Marczynski sums up the collective vision of the board, superintendent, administration, teachers, paraprofessionals, and support staff: "We're here to help students be successful, and we strive to provide as many opportunities as possible to make that happen." [NOTE: Each high school has developed its own unique enhanced opportunities to learn. Space does not permit describing all of the programs, interventions, and opportunities for learning at CVHS and UHS. Furthermore, there are multiple enhanced opportunities for advanced students who are ready to tackle more challenging coursework. The strength of programs for all types of students is characteristic of highly effective schools.]

Highly effective schools also address the needs of students who temporarily fall behind in one or more classes or need an extra push to master a particularly challenging standard. Although most teachers readily offer their students help, either in class or before and after school, failing students rarely, if ever, voluntarily subject themselves to more of the same embarrassment they face in the classroom. They just leave school.

In highly effective schools, there is a well-established process that mandates and ensures that students who fall behind in a course attend a study hall tutorial during the school day or after school to get help immediately. Processes are in place to shepherd failing students to the right place at the right time and to provide them with intensive instruction that is appropriate to their needs.

Unique Opportunities to Learn

Many urban high schools are providing unique opportunities to learn, coaching students in going-to-college skills that more affluent students learn from their college-educated parents. Schools are taking urban students on spring break college trips, walking them around campuses in their area that they might never think of visiting on their own.

One South Boston high school took the students who were planning to take the SAT on a walking field trip to find the building where they would be tested, making sure no students would get lost and miss the start of the test. In some districts and schools, advanced placement classes and tests are no longer for the privileged students. In Chattanooga, TN, there are no tracked students. Every student is now on a college track (Rimer, 2008).

On other campuses, teachers wear their college sweatshirts one day a week, and students are encouraged to do the same. Counselors visit freshman English classes to give their college pep talks, making sure that students understand about the fine points of getting into college: a high grade point average, tough classes, and extracurricular activities.

SUMMING UP

The variety of ways in which highly effective schools provide their students with opportunities to learn speaks to the creativity and resourcefulness of educators when they have a passion for raising the achievement bar. Without the types of opportunities to learn described in this chapter, educators limit the academic capacities of their students and diminish their own capacity as teachers.

WHAT'S AHEAD?

In Chapter 8, we investigate alignment—how content standards, curriculum, instruction, and assessment are linked. When these four components of a school's academic program are tightly aligned, achievement soars. Alignment in a school is not as easy to detect as lack of trust, instructional leadership, or low expectations, but without it, educators are working hard and going nowhere.

Alignment

A good school is not a collection of good teachers working independently, but a team of skilled educators working together to implement a coherent instructional plan, to identify the learning needs of every student, and to meet those needs.

—Boudett et al. (2005, p. 2)

Keeping a group of teachers articulated and coordinated is no small accomplishment, particularly if they have had years of instructional and curricular autonomy. I can recall a conversation I had with a somewhat desperate California principal during one of my workshops. He told me during a break that he was in danger of losing his job because achievement in his school was so low. I asked him what was happening in the first-grade classrooms.

He thought for a moment and then said, "Eight different things." When I looked puzzled, he explained in more detail. "I have eight sections of first grade," he said. "Each teacher is doing her own thing."

"Aha," I said to him. "If you want to save your job, you'd better get them all singing the same song." His school badly needed an alignment.

THE ALIGNMENT OF A HIGHLY EFFECTIVE SCHOOL

The highly effective school's content standards, curriculum, instruction, and assessments (formative and performance based) are in alignment and ensure a coherent and consistent academic program that meets the needs of all students.

The alignment of a school is somewhat like the alignment of an automobile. There are four wheels on most vehicles that need to be moving in precisely the same direction for optimum performance, and there are four components of a school's academic program that need to be similarly calibrated to ensure maximum student achievement: content standards, curriculum, instruction, and assessment. Figure 8.1 defines the components.

School alignment is the linkage between content standards (as set by state, district, or school), curriculum, instruction, and assessment that ensures consistency within and coherence across grade levels. The stronger the consistency and coherence, the more aligned a school's program is. The tighter the alignment, the greater likelihood that achievement will be high. Students of all ages learn more readily when they know what they are learning, how it is related to the content standards, and why they are learning it.

Alignment produces consistency and coherence for both teachers and students. A consistent program has similar outcomes and curricula at every grade level (elementary school) or in every content area (secondary school). If a program is inconsistent, it will be characterized by the "Julie Andrews syndrome": Each teacher in a grade level or department is doing his or her favorite things. With a consistent program in place, all students in a grade level or department will have similar opportunities to learn. For example, students enrolled in freshman English with Mrs. Bequeath will encounter the same expectations regarding the quantity and quality of literature they read as the students enrolled in Mr. Smith's section across the hall. The essays written by both classes will be graded using the department's collaboratively developed scoring rubric, and students will be expected to write the same number of book summaries during the semester.

A *coherent* program is connected from beginning to end in a district (PreK–12) or whichever grade ranges are found in a particular school. In a coherent program, preparation for the third-grade writing assessment does not begin with a mad dash for the finish line at the beginning of third grade but at the beginning of kindergarten. When coherency is present, teachers at every grade level know the expectations for students in both the preceding and succeeding school years. Ensuring that school and classroom activities are consistent with adopted or mandated standards as well as consistent and coherent with other grade levels or courses in their school necessitates the type of collaboration described in Chapter 5's case

Figure 8.1   Definitions of Academic Program Components

Content Standards

A statement of what students are expected to know, understand, or do as a result of completing a specific grade level, course of study, or range of grades (elementary school, middle school, or high school). More commonly, standards are referred to as "the state standards," meaning that the standards have been adopted by a state and will be assessed on some type of summative test at all or certain grade levels.

Curriculum

The overall plan developed by or for teachers to use as a guide to instruction in a content area or grade level. It is directly informed by content standards and generally includes a list of materials, textbooks, technology, and trade books that support the content standards. It may contain a scope and sequence and pacing guides as well.

Instruction

Teaching that must be aligned in two ways: (1) with content standards, curriculum, and assessment and (2) with the diverse needs of learners.

Assessment

The process of determining what students have mastered, which includes a range of tests to include formative classroom assessments to determine the effectiveness of a lesson (i.e., learning-centered assessments), benchmark tests designed by teachers and instructional specialists to measure what students have mastered in a specific units, and summative tests administered by the state as part of its accountability program. Also includes rubrics used by teachers to assess student work products in a standardized way and used by students to assess their own work products prior to submitting them to teachers.

Reproduction of material from this book is authorized only for the local school site or nonprofit organization that has purchased *Ten Traits of Highly Effective Schools: Raising the Achievement Bar for All Students*, by Elaine K. McEwan. Thousand Oaks, CA: Corwin Press, www.corwinpress.com.

study of the Alief Hastings High School PLC. In some cases, teachers may have to give up treasured units and curricular autonomy to support the common aims of the grade level and school.

BENCHMARKING ALIGNMENT

Benchmarking is a process by which an individual teacher or principal, grade-level team, or school undertakes an investigation to determine how a similar counterpart has managed to do something very successfully and then systematically learns how to replicate that success in its specific workplace. Here are three examples showing how two countries (France and the Netherlands), one school, and a group of highly effective principals in one district have conquered a chronic educational problem: lack of alignment.

Benchmarking Mathematics Attainment

An article titled "Benchmarking Education Standards" (Resnick, Nolan, & Resnick, 1995) reveals a surprisingly powerful way to attain high achievement. The goal of this study was to discover the secrets of Mathematics attainment in two countries that are noted for the achievement of their students. It was conducted to assist the New Standards Project, a consortium of 17 states and 6 cities.

The researchers investigated the standards, curriculum, instruction, and assessments used in Mathematics classes in France and the Netherlands. They discovered that although achievement was comparably high in both countries, each organized its curriculum differently, used completely different approaches to instruction, and tested its students using totally different types of assessments.

The authors were puzzled, wondering what, if anything, the Mathematics programs of these two countries had in common. They concluded that the convergence toward excellence that arose from two such divergent combinations of curriculum, instruction, and assessment was likely because "each of these countries uses a systemic approach to the teaching of Mathematics, in which texts, exams, and curriculum [standards] are all tightly linked, [giving] their students . . . a clear, consistent conception of what they are expected to know and be able to do" (Resnick et al., 1995, p. 459). The investigators had been looking in the wrong place for answers. They expected to find commonality in standards, curriculum, instruction, or assessment. Instead, they found that the secret lay in tightly linked program components—alignment.

Benchmarking Overall School Achievement

There have been several references in earlier chapters to Dale Skinner's approach to school improvement called the Formula for Success (FFS). A careful examination of how Dale taught his formula to teachers at two schools in Texas and how he presently teaches and models it for teachers and administrators in low-performing schools in California provides a plan for how to align an elementary school. Louise Sekula, Language Arts Specialist at Villarreal School, describes the process this way:

> Before we could be successful, we [the teachers at Villarreal School] had to learn three things: (1) the specific standards that the students at each grade level were expected to know; (2) how to design model lessons to teach those standards in rigorous, relevant, engaging, and meaningful ways at each grade level; and (3) how the standards were tested on our state's summative test—how our

students would be expected to read, write, think, or problem solve in order to demonstrate mastery.

Alignment is best achieved when grade-level or content-area teams work collaboratively to unpack one standard at a time to determine its essence, examine precisely what kind of instruction is needed to convey that essence to students in such a powerful way that they are able to demonstrate mastery on a required assessment, and then design a model lesson.

Professional development programs that feature only one aspect of the alignment process, like the development and use of formative assessments, curriculum mapping, or instructional design, are worthwhile and important. However, when removed from their context, the topics are viewed as innovations that will fade away, not essential components of a highly effective school. The lesson to be learned from examining FFS schools is this: Only teachers provided with sufficient amounts of time to engage in collaborative inquiry as well as leadership and support from instructional leaders and specialists are able to achieve the tight alignment that is essential to raising the achievement bar.

Benchmarking Instructional Leadership

Greg Fancher, Assistant Superintendent for Elementary Education in the Kennewick (WA) school district, where reading achievement has soared over the past 13 years, was asked by the school board to determine what the most effective principals in the district routinely did that enabled them to get spectacular results with nearly all of their students year after year, regardless of demographics. "At the time, we were experiencing a wave of principal retirements," Greg explained, "and board members wanted to make sure that the individuals we hired to replace the retirees would have similar profiles." After interviewing a group of the district's high-achieving principals, Greg discovered that the defining difference between being good and great was the ability to implement—the ability to get results. Greg compares implementation to a three-legged stool. It is an apt analogy. All three legs of a stool are of equal importance in supporting the body weight of the person who is sitting on it. The three legs of Greg's implementation stool are (1) curricula aligned to the standards in the state of Washington, (2) instruction that is differentiated for students in terms of instructional time, and (3) a district assessment that is aligned with their specific reading goals.

Greg says, "Anybody can make a plan. But not everybody is able to operationalize that plan and make sure that all of the critical pieces of the plan are put into action and that those actions are sustained year after year." Greg found that the star principals were able to do that. "They had the knowledge and skills to keep curriculum, instruction, and assessment aligned and on target and were able to do it in a culture of trust and collaboration." Star principals had the discipline to monitor alignment on a daily basis and to take immediate action to reconnect loose curricular or instructional pieces or pull things back into alignment when they observed an element slipping in a classroom or grade level or even schoolwide.

The lesson to be learned from high-achieving principals in the Kennewick district is this: Alignment must be monitored and supervised on a daily basis. Monitoring involves daily visits to classrooms; frequent drop-ins on grade-level, department, or PLC meetings; regular review of meeting minutes, short-term goals, and action logs; and ongoing conversations with teacher-leaders and instructional specialists to determine where support or resources are needed.

Supervision differs from monitoring in that it involves taking some kind of corrective action with individuals or a grade level or department whose behavior or attitudes are interfering with the mission. For example, the following problems need immediate attention from an administrator: a teacher whose absenteeism is impacting achievement in the classroom, a teacher whose students are frequently off task, or a team who has become bogged down in petty arguments over their roles. Without supervision and some type of corrective action, problems like these will take the academic program out of alignment.

STEPS TO ALIGNING AN ACADEMIC PROGRAM

There are four steps to aligning an academic program:

1. Understand and unpack the content standards of each grade level or content area, translating the standards into teacher-friendly and student-friendly language.

2. Select curricular materials (textbooks, Internet sites, media, trade books, and instructional activities) that align to the content standards and the needs of diverse learners. Include tie-ins to district-recommended or -mandated instructional approaches and strategies. Develop a pacing guide.

3. Aligning instruction is a two-part task: (1) Align instruction to the content standards and (2) align instruction to the needs of diverse learners.

4. Aligning assessment is a three-part process: (1) Unpack the summative assessment to determine the kinds of questions and levels of cognitive difficulty required as well as any published performance standards, (2) design formative assessments and use daily to improve instruction and provide feedback to students, and (3) design and use performance assessments, like scoring rubrics, to evaluate student work and to teach students how to evaluate their own work in advance of turning it in.

Some collaborative teams find that choosing one standard and working through all of the steps for it is a good orientation to the alignment process. A content department could choose to organize their work much like the Biology PLC at AHHS did as described in Chapter 5, examining the standards, lessons, and assessment results unit by unit. A more comprehensive description of each of the four steps follows.

Step 1: Understand and Unpack the Content Standards

Content standards specify the purpose and direction the content of a subject is to take when taught—what students should know and be able to do by the completion of a grade level or a secondary school course. Marzano, Kendall, and Gaddy (1999) provide three compelling reasons for having a well-defined set of rigorous academic standards in each content area and at every grade level: (1) Without an agreed-upon set of standards, getting results is impossible, (2) standards with a rigorous academic focus are necessary for maintaining uniformly high expectations, and (3) there is a strong public demand for education results—evidence that students have gained knowledge and skills from their schooling experiences.

There are some who would argue that standards, whether state or national, are not necessary to create highly effective schools. I can't disagree with that statement because there is nothing inherently magical in a binder of standards. However, in the absence of rigorous state or national standards, districts and schools must create and mandate their own set of academically focused standards or there will be as many curricula as teachers in a school, a practice that is still the norm in many schools.

Many districts and schools no longer have the freedom to choose what their teachers will teach or how and when their students will be assessed. Most states have developed academic standards and administer periodic assessments in every curricular area and at most grade levels. This fact of educational life in the 21st century drives our instructional efforts and is most assuredly a mixed blessing, for all standards and their concomitant assessments are not created equal. If a standard is fuzzy, indefinite, or incapable of being evaluated, as many current standards are, most teachers will ignore them or substitute learning outcomes of their own choosing. A teacher-selected set of outcomes may or may not be connected and articulated with any other teacher's chosen standards. A verbose or repetitive standards document invites teachers to tuck it away on a shelf to gather dust, rather than consulting it daily as a road map for where to head next. Some teachers may profess adherence to the standards but fail to prioritize instructional objectives or bring lower-achieving students to mastery in the essential outcomes before moving on to "cover" more material.

Strong instructional leaders work with teachers to translate fuzzy standards into plain English so they have detailed and understandable directions for instruction and communicate with both staff and students to explain the relevance and importance of assessments. Effective instructional leaders facilitate the translation, consolidation, coordination, and integration of state or district standards into a coherent set of school-level marching orders. Some principals even publish an abbreviated version of their school standards in a booklet for parents or develop Goals at a Glance summaries for teachers, to keep them focused on the essential outcomes for their grade or subject.

When I first interviewed Dale Skinner several years ago, I was intrigued by how much time he spent personally mastering the Texas standards in preparation for working with teachers. A former high school biology teacher and assistant principal, he was unfamiliar with the elementary school standards. I asked him how he was able to make the transition from the secondary school so readily. He told me that his first undertaking was the memorization of all of the standards for every subject at every grade level. When I expressed amazement, he said, "How could I possibly hope to raise student achievement in a low-performing school without knowing precisely what students were expected to know and do at every grade level?" That was Dale's first step in unpacking the standards.

Effective teachers translate the standards into more student-friendly language. Middle school Language Arts teacher Margaret Lawrence has developed student versions of the Kentucky state standards. Every time she gives students an assignment or a rubric, it contains a statement of the relevant standard in language that students can understand. Margaret describes her teaching as more intentional now that she has standards to inform instruction (as cited in Norton, 1999).

The first step to aligning any academic program is to unpack the content standards. Only when teachers take personal ownership of the standards at their grade levels or in their disciplines will they be able to translate them into effective instruction and solid learning for all of their students. If used creatively, well-developed content standards are a powerful tool for bringing about instructional and curricular change in a school. Rather than bemoaning their limitations or ignoring their mandates, effective instructional leaders use state standards as leverage to improve instruction and increase student learning.

Unpacking a standard necessitates a thorough understanding of it on multiple levels:

1. Translating the standard in language that is meaningful to teachers and students and using this reworded definition in all classrooms

2. Determining what the critical attributes of the standard are

3. Defining all of the related terms and concepts that are needed to both teach and master the standard

4. Acquiring student-friendly examples and nonexamples of work products related to the standard

5. Designing a model lesson sequence to teach the standard

6. Developing a scoring rubric using the performance standard required in the summative assessment

7. Determining how students will be expected to give evidence of their mastery of the standard on the summative assessment (how to apply the standard in a real-world application: multiple-choice test, writing in response to reading, problem solving, writing an original essay)

Ideally, a standard is unpacked with a collaborative team of colleagues who teach the same grade or course. In the typical collaborative team, there will be people who have taught a standard for decades as well as brand-new teachers who have never taught it. Heterogeneity in a teacher team is beneficial to the unpacking process. Different viewpoints will generate more examples and possibilities for future lessons and interventions.

When educators unpack a standard for the first time, it feels awkward, particularly if they have taught a grade level or content discipline for several years. They may even feel that the process is a waste of time because they have been teaching a skill for 20 years. However, this step is essential to

> For too long American teachers were given an overwhelming amount of curriculum to cover and, paradoxically, a great deal of freedom to decide what they taught. This resulted in an unhealthy curriculum anarchy, in which many students graduated with huge gaps in their knowledge and skills and many teachers operated in isolation from their colleagues.
>
> —*Marshall (2003)*

helping all students attain mastery. When a sizable number of students are failing to master certain skills or concepts, the problem lies not in the students but in the instruction. Unpacking helps teachers to master the standard themselves so they can more clearly teach it to students.

Step 2: Select Aligned Curricular Materials and Develop a Framework

There are some districts where teachers are still doing curriculum the hard way—writing it in summer workshops. Teachers simply do not have the time or expertise to write curriculum for every subject or content area at every grade level. My experience as a central office administrator matches this description of the process by Fenwick English (1992): "What often emerges from such projects is a vague set of platitudes and cookbook-type lessons that are unrelated, that are incoherent in terms of overall focus, and that remain unevaluated or assessed" (p. 75). Others are doing curriculum the wrong way—choosing a textbook and teaching it from start to finish, without regard for how the textbook aligns with the required content standards.

Teachers' valuable time is better spent finding or creating materials that assist them in differentiating instruction for diverse learners. For example, at Alief Hastings High School, the librarian has built a collection of easy-reading books about key concepts in the major content areas to scaffold instruction for ELLs and struggling readers. K–3 teachers in many districts have supplementary programs to use with students who need one or two periods of extra instruction.

Here are some important questions to ask during Step 2 of the alignment process:

- Does the chosen curriculum support the achievement of the standards?
- Are supplementary materials available to teach standards not covered in the textbooks?
- Is the curriculum vertically aligned K–12?
- Is the curriculum horizontally aligned across grade levels and content departments?
- What programs are known to get results in teaching the skills, strategies, or knowledge of specific standards that students are expected to master?
- What programs might be used to differentiate instruction for students who are faster paced and for those who need additional time to learn?

Step 3: Design Instruction Aligned to the Standards and the Learners

Standards-based teaching requires moving from an instructional paradigm that for decades has given classroom teachers unlimited curricular autonomy to a paradigm that spells out what students are expected to master in every content area and at every grade level. For some educators, this shift has been traumatic. Under the old paradigm, teachers evaluated their instruction using subjective guidelines: (1) How do I feel about the lesson? (2) Did my students seem to have a good time?

The new paradigm—standards-based teaching—gets mixed reviews. Some view the new paradigm as the cure for what's ailing education. Others see standards-based teaching as nothing more than a mind-numbing test preparation exercise that takes the joy out of teaching. Others worry that the standards are too high and will create too many dropouts, while others think the standards are too low and advanced students won't be challenged. Highly effective schools have embraced standards-based teaching as a way to align instruction with a specific set of standards, thereby ensuring that students across the grades and across the curriculum have the same opportunities to learn.

> The conflict between focusing on standards and focusing on individual learners' needs exists only if we use standards in ways that cause us to abandon what we know about effective curriculum and instruction.
>
> —*Tomlinson (2000, p. 6)*

In highly effective schools, instruction is both learner centered (differentiated according to the needs of the learner) and content centered (organized from a deep conceptual understanding of the skills and content of the discipline as well as the way in which it is organized).

The standards are nonnegotiable. Learning-centered instruction begins with the standards to be mastered, continues with the selection of appropriate materials to support instruction, and then goes on to apply research-based strategies that incorporate the following principles of learning:

- New learning is invariably shaped by the learner's prior knowledge. Therefore, the lesson must include some assessment of students' background knowledge as well as the provision of information and concepts that are essential to understanding the new material.
- All learning consists of connecting the new to the known. The moment of integration is when learning occurs. Therefore, the lesson must include opportunities for learning that include social interaction, discussion, writing, explaining, defending, or questioning.

- Learning occurs more readily when learners see assignments, tasks, or activities as being purposeful, meaningful, and relevant to their lives. (Burnett & Lowery, 2006)

Designing lessons in collaborative work groups has only recently come to be a part of professional development in the United States, but it is catching on. Lesson Study Groups have long been part of Japanese professional development. During the first year of implementation, Dale Skinner's FFS schools set aside one afternoon per week for professional development sessions that are similar to *jughokenkyu* (the Japanese lesson study approach). The agenda is usually constructed around a standard that has been particularly challenging for a large percentage of the students to master (e.g., estimating, summarizing, cause and effect, inferring). To begin, the principal, coach, or instructional specialist often leads a discussion about the critical attributes of the standard, perhaps modeling ways that adults might use it in their professional lives. Next, a sample lesson appropriate for third grade would be taught. Then the faculty would divide into grade-level groups to unpack the standard and design a lesson to teach it at a specific grade level. In Japan, the process looks like this:

For example, fifth-grade teachers at a school might come together to plan a lesson on how to find the area of a triangle, a typical mathematics benchmark or standard. They meet several times as a group to draft a plan for this lesson, and ultimately one of the teachers in the group will teach the lesson with all other group members present in the classroom. The teachers will then reflect on lesson implementation and try out improvements by having a second group member teach a revised version of the lesson. Often all teachers from the school, and sometimes the entire district, are invited to see this revised version of the lesson. At the end of the school year, a booklet containing the results of the lesson study is often printed by the school (Yoshida, 1999, p. 6).

The lesson study process requires teachers to articulate the "big ideas," define important vocabulary, tease out critical attributes, and find or create perfect examples and nonexamples. Relevant and rigorous examples and nonexamples of student work and thinking are needed so that students can judge their own work and that of their peers. During the lesson study process, teachers practice teach in front of each other and practice modeling and thinking aloud for students. Another aspect of the lesson study process is the development of intervention strategies to help struggling students as well as the development of alternative materials and approaches that are motivating and engaging.

Using standards as a basis for choosing curriculum and designing lessons does not mean standardizing your teaching or curriculum to a one-size-must-fit-all mode. Standards provide the direction; standards-based teaching must be aligned to the needs of the students. The enhanced opportunities to learn described in Chapter 7 are excellent examples of standards-based teaching that is designed for diverse learners. Recursive teaching, mastery learning, response to intervention, and adjusting quantity of time are other ways to differentiate instruction that enable diverse learners to meet standards.

However, achievement for all students will soar when individual teachers meet the academic needs of *all* of their students on a daily basis using a variety of instructional strategies to include the following:

- Provide "advance organizers" for all lessons.
- Use the "I Do It, We Do It, You Do It" lesson plan when introducing new material or especially difficult skills and concepts.
- Preview and preteach critical concepts and vocabulary, especially for English language learners and students who are at risk.
- Check for understanding frequently.
- Assess for learning *and* for grading.
- Use graphic organizers and concept maps.
- Use easy-reading nonfiction to build background knowledge.
- Use the cooperative learning model, creating content-based cooperative games and activities.
- Provide models, examples, and nonexamples for students.
- Increase wait time to give all students time to process questions.
- Build in frequent processing "breaks" to give students opportunities to think about, talk about, and write about the "big ideas" of the lesson.
- Think aloud regularly for students, showing them how teachers use cognitive strategies to make sense of difficult text, summarize and remember what they read, and connect what they read to prior learning and experiences.
- Expect all students to think aloud regularly.
- Teach students how to mark text as they read using highlighters, hand-written comments, or "props" like sticky flags, arrows, or notes.
- Teach students how to graphically organize text and concepts by "chunking" (dividing) large text selections into smaller sections.
- Teach students the power of visualizing what they need to remember.
- Teach students how to use mnemonics to remember important factual material.

> While a focus on testing can illuminate potential learning issues, testing alone cannot move learning forward: To improve student performance, classroom instruction needs to improve.
>
> —*Ciofalo and Wylie*
> *(2006, p.1)*

- Vary teaching models, approaches, and strategies from day to day.
- Determine what's hard for students about certain skills or concepts and collaboratively design lessons to overcome specific learning difficulties.
- Expect students to summarize (either in writing, verbally, or visually) what they have learned during a specific class period. (McEwan, 2007)

Step 4: Align Assessment

Recall that there are several steps to aligning assessment: (a) Unpack the summative assessment, (b) design and use daily formative assessments, and (c) design and daily use performance assessments.

Unpack the Summative Assessment

While there are many educators who rail against the evils of teaching to the test, I must once again defer to Fenwick English who said, "There is nothing wrong in teaching to the test if the test 'matches' the objectives contained in the curriculum designed for delivery. In cases where tests are to be used as accurate and valid measures for determining whether pupil learning has occurred as intended, one always teaches to the test. If this were not the case, the test data would not have much to do with any specific curriculum and would be useless as a source of information to improve learning" (English, 1992, p. 18). In highly effective schools, teaching to the test means delivering rigorous and relevant instruction to all students all day every day (and even after school when necessary, for students who need to catch up) and then confidently watching those students tackle the summative tests with enthusiasm and motivation to demonstrate how much they know and can do. Unpacking the summative assessment is a two-step process: (1) Determine how students are required to respond to the questions and (2) establish the cognitive levels of the test questions (fact and recall, or analysis and synthesis). Knowing how the assessment is structured enables teachers to align their instruction with the assessment. For example, prior to renewing one's driver's license, it is helpful to know whether it will be necessary to take the examiner for a two-mile drive or simply answer multiple-choice questions. The type of test dictates how to prepare, and smart students go prepared.

Design and Use Formative Assessments Daily

In highly effective schools, formative assessment is used on a daily basis to improve instruction. Increasing the number of informal assessments can improve student achievement. Formative assessments enable teachers to make midcourse corrections, thereby enabling students to more readily understand. One relatively new approach to formative assessment is the use of diagnostic items (Ciofalo & Wylie, 2006).

The samples shown in Figures 8.2 through 8.5 might appear to be ordinary multiple-choice questions at first glance. But as you look more closely, you will discover that they have been designed to help teachers identify common misconceptions that students may have regarding specific learning goals. Diagnostic items can serve as powerful formative assessments, particularly when every student in the classroom is required to commit to what they believe is the correct answer, via a 3×5 card or a whiteboard. If students are using cards, the group can quickly be divided for further instruction. One teacher said of her experience in writing diagnostic items, "Creating the diagnostic item helped me to predict possible student answers in a systematic way. I had already thought ahead enough that I had a good understanding of what each answer would reflect about the student's understanding." Creating a bank of diagnostic items similar to the examples shown can help a grade-level or department team diagnose and differentiate instruction in very specific ways. In addition to the four samples, a template is included, Form 8.1.

Create Performance Assessments

Performance standards describe in detail for both teachers and students "what a good one looks like." The most common performance assessments are rubrics. Raising expectations and achievement entails far more than teaching students the right answers, although all teachers focus on content and background knowledge in their daily lessons. Grading true–false or multiple-choice tests is relatively simple. The answers are either right or wrong. However, to raise the achievement bar, educators in highly effective schools create performance assessments in which students' work products or performances

> I was holding a site council meeting and a parent asked if the teachers felt there was too much testing happening in schools today. I sensed that she felt I was making teachers do something that was taking time away from their teaching. But before I could respond, one of the teachers said, "No. If we don't give students frequent formative tests, we won't be able to help some children learn, because we won't know what they don't know. Teaching is no longer a guessing game. With information from the tests, I can teach students what they don't know. It works." The parent was taken aback, realizing that assessment was something that the teachers would do, no matter what.
>
> —Teena Linch, Principal

Figure 8.2   Sample Diagnostic Item: English–Language Arts, Grade 10

Standard

Rely on context to determine meanings of words and phrases such as figurative language, idioms, multiple-meaning words, and technical vocabulary

Sentence

Lucinda wrote an essay about the <u>impact</u> other people can have on our lives.

Which dictionary definition below most correctly defines the underlined word in the sentence above?

Multiple-Choice Answers	Teacher Reflections About the Answer Choice
A. Lucinda's friends and family	If students select A, they have not understood the directions; possibly they are not certain of what a dictionary is or how terms are typically defined in a dictionary.
B. To hit with force	If students select B, they are not able to use the context clues embedded around the word *impact* in the sentence sufficiently enough to determine which meaning to use. They may not understand that a single word can have multiple definitions and that it is their task to find the definition that relates to the context they have been given. They may not understand that the way a word is used determines whether it is a noun, verb, and so on.
C. Influence	If students select C, they are able to use the dictionary to look up words, and they are able to use context clues to determine which definition most closely relates to the way *impact* is used in the sentence.
D. To have an impact	If students select D, they do not understand that the best definition does not use the word that is being defined.

SOURCE: Used with permission of Allyson Burnett.

Reproduction of material from this book is authorized only for the local school site or nonprofit organization that has purchased *Ten Traits of Highly Effective Schools: Raising the Achievement Bar for All Students*, by Elaine K. McEwan. Thousand Oaks, CA: Corwin Press, www.corwinpress.com.

are evaluated along a continuum of excellence, thereby enabling them to see precisely what they must do to be successful. "Rubrics are scoring guides, consisting of specific pre-established performance criteria, used in evaluating student work on performance assessments" (Mertler, 2003, p. 126). Skilled teachers teach students the rubrics they will use during the school year to evaluate their written work, problem-solving abilities, and individual content assignments.

Figure 8.3   Sample Diagnostic Item: Math, Grade 6

Benchmark 1

Understands exponentiation of rational numbers

Benchmark 2

Understands the correct order of operations for performing arithmetic computations

Problem

$$5 + 3^2 \cdot 2$$

Multiple-Choice Answers	Teacher Reflections About the Answer Choice
A. 28	If students select A, they know how to work with exponents but do not know their order of operations (i.e., multiply before adding).
B. 17	If students select B, they know how to apply the order of operations but not how to use exponents.
C. 23	If students select C, they know how to apply the order of operations and how to use exponents.
D. 22	If students select D, they do not know how to apply the order of operations or how to use exponents.

SOURCE: Used with permission of Kathy Hoedeman.

Reproduction of material from this book is authorized only for the local school site or nonprofit organization that has purchased *Ten Traits of Highly Effective Schools: Raising the Achievement Bar for All Students,* by Elaine K. McEwan. Thousand Oaks, CA: Corwin Press, www.corwinpress.com.

ALIGNMENT IN A HIGHLY EFFECTIVE SCHOOL

Determining how to bring a school into alignment can be confusing. There are multiple experts, dozens of programs, and nearly as many sets of content standards and summative tests as there are states in the union. A single principal in a very small school might seem to be at a disadvantage without scores of instructional specialists and a generous budget for professional development. However, in a larger district with a bigger budget, there is less opportunity for hands-on involvement by the teachers who teach the content standards. Alignment can't be achieved overnight. In the elementary school, begin with reading. In the high school, find a department with strong leadership and excellent teachers and provide time for them to develop a PLC.

During and after the alignment process, someone has to monitor its implementation. Are teachers faithfully implementing the standards,

Figure 8.4   Sample Diagnostic Item: Reading, Grade 4

Standard

Demonstrates competence in general skills and strategies for reading a variety of texts

Benchmark

Makes inferences regarding character traits and motives and the consequences of their actions

Problem

Jessica walks home from the library after school feeling dejected. She was hoping that her special day would have turned out better. As she nears her home, she's surprised to see many more cars than usual on the street. Then she detects the aroma of fresh-baked sweets that permeates the air. She hears music and the sound of laughter coming from somewhere and her pulse quickens as she spots colorful objects dangling from the ceiling of her living room. "Could it be that this day will turn out better than I thought?" she asks herself.

Question

You can conclude that . . .

Multiple-Choice Answers	Teacher Reflections About the Answer Choice
A. Jessica's mother is having a family reunion for all of the relatives.	If students select A, they have concluded that there is a party, but they did not read carefully or did not pay close attention to the beginning and ending sentences of the text.
B. Jessica is a very unhappy person.	If students select B, they did not read the entire passage carefully and jumped to the wrong conclusion.
C. It is Jessica's birthday today and her family is having a party for her.	If students select C, they have figured out both the "what" and the "why" based on clues in the text.
D. Jessica's family is planning a party for her because she got all A's on her report card.	If students select D, they have concluded that a party is being held for Jessica but missed the reason for the party.

SOURCE: Used with permission of Dale Skinner.

Reproduction of material from this book is authorized only for the local school site or nonprofit organization that has purchased *Ten Traits of Highly Effective Schools: Raising the Achievement Bar for All Students*, by Elaine K. McEwan. Thousand Oaks, CA: Corwin Press, www.corwinpress.com.

Figure 8.5   Sample Diagnostic Item: Math, Grade 10

Benchmark

Uses the Pythagorean theorem and its converse and properties of special right triangles

Problem

A triangle has a hypotenuse of length 10 cm and one leg of length 6 cm. What is the length of the other leg? Round to the nearest centimeter, if necessary.

Correct Solution

$$6^2 + x^2 = 10^2$$
$$36 + x^2 = 100$$
$$x^2 = 64$$
$$x = 8$$

Multiple-Choice Answers	*Teacher Reflections About the Answer Choice*
A. 64 cm	If students select A, they either did not know how to eliminate the exponent in the equation or did not understand that they needed to do so; they did not know how to take the square root of 64.
B. 13 cm	If students select B, they did not understand the meaning of a, b, and c in the Pythagorean theorem formula ($a^2 + b^2 = c^2$).
C. 164 cm	If students select C, they made both of the mistakes described above.
D. 4 cm	If students select D, they did not understand how to square the lengths or did not understand that they needed to do so; they just subtracted 6 from 10.
E. 3 cm	If students select E, they thought that squares are found by adding a number to itself instead of multiplying it by itself.
F. 8 cm	If students select F, they have solved the problem correctly.

SOURCE: Used with permission of Daniel Rosenthal.

Reproduction of material from this book is authorized only for the local school site or nonprofit organization that has purchased *Ten Traits of Highly Effective Schools: Raising the Achievement Bar for All Students*, by Elaine K. McEwan. Thousand Oaks, CA: Corwin Press, www.corwinpress.com.

Form 8.1   Diagnostic Item Template

Standard or Benchmark

Question or Problem

Multiple-Choice Answers	Teacher Reflections About the Answer Choice
A.	If students select A, they . . .
B.	If students select B, they . . .
C.	If students select C, they . . .
D.	If students select D, they . . .

Copyright © 2009 by Corwin Press. All rights reserved. Reprinted from *Ten Traits of Highly Effective Schools: Raising the Achievement Bar for All Students*, by Elaine K. McEwan. Thousand Oaks, CA: Corwin Press, www.corwinpress.com. Reproduction authorized only for the local school site or nonprofit organization that has purchased this book.

Figure 8.6   Implementation Scan

Directions: Check each item for which evidence of implementation is found in this classroom.

Standards or Curriculum

_____ Is a student-friendly version of the lesson objective readily apparent (board, overhead, poster, or student notes)?

_____ Is the objective of the lesson tied to a required standard of the grade level or course?

_____ Are the instructional materials closely aligned with the standard or objective?

_____ Are new objectives connected to prior learning or background knowledge with an advance organizer?

_____ Is the pacing and sequencing matched to school or district guidelines?

_____ Is there evidence of the faithful implementation of an adopted curriculum?

Instruction

_____ Do the instructional approaches being used engage and motivate students (e.g., appropriate use of technology, constructive feedback, relational teaching)?

_____ Are the instructional approaches being used well matched to the learning objective?

_____ Is there evidence of district-mandated or school-mandated practices being used (e.g., cooperative learning, thinking or concept maps, graphic organizers)?

_____ Do students have adequate time to process (talk about, write about, or graphically organize) new learning during class time?

_____ Do students have opportunities to both teach others and learn from others in a cooperative group?

_____ Is there evidence of recursive teaching of essential skills (e.g., cognitive strategies for reading)?

_____ Is there evidence of rigor and relevance in learning activities (e.g., in questioning, use of challenging vocabulary)?

_____ Is there evidence of scaffolded instruction for struggling students (differentiated materials, assignments, cooperative groups)?

_____ Is there evidence of organizational and academic routines having been taught to students?

_____ Is there evidence of higher-level thinking and questioning?

Assessment

_____ Is there evidence of diagnostic or formative assessment taking place (e.g., various ways of checking for understanding being used as well as diagnostic items)?

_____ Are students able to articulate what they are doing and why?

_____ Is there evidence of how students' work products will be evaluated (e.g., rubrics, checklists, samples against which to evaluate work)?

_____ Are rigorous and relevant student work products displayed and labeled with the objective?

_____ Is there evidence of formative assessment being used to motivate students?

_____ Is there evidence of formative assessment being used to modify instruction?

Copyright © 2009 by Corwin Press. All rights reserved. Reprinted from *Ten Traits of Highly Effective Schools: Raising the Achievement Bar for All Students*, by Elaine K. McEwan. Thousand Oaks, CA: Corwin Press, www.corwinpress.com. Reproduction authorized only for the local school site or nonprofit organization that has purchased this book.

curricula, instruction, and assessments that have been agreed upon by grade-level teams in their PLCs or through any other alignment process? Figure 8.6 contains an Implementation Scan that can be used by administrators, teachers-leaders, or department chairs to keep the school tightly aligned.

Smithfield High School: How Lack of Alignment Can Result in Low Test Scores

Smithfield High School (a pseudonym) is a large urban comprehensive high school of 3,500 students and more than 250 teachers. It is a Title I school with multiple resources available to fund school improvement. Instructional specialists and department chairpersons support teachers with a variety of embedded professional development opportunities. The teachers are knowledgeable and experienced and count themselves privileged to work in an environment where they are appreciated by parents and the administration. They have been organized into PLCs and regularly engage in reflecting upon and evaluating the teaching and learning in their school.

The leadership of the school has recently changed, however. The former principal was greatly beloved but unwilling to be assertive and performance driven. The newly appointed principal has his eye on stagnant test scores. Smithfield is stuck in the third quartile of a four-part rating scale where they have been for the past five years. There is a sense of complacency and satisfaction in the faculty that needs to be disturbed. Dr. Stanton, the new principal, wisely decides to engage a well-known data consultant to work with a newly formed Data-Smart team to look for possible root causes of stagnant test scores.

At the first meeting of department chairpersons and instructional specialists, the consultant doesn't pull any punches with the group. "Stop drawing quick conclusions about what you think the data means. The data can't give you answers. The data can only give you questions. Then you have to find the answers to those questions."

One of the senior faculty members said, "For me, the big question is, Why can't this faculty of fabulous teachers do any better than this? We have every technology and professional development opportunity available at our fingertips. We've heard all of the national speakers talk about this issue. And we've had dozens of people in the building and in central office working on this problem for years. Why are we so stuck?"

"It's true," said someone else. "We've got pacing guides, common assessments that every department gives. Everything in this school is better aligned than a brand-new car. We've got some of the best minds in the city working on this problem. Frankly, I just think our kids have maxed out. We're doing the best we can with the raw material we get."

"We've had these meetings every year in the fall," said George, the Social Studies department chair. "The names and the faces change, but the conversation is always the same. I, for one, am tired of being kicked around because of our low scores. We're smart people. Why can't we figure this out?"

At this point, the consultant jumped in. "I think you are assuming way too much. You are assuming that everyone is teaching the standards. I can tell you from prior experiences with this problem in other schools like yours that when test scores are low, it's because teachers aren't teaching the standards."

"But I don't think you understand," the English department chair said. "We have had so many committees and specialists and district office staff working on this problem. If we were the problem, don't you think we would have figured that out before now?"

The consultant smiled patiently and said, "Well, let's do it one more time together. The first thing you need to do is unpack the standards more thoroughly. Before you can teach the standards, you must know them intimately. Then you need to figure out if every teacher in each department is actually teaching the standards. Perhaps there are some teachers who are still doing their own thing." There were furtive glances around the room and some eye rolling in the English department.

"Then," the consultant said, "you need to look carefully at all of the materials available to you from the State Department of Education regarding past tests to determine precisely how your students are being asked to demonstrate mastery of certain skills and knowledge. There are some subtleties that you may be missing. I'm not saying you are missing them. But my prior experience tells me you may be."

Each department met individually with the consultant during the next week, and then the Data Team gathered a second time to share their findings. The Science department was the first to report. They had discovered two problems. The state assessment asked four to five questions every year about setting up experiments. At Smithfield, the teachers set up the experiments in the interests of time and safety, so students had no firsthand knowledge about setup procedures, nor had they ever received any instruction in how to set up experiments. The consultant said, "If every student misses those five questions, it could be huge in terms of your students' scores in science. Capture those five questions and you'll see a difference in your scores immediately."

Another problem uncovered by the science teachers dealt with the amount of difficult scientific vocabulary used on the test. The teachers immediately recognized a problem. When science teachers across the district met to construct their common assessments, they purposely avoided using more difficult scientific terms so that their students who had mastered the science concepts wouldn't be penalized by not knowing more difficult vocabulary. In the interests of making things easier for themselves and their students, they had lowered expectations.

The English department was embarrassed about what they discovered as they unpacked the standard dealing with figurative language. Teachers had been completely focused on having students simply pick out or identify examples of figurative language in a text. For example, "Point out the metaphor or simile in this passage." The standard actually required students to determine the author's purpose in using a specific kind of figurative language, a far more difficult cognitive task than merely identifying the figurative language. Teachers were not teaching to the required cognitive level and their common assessments did not test it.

Other departments shared similar examples of misalignment. The Math department discovered that content from only one of the courses taught in high school appeared on the test. The remaining content is material assumed to have been mastered in earlier grades. Students had either never mastered the material or had forgotten a great deal. Math teachers had always known that their students didn't have

(Continued)

(Continued)

complete mastery of earlier standards, like fractions, for example, but felt pressured to keep covering the material because of the pacing guides.

The same issue was discovered by the Social Studies department, who reported that the state test contained numerous items on the U.S. Constitution, a unit taught in eighth grade. If the Smithfield faculty is intent on becoming a more highly rated school, there are multiple alignment issues to resolve. Before the meeting adjourned, the consultant questioned each department chair and the principal about precisely who would be responsible for implementing changes to instructional practice and when they expected those changes to be put into place. The group agreed on a time line, and the consultant promised to be available by phone and e-mail to answer any questions that might arise in the process.

SUMMING UP

Alignment is about coherence and consistency. Without these qualities, teaching and learning are random: Some teachers teach and some students learn. Some students in a school are fortunate to get teachers that teach every year and some aren't. Some teachers get some kids that know one thing, a second group of kids that knows another thing, and a third group that doesn't know anything. Without alignment, there are no guarantees that any child will get a connected and articulated Reading or Math program. Without alignment, students can't be sure that what they learned in one class will ever be mentioned again in the future. Alignment tightly links content standards, curricula, instruction, and assessment.

WHAT'S AHEAD?

In Chapter 9, we examine the trait called results. Results represent the payoff for the commitment and effort that administrators, teachers, students, and their parents have invested in the enterprise of student learning. Rising test scores are tangible evidence of the results obtained by a school. But as many educators point out, a test score is only a snapshot of the student body on one day out of the school year. The most significant evidence of results for educators is the growth and progress that individual students make during the school year—jumping three grade levels in reading comprehension, achieving an Advanced rating in two different academic subjects, or passing a high-stakes test needed for high school graduation after a disastrous freshman year. The testimony of the students themselves is often all of the evidence of results that teachers need: "You've built my confidence and now I know I can do anything."

Results

The litmus test for a good school is not its innovations but rather the solid, purposeful, enduring results it . . . obtain[s] for its students.

—Glickman (1993, p. 50)

Anyone who has breathlessly waited for results—the opening of the envelope or the counting of the votes—knows the routine. You're rooting for your favorite contestant or nominee with a nervous feeling in the pit of your stomach, especially if a family member or friend is in the running. Waiting for test scores in the spring or summer evokes similar feelings in educators. There's the moment when we find out: We did it or we didn't. Getting results is achieving a favorable outcome in an endeavor. In education, the endeavor is student learning, and the results come packaged in different data sets: (1) in the achievement or yearly growth of individual students who may be placed in various categories, such as Proficient or Basic, based on their scores; (2) in the overall scores of the entire student body that are often translated into a letter grade, label, or numerical academic performance index; and (3) in percentages of students achieving a required AYP goal.

> School improvement generally proceeds in phases rather than a steady linear fashion. Each phase involves more complex and demanding challenges than the prior phase and thus more skill and knowledge on the part of the people in the organization.
>
> —Elmore (2003, p. 12)

STAGES OF SCHOOL IMPROVEMENT

When educators commit to improving their schools, they are eager for results and the sooner the better. They desire data that will document the effectiveness of their initiatives. They should be prepared, however, for the inevitable and even predictable setbacks, according to Harvard scholar Richard Elmore (2003). He hypothesizes eight stages of school improvement: (1) problem recognition, (2) low-hanging fruit, (3) stagnation, (4) external help, (5) barrier resolution, (6) impossible work, (7) transformed organization, and (8) self-management of improvement (pp. 12–13).

When the leadership team at Lincoln set its first measurable goal in 1983, I was a brand-new principal, but I had no problem recognizing the problem. Reading achievement on the Iowa Test of Basic Skills (ITBS) was at the 20th percentile. Using the data as leverage, I convinced a sizable percentage of the faculty that we had a problem and that together we could do something about it. Recognizing a problem and taking ownership of it is the first stage of school improvement. The norm-referenced ITBS was not an ideal test for tracking student achievement, particularly in a school where 50% of the students were at risk for reasons of poverty and limited English proficiency, but it was all we had. I reasoned that if we taught the students who couldn't read how to read and taught the students with a fair amount of reading skills how to read more strategically, we had to improve. And we did. Elmore (2003) calls what we accomplished that first year "picking off the low-hanging fruit" or the "some teaching versus no teaching" phase. He says, "If schools succeed in choosing the right target and developing the initial knowledge and skill in teachers and students to reach that target, they typically see a modest bounce in students' performance" (p. 12).

We moved 17% of our students out of the bottom quartile. Our goal had been 15%. The superintendent was so thrilled he threw a party for us at a local restaurant. Compared to the research-based curricula, sophisticated interventions, standards-based tests, and sophisticated data-analysis methods that are now a part of school improvement, our efforts were rather amateurish. However, we all have to begin where we find ourselves, take stock of our resources, build on the available instructional capacity, and confront the issues that are holding the school back, with courage and vision.

Our upward achievement trend hit a bump in the road three years later. We opened the envelope and found what Elmore (2003) calls "stagnation." He explains that what is needed at this juncture is "internal accountability" and a focus on "adopting specific curricula and instructional practice." Although the teacher-leaders at Lincoln didn't articulate our dilemma in Elmore's words, they knew exactly what our problem was. So we developed learner outcomes to standardize what we were teaching. We read the research on cooperative learning and decided to adopt Robert Slavin's (1978) Cooperative Integrated Reading and Composition (CIRC) model to meet the needs of diverse learners in heterogeneous classrooms. We received training in CIRC and cooperative learning. We moved into the stages that Elmore (2003) calls "external help" and "barrier resolution," periods during which educators in low-performing schools need more resources and outside expertise to make it through the "impossible work" phase. We never made it through the impossible work phase. We were getting close when the Illinois State Board of Education began tinkering with school improvement. Suddenly, principals and teams in our small district were deluged with paperwork and mandates that distracted us from our internal accountability system.

In spite of the distractions, we managed to boost our student achievement into the low 70th percentile, but we most certainly did not reach the "transformed organization" or "self-management of improvement" stages—the final stages in Elmore's model. At that point the Board of Education decided to sell our 100-year-old school to the high school that adjoined our campus; the teachers and students were assigned to other schools, and I moved to central office. It was like putting a book on the shelf before finishing it.

Educators who are engaged in school improvement in the 21st century face the same issues that we did at Lincoln School—stagnation, barriers, and impossible work. The good news is that we now know more than ever about how schools can become transformed organizations.

> We must remember that if we make 15% improvement, it is only important because there is a face behind every percentage point. Fifteen percent is meaningful because 15 kids are doing better because of what we did. Too often people celebrate the improvement of test scores without realizing that it is only important because we have made things a little better for a child.
>
> —*Dave Montague*

GETTING RESULTS

Results are evident only through data—student achievement data on a standardized test (quantitative) or in some cases through observational and anecdotal data (qualitative). Whether our goal is increased learning for one student or 1,500, the process is still the same: (a) Assess and evaluate the data, (b) set measurable and attainable goals, (c) implement a plan to meet the goals, and (d) assess and evaluate the data once more. Recall the story I shared earlier in the book about my granddaughter,

Lizzie. Lizzie's reading achievement was three grade levels below her grade placement. Since the school and district had no answers for us, I recommended that her mother enroll her in a nearby Sylvan Learning Center for at least the summer and perhaps even longer. The diagnostic assessment she was given at Sylvan validated the informal tests I had given her. Her decoding, fluency, vocabulary, and overall comprehension of grade-level text were very low, compounded by her penchant for wild guessing. The specialist at Sylvan put together a program for Lizzie—one-to-one tutoring for two hours per day for two days a week. Lizzie complained bitterly about how we (her mother and I) were ruining her summer and spoiling her life. We knew better. The experience was so positive and improved not only her skills but her attitude toward reading in general that Lizzie ended up making a short commercial for the Sylvan Web site. Oh, that we could give every child the same opportunity to learn.

Getting results with one child, particularly when there are economic and social resources to draw upon, is easy. Getting results in a whole school of Lizzies takes more than good intentions. It takes implementation. Bossidy and Charan (2002) define implementation as "a discipline for meshing strategy with reality, aligning people with goals, and achieving the results promised" (p. 1). In highly effective schools, implementation is the attainment of a compelling and measurable goal as verified by quantitative or qualitative data. Implementation to raise the achievement bar begins and ends with data. It's a continuous cycle.

There are depressing examples of schools where teachers are instructed to divide their pupils into three groups, similar to triage in the emergency room (Definitely, Maybe, and No Hope) and to intensively "treat" only those students who show promise of passing the test. At the high school level, there are often limits for how many students can be placed in remedial or intervention classes, with students who have the best chance of making the mark given the available spots. Schools are savvy about the need to avoid negative coverage in the newspaper, a by-product of the very accountability systems that were designed to provide achievement opportunities for at-risk subpopulations. These regrettable attempts to beat the system are no reason to approach school improvement with cynicism. There are plenty of individuals who cheat on their income taxes, but this fact does not deter the rest of us from doing what we know is the right thing to do.

> We must remember that if we make 15% improvement, it is only important because there is a child's face behind every percentage point. Fifteen percent is meaningful because 15 kids are doing better because of what their teachers did in their classroom. Too often people celebrate the improvement of test scores without realizing that scores are only important because we have made things a little better for a child.
>
> —Dave Montague

WHAT TO DO WHEN YOU DON'T GET CLASSROOM RESULTS

Stiggins (2001) suggests five possibilities for why students might do poorly on formative and benchmark assessments:

1. They lacked the prerequisite skills or background knowledge needed to achieve what the teacher expected of them.

2. The teacher didn't understand the target [standard] to begin with, and so could not teach it appropriately.

3. The teacher's instructional methods, strategies, and materials were inappropriate.

4. The students lacked the confidence to risk trying—the motivation to strive for success.

5. Some force(s) outside of school and beyond the teacher's control (the environment, for example) interfered with and inhibited learning. (p. 62)

I advise educators to eliminate Reason 5 from consideration when they are investigating possible reasons why students are failing in classrooms. Blaming inalterable variables for low achievement is the state of mind that got educators in trouble in the first place. We must concentrate on the things we can control. The first four possibilities suggest several things teachers and principals can do to get results. Here are just a few examples.

Lack of Students' Background Knowledge

Find out what students don't know and teach it to them. Step into the shoes (or the brains) of your students, whether struggling or gifted, and figure out what is most difficult about the text or topic you are planning to teach. Or better yet, ask them what's confusing to them. With this information in hand, you can decide what approach will make the information more accessible. Even the brightest students may lack background knowledge or be confused by poorly written text. After you have determined the most difficult aspects of your content, directly teach students what they need to know to be successful. For example, using the text, think aloud for students regarding how you distinguish between important and trivial information when you are reading. Show a video clip, draw a diagram on the board, or read aloud from a primary-source document to provide background information that students may not have. If the main idea is especially difficult to understand, make a summarizing statement in advance of giving the reading assignment. Make difficult content as accessible as possible (McEwan, 2007, pp. 97–98).

Lack of Standards Knowledge by Teachers

Just as it is a mistake to assume that students have the necessary background knowledge to be successful in a subject or class, it is also dangerous to assume that teachers have unpacked the standards required for that subject or class. Unpacking the standards and designing lessons that actually teach the standards is an assignment for collaborative work groups. In highly effective schools, principals and teachers regularly examine the linkage between the content standards and what is actually being taught in classrooms. Also, recall the English teachers at Smithfield High School, described in Chapter 8. Although they were an experienced and highly trained group of educators, somehow they all assumed they understood what they were supposed to be teaching. Follow the lead of the Alief Hastings High School biology team and develop a set of reflective questions to use collaboratively after your next common assessment. Explore what's working and what's not. Share lessons and invite peer observations.

Lack of Appropriate Instructional Methods

For educators desiring to create highly effective schools, the improvement of instruction is "the toughest nut to crack," (Connell & Broom, 2004). Any administrator, instructional specialist or coach who has engaged in the hands-on improvement of instruction knows what a challenge it can be (McEwan, 2005). When I first interviewed Dale Skinner in 2002 for *Ten Traits of Highly Effective Principals*, I asked him how he approached a teacher who was having a difficult time teaching. Here's what he said: "If I have a teacher who is struggling, I get a substitute for that person, and we work on teaching each other all day. I teach, the teacher teaches, we just play with instruction. I believe that I can help almost any teacher who is willing to work with me to be successful, if I can work with them one on one like that." In spite of Dale's willingness to work with teachers one on one, 40% of the Villarreal teachers decided that they just weren't willing to do the difficult work of school improvement. The willingness and ability of teachers to change and how it impacts the faithful implementation of a plan is an issue that administrators, instructional specialists, and coaches must confront with courage and directness.

As PLCs collaboratively and systematically examine the reasons why their content team or grade level isn't getting results, there are opportunities to acquire research-based practices from teammates through embedded professional development. Teachers and coaches can hold their colleagues to high expectations but only to a certain point. In the end, when teachers can't or won't improve, instructional leaders must step up.

Unquestionably, teacher performance impacts results. Unsatisfactory teacher performance requires intervention from the principal, resources and support from central office, and the courage to confront individuals who may have been told in written evaluations by other administrators for years that they were satisfactory or even excellent. The norms for what teachers need to know and do have drastically changed. The ability and courage of administrators and their central office supervisors to deal with this change need to catch up.

> Teach your [students] to form vivid mental pictures of how they are going to reach their desired goals. . . . Children hunger for hope and respond to an environment that allows and nurtures it. . . . A good role model provides a lighthouse of hope for a safe passage.
>
> —*Snyder (1994, p. 209)*

Lack of Students' Motivation

Dale Skinner believes that unless students are fully invested in their own learning, educators are failing to maximize their academic capacity. His agenda for engaging students in the improvement process includes the following steps:

- Teach students to visualize wonderful things in their future lives using Dream Boards.
- Teach students to understand that goals are bridges that span their dreams.
- Teach students that the key to their academic success is effort. Then teach them how to make plans and give them opportunities to learn so they can achieve their goals.
- Teach students to visualize doing what needs to be done to reach their goals (studying, attending tutoring sessions, reading more books, practicing a skill that is required).
- Teach students how to visualize and organize to implement their plans.
- Give students hope for the future by sharing motivational stories, showing inspirational video clips, and featuring exemplary efforts and achievement of classroom teams or team members.

> Data almost always point to action—they are the enemy of comfortable routines.
>
> —*Schmoker (1999, p. 39)*

WHAT TO DO WHEN YOU DON'T GET SCHOOL RESULTS

Tracking down the sources of low achievement is often a process of elimination, but the ground rules for doing so are the same as uncovering classroom sources—concentrate on the alterable variables (Bloom, 1980). Here are the variables that we concentrated on changing at Lincoln:

- Change your focus. Zoom in on what's most important. Don't become distracted.
- Change how teachers teach. If teachers have unfocused lessons, poor classroom management, lack of time on task, and a devotion to their favorite things, their instructional effectiveness must be notched up.
- Change how implementation is monitored and supervised. If everybody's accountable but nobody is monitoring and supervising, anything that happens will be by accident, not by design.
- Change how you choose curriculum. Choose programs that get results, especially when it comes to reading instruction for any level.
- Change the alignment in your school. Check out the alignment between content standards, curriculum, instruction, and assessment. Tighten it up.
- Change the amount of time students are engaged in interactive learning with teachers or paraprofessionals. More direct instructional time equals results—if your alignment is tight.
- Change how learning is assessed. Use more formative assessments to make midcourse corrections in lessons and provide feedback to students about their progress and what they need to do to improve.
- Change your expectations for students. Eliminate teacher behaviors, attitudes, and language that communicate low expectations for students.
- Change how professional development is provided. Begin embedding professional development so that it hits the targets that teachers need today in their classrooms. Forget sending teachers to one-day workshops they choose from a catalog. It may make them happy, but it won't get results.
- Change how you treat students. Treat students as partners in teaching and learning—individuals who can have dreams, set goals, and work to meet them.
- Change how you deliver interventions to students. Make sure that targeted students aren't receiving interventions that are unintentionally canceling out learning. At-risk students need to receive aligned interventions.

THE KEY TO RESULTS: DATA

When someone says *data*, most educators think of the summative test. In many instances, however, this test can only tell you that something is wrong. It often cannot tell you precisely *what* is wrong. Some types of data communicate the status of achievement: state tests, benchmark assessments, graduation and drop-out rates, and individual student growth profiles. In order to determine exactly what is wrong, other kinds of data are needed: attendance, time on task, grades, homework completion, percentage of students failing in individual classes, the praise-to-criticism ratio in certain classes, observations of students, student work products, performance rubrics used by teachers, information about alignment in the form of content standards documents, curricular framework documents, faculty evaluations of the principal, principal evaluations of teachers, student evaluations of teachers, parent complaints, students complaints, disciplinary referrals, suspensions, and expulsions. Various types of data can help to uncover the root causes of low achievement.

Uncovering the Root Cause of Very Low Student Achievement

The average daily attendance at Marshall High School is 70%, clear evidence of a problem. If data point to action as Schmoker (1999) suggests, the question is, What kind of action should the staff at Marshall High School take? The school is failing and the teachers are trying to save their jobs. They have hired a consultant and the first assignment is a root cause analysis. The term *root cause* comes from the business world and *root cause analysis* is a problem-solving method that seeks to get to the bottom of a problem and then identify the real cause for the observed effect (Andersen & Fagerhaug, 2006). Data regarding student attendance at Marshall High School point to the need for action. On any given day, only about 70% of the enrolled students are actually in classes all day. That means that in any given classroom, at least one-third of the students are not there. When students are absent, they cannot achieve. Teachers never know which students will show up and soon grow careless about planning comprehensive lessons. What's the point if nobody comes?

Getting at the root cause of this problem will require some collaborative inquiry and deep soul searching. If students don't attend, they can't learn. What is the root cause of low attendance? The process consists of a questioner who keeps asking question after question until the group actually gets to the bottom of the problem—the root cause.

The questioner is a guest facilitator. The group is the faculty leadership team of 15 individuals. Various individuals on the team are answering the questions posed by

(Continued)

(Continued)

the facilitator. There is a comfortable back-and-forth interaction between the facilitator and group members.

Q. Why is attendance so poor at Marshall?

A. Because there's no one at home to hold these kids accountable for coming to school. We get absolutely no parental support.

Q. But why don't kids just come on their own? They *are* capable of feeding and dressing themselves. They do other things without their parents holding them accountable, don't they?

A. They don't care about school. They just don't see the point of education.

Q. Why don't they get the point?

A. Because they never listen to their teachers. We talk all the time about the value of education. Every one of us has a speech that we must give about 50 times a week.

Q. *Why* don't kids listen to teachers?

A. Well, maybe because they don't trust us.

Q. So why don't they trust you?

A. Maybe because they don't like us. We're the enemy.

Q. Why don't they like you? I've just met you today and I like you. Why don't your students like you?

A. Because they think everything I make them do is a waste of time and pointless. If I hear that word one more time, I'll scream.

Q. Why are you giving them pointless things to do?

A. I didn't say *I* was giving them pointless things to do. I said they thought the things I was giving them to do were pointless.

Q. Why would they think the things you're giving them to do are pointless?

A. Well, I guess maybe a lot of what we do *is* pointless to kids.

Q. So I ask you again, why are you giving kids pointless things to do?

A. Because we've always done it this way.

Q. Why?

A. Because I've never really thought about the relationship of what I do in class having anything to do with kids not coming to school. I really thought and maybe still do that their attendance is not my problem. I teach to the kids who come. I can't worry about the ones who don't come.

Q. So could one of the root causes of poor attendance have something to do with the fact that we're not giving students anything to do or think about that's actually relevant to their lives?

A. Yeah, I guess so.

Q. Have you ever asked kids why they don't come to school?

A. No, because I didn't really care.

Q. Do you care now?

A. Well, if we frame poor attendance as a teacher problem rather than a student–parent problem, although they do have to take some of the responsibility, then I guess I do want to know what they're thinking.

The first action the leadership team will take is to develop and administer a student survey to find out why kids do and don't come to school. They'll use those data to set a goal to increase student attendance.

DETERMINING WHY GOOD SCHOOLS AREN'T GETTING RESULTS

Some schools appear to be doing all of the right things. They make school improvement plans, set goals, adopt new curricula, send teachers to training, and bring in experts from everywhere. Their sports teams win. Their halls are bright and shiny. Everything looks good on the outside. However, their achievement is stuck. They may need to collect some qualitative (observational) data to uncover the reasons for low achievement. Here are some places to start looking:

1. There are too many goals, plans, initiatives, and innovations going on simultaneously resulting in what Bryk and his colleagues term a "Christmas tree school" approach (Bryk, Camburn, & Louis, 1999).

2. Central office curriculum administrators are inadvertently undermining the implementation with mandates that are designed to enhance the status of central office staff with no regard for implementation at the building level.

3. No one person has been charged with or is taking the responsibility for monitoring the implementation. Either the principal is not committed to the implementation and has delegated it to someone else for the express purpose of letting it fail or the principal is not spending at least 10–15 hours weekly in classrooms monitoring, model teaching, coaching, and supporting. Even more time may be needed during the first year of implementation.

4. The implementing teachers have not received adequate preimplementation training and are not receiving embedded professional development on a weekly basis to scaffold their success.

5. There is a critical mass of politically connected teachers who have systematically sabotaged the implementation by circumventing the administrator and going directly to school board members or the superintendent.

6. More than 20% of the staff believes that they are not accountable for student learning.

7. Teachers have been given directives to implement, in the absence of background knowledge and collaborative goal setting. No short-term goals exist to create up-front enthusiasm and momentum for the initiative.

8. Teachers have been told to implement at the last minute. There was an ill-conceived training done by a poorly prepared trainer, and the teachers feel justified in undermining the implementation.

9. The implementation has resulted in totally unforeseen circumstances, and chaos has ensued, distracting everyone from the implementation.

10. There are too few administrators with evaluative power to adequately monitor the number of teachers implementing.

11. The school hasn't stuck with its compelling goal for a long enough period of time. They have quit too soon. As one teacher told me, "Just about the time the tree should realistically start to bear fruit, we chop it down and plant a different one." A school board member in the Kennewick School District said this about their 90% reading goal: "It took several years for principals to get the focus off demographics, which they could not control, and onto curriculum, increased time, and quality of instruction, which they could control" (Fielding et al., 2007, p. 108).

12. The majority of teachers do not believe that their students are capable of learning or that they and their colleagues are capable of teaching. The goal is incompatible with the culture of the school. No efforts were made to modify the change or to alter the culture, and so the implementation has failed.

> All organizations are perfectly aligned to achieve the results they are getting.
>
> —Covey (as quoted in Miller, 2007, p. 9)

DATA-DRIVEN SCHOOLS GET RESULTS

We know that highly effective schools (and the educators who staff them) routinely make decisions based on data (Datrow, Park, & Wohlstetter, 2007; Fielding, Kerr, & Rosier, 1998, 2004, 2007; Supovitz & Taylor, 2003; Togneri & Anderson, 2003). Data-driven schools or systems are not just places where number crunchers rule. They are superbly managed organizations in which implementation is supported and driven by data (Boudett et al., 2005; Datrow et al., 2007; Holcomb, 2004).

Characteristics of Data-Driven Schools

The degree to which data can be used effectively in a school is dependent on the strength of the following characteristics in that school, many related to the traits we have already discussed.

1. Explicit, targeted, measurable achievement goals

2. A curriculum that is aligned to standards with a pacing plan that allows for some flexibility

3. Assertive leadership at the school level that communicates the value and nonnegotiable use of data

4. A climate of trust and collaboration that allows colleagues to talk about critical issues of instruction and achievement with the best interests of students at heart

5. The existence of multiple types of data (e.g., student achievement, student and teacher attendance, graduation rate, student and teacher performance assessments, faculty and parent evaluations of instructional leadership)

6. Schoolwide interim benchmark assessments that are tightly aligned to standards

7. A schedule of regular observations and walk-throughs by administrators, teachers, and groups from other schools or districts that are designed to focus specifically on student learning as opposed to evaluative observations for summative teacher evaluations

8. Collaborative grade-level and department teams that are charged with monitoring data and setting short-term achievement goals

9. Embedded professional development to assist teachers with the technical aspects of data collection and interpretation

> Once teachers can admit that children are not the problem but that instructional strategies are, then learning is going to happen for every child.
>
> —Datrow et al. (2007, p. 26)

10. Explicit data analysis protocols and goal-monitoring reports for administrators, teachers, and students to use

11. Software and data management systems that are user-friendly and specific to the needs of the school

Using Data to Improve Teachers' Instruction

Effective schools use data in a variety of ways, including but not limited to the following: identifying trends in longitudinal achievement, identifying individuals or groups who are failing to achieve, evaluating current programs or curricula, and selecting programs that get results. One of the most underused yet powerful ways of using data is the improvement of instruction in the classrooms of individual teachers.

In effective schools, strong instructional leaders use data, particularly in the beginning stages of turning around a low-performing school, to show teachers how *their* instruction impacts student learning generally and also in comparison to other teachers at that grade level. This approach can be taken only when there are at least four sections of a content class or grade level and students have been randomly assigned so that the class groups are heterogeneous and relatively similar. This is to avoid the inevitable "Her class is a much better group of kids." This process is by no means a *genuine* experiment in which there is a randomly selected experimental group and a control group and each group receives a different treatment. However, experienced administrators know that some teachers routinely achieve spectacular results with all types of students and some teachers regularly have overall lower scores, no matter what kinds of students they are teaching.

Strong instructional leaders are not afraid to use test scores as leverage when working with ineffective teachers. Cathie West, an experienced instructional leader, specializes in bringing out the best in teachers, albeit with very high expectations. She describes an experience with a marginal teacher who was quite resistant to making instructional changes until she was presented with the data.

Cathie said, "This teacher was finally motivated to improve when I showed her my rank order of classroom state test results—ranked from high to low by teacher, without names, of course. I highlighted the scores of her class; they fell right near the bottom. She is bright and competitive. Her unfavorable ranking motivated her to improve her instruction and raise her students' achievement."

Principal Lorraine Fong explains how she uses data to notch up teachers' performance. "If there are five teachers at the third-grade level and only three of them are getting top-notch results with their students in a specific area, these three teachers and I have a responsibility to help the other two teachers figure out what to do differently, and we have to do it in a collaborative way. We're at the point in the process where our teachers are able to be up front and honest with me and with each other, saying, 'My scores are lousy. What can I do? What did you do? How did you teach that lesson to get such good results?' My job is to facilitate that kind of dialogue" (McEwan, 2003, p. 129).

Kathie Dobberteen says, "Data is irrefutable. It's not a matter of, 'You're a bad teacher.' I don't have to judge the teacher. I let the data do the talking. Teachers are either producing results or they're not, and the data tell the story. My role as a principal is one of meeting with a teacher as a colleague to look at the data and ask questions about what we see. The focus becomes, 'How can we work together on this? What are we going to do for this child or for your class?'" (McEwan, 2003, p. 127).

> When there is no data to show how kids and teachers are doing, you are left with opinions. Data doesn't offer an opinion or an excuse. The data is what the data is. We cannot continue to blame our kids for our inability to teach them. If the "greatest" teachers in the world are failing to teach half of their students, the teachers need to change instruction.
>
> —Dave Montague

Using Data to Drive School Improvement: Joan Marble, Fourth-Grade Teacher, Washington School

When the WASL (Washington State Assessment of Student Learning) was first used, it was thought of only as an assessment for the fourth, seventh, and tenth grades. It is no longer viewed that way. Now it is viewed as a measure of academic achievement for Grades K–10. Therefore, all teachers feel responsible for their students' success or failure. At Washington Elementary, we collaborate and reflect every year during building professional development days to see what we can improve upon to ensure that more students are proficient.

The WASL is actually a minimum standard, and the state makes the expectations very clear through the Essential Academic Learning Requirements (EALRs) and the Grade Level Expectations (GLEs). The WASL directly correlates to the EALRs and GLEs. The trick for teachers is aligning the current curriculum with our state standards, because they don't always match. We are currently in the process of aligning Everyday Math with the GLEs and filling in the gaps that Everyday Math doesn't cover. This is a time-consuming task but an essential one, to make certain that more students are successful in passing the WASL.

(Continued)

(Continued)

It all comes down to accountability. The staff at Washington Elementary isn't satisfied with our current test scores; we realize they can be improved upon. We have to dig deep to identify which students did not pass and ask ourselves why. Then we have to provide extra services to those students so they don't fall through the cracks. The WASL holds us responsible for the number of students that are proficient. Therefore, under Dave's [Montague] leadership, we are constantly striving to increase the percentage of students that have mastered the state minimum standards and adjust our instruction as needed.

SUMMING UP

When I entered the principalship, getting results was something about which few principals lost any sleep. Choosing is no longer an option. It's required. Getting results is not about teaching to the test. It's about students learning to read, write, problem solve, understand the scientific method, and understand the responsibilities they have in their community and country. It's about raising the achievement bar for all students, those who are gifted and could be achieving so much more and those who need enhanced opportunities to learn and differentiated instruction.

WHAT'S AHEAD?

We have only one last trait—accountability. Accountability has to do with we how we feel about the fact that we may have left some students behind or let some students fall through the cracks. If we feel accountable, those students come back to see us in our dreams or haunt our memories. They don't find us on the Internet to write notes of appreciation for all we did for them. I still see a lanky fifth-grade girl from my first class. Cheryl barely read on a preprimer level. I didn't know then what I know now. She knew no more about reading when she left my classroom than when she enrolled. But I remember her name. I also remember Matthew, a first grader in my school. We kept waiting for him to bloom. He never did, and we sent him on to middle school with very few academic skills. I often wonder where he is now and what he's been able to make of his life. When you feel accountable, you care. The educators in highly effective schools operate in a framework of accountability and demand continuous improvement from themselves, their colleagues, and their students.

Accountability

Accountability systems that look only at process and effort will reward a fixation on meetings, plans, and strategies while ignoring results. [Initiatives] are only effective when they are built upon a foundation that soundly evaluates student achievement.

—Reeves (2000, p. 18)

The educators in highly effective schools are passionate about the achievement of their students because of their vision of a highly effective school, not because of No Child Left Behind (2002) or a directive from the superintendent. External accountability is surely a factor, but there is also a strong internal accountability woven into the culture of their schools. Initially, some staff members may have responded to someone else's vision or goal, but once they began to experience the excitement of rapidly increasing academic capacity, they became believers. Only when the majority of educators in a school (80% or more at the very least) believe that their students are able to master the standards and they have a responsibility to teach them does accountability become a cultural norm. When that happens, teachers no longer think in terms of excuses but of

> As an educator, I believe accountability means meeting goals, expectations, and mutual commitments. It's all about attitude. Teachers can't control all of the variables that affect students, but we can provide equitable opportunities for students to learn.
>
> —*Rita Root, Teacher, Washington School*

solutions. The highly effective school is characterized by high levels of internal accountability that when coupled with external accountability measures, ensure continuous improvement of instruction and achievement.

INTERNAL ACCOUNTABILITY

Internal accountability comes from within the school. It refers to doing the right thing based on a strong set of personal values, a commitment to colleagues, and a belief in the mission of the school.

The *Oxford American Dictionary* (Apple Software 1.0.) says of the word *accountable,* it is more positive than its synonyms, *responsible* and *answerable,* suggesting that something has been entrusted to someone who will be called to account for how that trust has been carried out. This is precisely the mindset that one finds in highly effective schools. Teachers feel accountable to parents, to their students, and to their administrators. But most of all, they feel accountable to their colleagues, knowing that they are collectively responsible for all of the students who attend their school.

Stephen Covey (1989) says that responsibility is actually *response-ability*—the ability to choose one's response to a given situation, to be proactive rather than reactive (p. 71). Using Covey's play on words, accountability could then be thought of as *account-ability*, the ability to examine one's teaching performance and give an accounting of its effectiveness—how well one's students perform—in the classroom as well as on external measures, like a state test. Having an account-ability mindset means recognizing one's personal responsibility to make a difference in the academic lives of students and feeling compelled to bring all students to mastery.

According to Covey, Merrill, and Merrill (1994), the way in which individuals *see* a problem impacts what they *do* in response to that problem, which in turn affects the results they *get* from their actions. The See-Do-Get Cycle gives us an intriguing way to examine two accountability paradigms. A *paradigm* is a set of assumptions or beliefs shared by those in a specific field of study or discipline (Kuhn, 1962/1996) that when firmly established, become self-sustaining, providing continuity and stability to those who embrace it. Paradigms change only through radical and sudden shifts that occur when new discoveries, knowledge, or concepts arise that cannot be rejected or assimilated by the old paradigm. The new paradigm then replaces the old one.

In education, we are still in the midst of a paradigm shift, and it has been going on for far too long. Those of us who shifted our paradigms in the early 1980s are still waiting for the rest of the educational world to catch up with us. The original paradigm, illustrated in Figure 10.1, rejects accountability altogether, refusing to accept any responsibility for students' lack of academic success. Teachers who reject accountability have the following script saved on their hard drives:

> I do the best I can with the students I have. I work hard and feel good about what I'm able to accomplish. But our students have too many deficits for me to overcome: learning problems, unsupportive parents, limited English-language proficiency, and poverty. If these kids can't learn, I refuse to accept the responsibility for that. Society ought to fix the problems of poverty. Parents should accept the responsibility for preparing their kids for school. The school district should put these impossible-to-teach students into special education. That's where they belong.

Figure 10.1   See–Do–Get: The Not-Accountable Paradigm

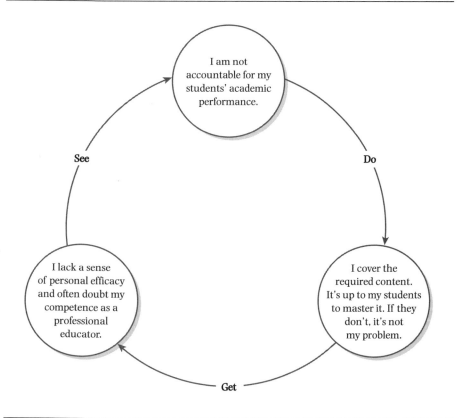

SOURCE: Adapted from Covey, Merrill, & Merrill (1994).

Reproduction of material from this book is authorized only for the local school site or nonprofit organization that has purchased *Ten Traits of Highly Effective Schools: Raising the Achievement Bar for All Students,* by Elaine K. McEwan. Thousand Oaks, CA: Corwin Press, www.corwinpress.com.

A teacher whose mindset is based on the *I Am Accountable* paradigm, shown in Figure 10.2, accepts responsibility for student learning and embraces the challenges and opportunities it affords to become a superior educator, an instructional virtuoso as described in Chapter 2:

> I have to get results no matter where my students are academically when they arrive in my school or classroom. My instruction is the most powerful variable impacting student learning, and I am committed to doing everything I can to ensure that my students learn. How hard we work or how good we feel about what we are doing is irrelevant if our school is not getting results for all students. Although there are bound to be temporary setbacks along the way, I remain focused on our goal: raising the achievement bar for all students.

Figure 10.2   See–Do–Get: The Accountable Paradigm

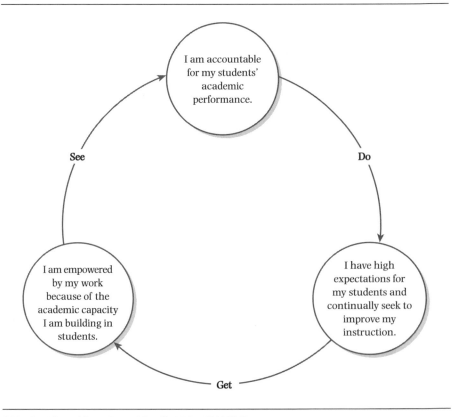

SOURCE: Adapted from Covey, Merrill, & Merrill (1994).

Reproduction of material from this book is authorized only for the local school site or nonprofit organization that has purchased *Ten Traits of Highly Effective Schools: Raising the Achievement Bar for All Students*, by Elaine K. McEwan. Thousand Oaks, CA: Corwin Press, www.corwinpress.com.

Teachers are not the only educators whose work is impacted by the old and new paradigms. Principals have had to shift their paradigms as well. For example, listen to this principal's lament: "Twenty years ago, all I had to do was keep the parents and the teachers happy. Now I have to get results."

Kathie Dobberteen, retired from the La Mesa-Spring Valley School District near San Diego, California, and now writing and consulting, shifted her paradigm long before NCLB. Her school was named a National Title I Distinguished School, and Kathie received a Change Award from the Chase Manhattan Bank and Fordham University for the accomplishments of her school. Here's how she sees accountability:

I believe the driving force for our school to improve so dramatically was that we not only felt accountable to parents and to our Board of Education but also to society. We did whatever it took to help our children become educated citizens who could participate fully in our society. We looked around and saw that many families could not catch a piece of the American Dream because they were not educated. We pulled out every stop to make sure that if our students had problems in their lives, it would not be for lack of an education.

We decided as a staff that we could make a difference in children's lives. We knew that if we didn't make children literate, we were handicapping them for the rest of their lives. We felt accountable to these children so they could have choices in their lives. We made up our minds that every child in every classroom could learn to read if we were willing to do everything we could to unlock learning. We had before-school, afterschool, and in-school intervention classes. We looked at every aspect of the reading process to determine where we might improve. We worked so hard to get every parent in for a parent conference and then worked even harder to get every parent of a below-grade-level reader in for an additional reading conference with one of the reading specialists. We had well-attended workshops for parents, to show them how to help their children with reading. The reading specialist had parties for parents and children to celebrate achievement. Our whole school went to Sea World to celebrate reading the number of books that matched the height of the Sea World tower. We also celebrated as a staff as we made those incremental improvements in the percentage of students who were reading at or above grade level. Seeing improvements in student achievement, and being accountable in this way, was the most exhilarating experience our staff had ever experienced in education.

Kathie's accountability paradigm stands in stark contrast to the principal who wasn't quite sure about getting results, but in reality, most schools have teachers and principals at various places along the continuum. One thing is certain: In a low-achieving school, improvement can occur only when the collective paradigm starts to shift, led by a principal with a vision for what the school can become. If all students are to achieve academic success, the shift has to start in the principal's office and move through the building like a tidal wave.

In my workshops, I use an activity called Agree or Disagree. I put a slide up on the screen with the title, Agree or Disagree? Underneath the title is this statement: Student performance is a measure of teacher performance. Before the workshop I put up signs in each of the corners of the room: Agree, Strongly Agree, Disagree, and Strongly Agree. I ask the participants to read the statement and then go to the corner that aligns with their belief. Some individuals stand up and quickly walk to a corner. There's no doubt in their minds what they believe. Then there are the individuals who want to put a foot in a couple of corners, leaving some wiggle room for excuses or special cases. When everyone has made a decision, I ask each group to talk together about why they chose the corner they did and then to select a reporter who can make the group's case to the rest of the participants. I have never been disappointed by the discussion that follows. Figure 10.3 contains the slide I use in the exercise.

Figure 10.3   Agree or Disagree Slide

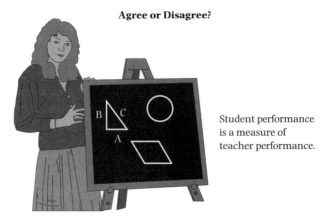

Reproduction of material from this book is authorized only for the local school site or nonprofit organization that has purchased *Ten Traits of Highly Effective Schools: Raising the Achievement Bar for All Students,* by Elaine K. McEwan. Thousand Oaks, CA: Corwin Press, www.corwinpress.com.

Educators in highly effective schools have built consensus around the "I Am Accountable" paradigm and are of one mind regarding who is responsible for student learning. Fourth-grade teacher Joan Marble describes accountability at Washington School this way:

Washington is a collegial and collaborative school that truly embraces accountability. We work together as a team to provide the best instruction for our students. Our building motto is, *All students can learn. We can teach them. No exceptions. No excuses.* Our expectations are clear and focused. Our students are the children we have for 180 days. We realize we have a short amount of time to bring *all* students up to grade level and understand that we are responsible for their success or failure. Therefore, our instruction is purposeful and deliberate.

Our professional development sessions are extremely productive as we work toward the shared goal of success for every child. Each staff member feels as valued as the next, knowing that he or she is part of the big picture. We don't accept the status quo; instead we focus on what we can do better to enhance student learning. It all relates to accountability. It is a state of mind, an attitude that benefits all the students in our school. I feel privileged to be part of such an organization. I realize I am accountable for the success of my students.

> In order to continuously improve, the whole campus had to be committed to the vision. The classroom teachers were not the only ones responsible for their students' learning. The principal, specialists, assistants, office staff, and cafeteria ladies all played a role in assisting the students. Everyone became a team player to realize the vision. If our colleagues were having a difficult time with one or more students, we did what was necessary to assist them. When our vision became a reality, our celebration was very meaningful to all of us because we united to make it happen.
>
> —*Mary Isabel Cissell, Kindergarten, Villarreal School (TX)*

EXTERNAL ACCOUNTABILITY

The external accountability systems in states are different from the internal accountability that is found in highly effective schools. Nonetheless, the installation of state accountability systems over the past 15 years has notched up achievement generally to a much higher level and caused quite a few educators to tweak their paradigms if not shift them altogether. In 1996, only 12 states had accountability systems that included statewide testing, a mandatory school report card, and a system of grading schools based on their performance as defined by the state. By 2000, 39 states had accountability systems in place. NCLB (2002) greatly expanded the accountability requirements by mandating the following: (1) annual testing of students in Grades 3–8, (2) disaggregated reporting of test data, and (3) sanctions for schools where student performance fell short of goals (e.g., the mandated Adequate Yearly Progress set forth by each state). Some states were well ahead of NCLB—Delaware, Texas, Massachusetts, New York, and North Carolina (Olson, 2006, p. 9)—and their improved test scores gave evidence of their commitment.

However, there is no uniformity among states regarding their implementation of the following benchmarks of accountability: required report cards for all schools, sanctions imposed on low-performing schools, rewards to high-performing or improving schools, participation in the state-level National Assessment of Educational Progress (NAEP), student promotion contingent on performance on statewide exams, and high school graduation contingent on performance on statewide exit or end-of-course exams (Olson, 2006, p. 10).

Researchers have found positive relationships between gains on the NAEP in states where standards and the tests that measure them count. After developing a zero-to-five index of the strength of accountability in the 50 states, Stanford University economists Martin Carnoy and Susanna Loeb (2003) used the 1996 and 2000 NAEP mathematics scores to determine the effects of external accountability on student outcomes. They concluded that students in high-accountability states averaged significantly greater gains on the NAEP Math test between fourth grade and eighth grade than did students in states with few or no state measures to improve student performance. Although accountability measures are frequently hypothesized to result in higher retention rates for ninth graders or lower high school completion rates, according to this research, students in high-accountability states do not have significantly higher retention or lower high school completion rates. Nor have more stringent accountability measures resulted in more Special Education placements, as was once hypothesized (Hanushek & Raymond, 2004).

THE KEY TO ACCOUNTABILITY: CONTINUOUS IMPROVEMENT

Getting there is hard work. Staying there is even harder work. After a four-game winning streak, a young basketball team gets full of itself and begins to feel that what they have done was pretty easy. They haven't yet figured out that every game is a brand-new contest. In schools, every school year is a brand-new challenge. In challenging schools, only "an unwavering commitment to progress" (Zmuda, Kuklis, & Kline, 2004, p. 17) will realize what Elmore (2003) calls the "self-management of improvement." To be improvement driven in the context of an effective school is to be focused on the academic success of all students. When schools have other priorities, like keeping teachers happy, having fun in the classroom, or keeping kids quiet doing worksheets, academic success always takes a backseat. Being performance driven doesn't guarantee that a school will soar to the top of the ratings chart overnight or never encounter roadblocks or detours that momentarily set them back. However, they will always bounce back and get results under strong and steady leadership.

Dave Montague is a performance-driven principal. The first clue is the school motto posted on his bulletin board: *All Kids Can Learn. We Can Teach Them. No Exceptions. No Excuses.* He frequently tells his teachers, "If our kids are successful, it is because of us. If they are not successful, it is also because of us. We have proven that we can produce successful kids, so if they aren't, it is our fault, not the kids'. We will not blame the students for our inability to teach them."

Dave doesn't worry about putting too much pressure on his teachers. "Performance pressure should build determination, not fear. If you know you are a good teacher, are willing to work hard and try new things, are willing to become part of a group dedicated to improvement, and have been provided with goals and direction (that's the principal's job), then you should never fear accountability. Accountability offers an opportunity to show others what can be done.

"The teachers at Washington know that our strength lies in our collaboration. When we have challenges, we tap the collective knowledge of 27 staff members to come up with solutions. This makes accountability much easier to accept, because you know you always have help if you need it."

School improvement is like running a race—with one major difference. The improvement race is never over. There is no clear finish where a winner is declared. Schools are in a constant state of flux. There *are* brief moments when we can celebrate marvelous milestones, and then the race begins anew with an entirely new group of runners. Teachers resign and new ones are hired. New students enroll and others transfer to different schools. New textbooks are adopted. Instructional leaders must continually monitor and adjust. Teachers must welcome new members into their collaborative groups.

Running the Race: Mark Stephens, Principal, Eastgate Elementary School, Kennewick (WA)

Mark Stephens, the principal of Eastgate Elementary School in the Kennewick (WA) District, has been an administrator for 11 years. He has never faced greater challenges and more accountability than in his current assignment. He is humble about the results that he and his faculty have produced over the years and remains quietly focused on his district's 90% goal in third grade and the upward-moving performance target of the fourth-grade WASL assessment.

Eastgate is one of 13 elementary schools in the Kennewick District where the 90% goal for third-grade reading achievement was adopted in 1995. The 90% goal was raised to 95% by the district in response to the accountability requirements of NCLB. In addition to the district's third-grade goal, Washington educators are also performance driven by the fourth-grade WASL, the test by which AYP is measured. The reading AYP benchmark set by the state was 52.2% in 2002 and increases every third year. In 2007, the benchmark rose to 76.1%.

The demographics of Eastgate are the most challenging among the district's 13 elementary schools. More than 90% of Mark's students receive free and reduced-price lunch. Almost 50% of the students are English-language learners, 78% of the students are Hispanic, and the turnover rate of students moving in and out of Eastgate fluctuates between 20% and 30%. Very early during Mark's first year (2002–2003), he and the staff took stock of the school. In the spring of 2002, previous to Mark's arrival at Eastgate, 53% of the fourth-grade students had met the state's Reading WASL benchmark. In 2003, it dropped to 44%. The pressure was on. One achievement advantage, in Mark's view, was the school's reading curriculum (Open Court), adopted two years previously. [NOTE: The elementary schools in Kennewick have curricular autonomy, and each school selects its own reading program and instructional methods.]

As Mark and his teachers carefully compared the state standards at each grade level with the curriculum, they found that every standard was either met or exceeded by the program. They have also integrated the use of systematic instruction in which each grade level builds on what students have been previously taught. Because vocabulary and phonemic awareness are two areas of student weakness, the explicit phonics and rigorous vocabulary components of Open Court serve as effective tools to scaffold struggling readers. Open Court also provides teachers with guidance in creating and teaching rigorous lessons, keeping expectations high for all students.

What was missing, in Mark's view, was a schoolwide assessment program that would give him and his teachers formative data about the three levels of learners at Eastgate: benchmark (students on grade level), strategic (students just below benchmark), and intensive (those students deemed to be in need of both increased instructional time and a slightly different instructional approach). The addition of the CORE Reading Assessment gave Mark and his faculty the crucial data they needed to build academic capacity at Eastgate.

At the end of Mark's second year, 80% of third graders were at or above grade level, up from 68% the previous spring, and 74% of fourth-grade students were at or above proficient on the fourth-grade WASL, up from 44% the previous year. Scores at both third and fourth grade continued to move upward in subsequent years as Mark and the staff tweaked their instructional approaches and used assessment data to guide the provision of more time for intensive interventions at first and second grades.

Mark had some forewarning that the 2006–2007 fourth-grade class would have some difficulty with the WASL. Although 84% of the prior year's fourth graders had scored proficient, he expected the results for this particular class to dip to perhaps 70%, based on the benchmark assessment scores they had received. He and his staff were stunned, however, when they opened the envelope: only 50% of Eastgate's fourth graders had achieved a proficient rating.

When achievement temporarily dips and the news is discouraging, highly effective schools take only 24 hours to feel the pain. Then they hit the road again with renewed focus. Mark and his staff members agree that building academic capacity in a very challenging school starts anew every year and that they are accountable for doing it. Each new student brings instructional challenges and academic deficits. In schools with few minority or disadvantaged students, student achievement is taken for granted. However, in challenging schools like Eastgate, staff members must maintain an intense focus on the compelling goal that is still before them: bringing all students to mastery.

Continuous Improvement Cycles

Creating and sustaining highly effective schools is not an event. It is a process that requires close adherence to a continuous improvement cycle. The term *continuous improvement* suggests that there is already evidence of improvement and that an individual or school desires to use that improvement as a push-off to even greater improve-

> The more explicit and targeted the goals are, the more likely they are to provide focus for data-driven decision-making.
>
> —*Datrow et al. (2007, p. 71)*

ment. The steps to getting improvement in the first place are more complex and require the creation of a shared vision, the articulation of a compelling mission, and a variety of intentional culture-building activities to lay the foundation for improvement.

Once there is solid evidence of increased academic capacity, continuous improvement can be sustained by adhering to a continuous improvement cycle like the one shown in Form 10.1.

Continuous Improvement for Principals

Dave Montague believes that if he expects his teachers to be accountable for student learning, he must also be accountable for student learning, ultimately shouldering the responsibility in front of the annual

Form 10.1   Continuous Improvement Cycle Form

Copyright © 2009 by Corwin Press. All rights reserved. Reprinted from *Ten Traits of Highly Effective Schools: Raising the Achievement Bar for All Students*, by Elaine K. McEwan. Thousand Oaks, CA: Corwin Press, www.corwinpress.com. Reproduction authorized only for the local school site or nonprofit organization that has purchased this book.

report to the Board of Education. He explains, "Principals who think it's unfair that they are the ones who are responsible for how well their school performs should probably look for another job." Dave is correct. The paradigm is shifting much faster now than it was five years ago.

Principals are the only educators who have both e-power (the power to evaluate teacher performance) and access to classrooms, prerequisites to motivating teachers to improve. Principals whose paradigms are in the right place but are tentative in their approach to accountability, fearful of making waves or offending, will not succeed in moving a school from underperforming to highly successful.

Continuous Improvement for Teachers

Continuous improvement for individual teachers should be focused on the improvement of instruction. During any given school year, committed and competent staff members are likely to be situated at about six points along a continuum in their educational practice (Leithwood, 1990): (1) developing survival skills, (2) becoming competent in the basic skills of instruction, (3) expanding their instructional flexibility, (4) acquiring instructional expertise, (5) contributing to the growth of colleagues' instructional expertise, and (6) participating in a broad array of educational decisions at all levels of the educational system (pp. 74–75). Knowing where staff members are on that continuum is essential to guiding each one toward setting instructional improvement goals as well as leading teams and grade-level PLCs toward specific

> We have to teach the kids we have right now. Not the ones we used to have, or the ones who were like us when we were in school, or like the ones in the upscale school across town. We have to teach the kids we have right now.
>
> —Dave Montague

embedded professional development experiences. Unfortunately, there is always the possibility that some staff members aren't even on the continuum. They may fall into the categories I refer to as angry, troubled, exhausted, or just plain confused (McEwan, 2005) and will require more intensive interventions and possibly even remediation. One principal said of her first year in a failing school, "I'm not always the most popular person. I've had to do eight Letters of Concern with various teachers, two Counseling Reports with custodians, one Counseling Report with an office worker, and several conferences with others (P. Bradley, personal communication, May 5, 2006).

However, continuous improvement for the majority of teachers demands that principals be diligent about motivating, energizing, renewing,

> I can with absolute certainty say that my best teaching paralleled the years that I was accountable to nine professional teammates within my grade level. I was fortunate enough to be part of a team who respected the boundaries, agendas, and insecurities of others. The energy generated from those team efforts fed me, stretched me, and caused me to flourish like never before. It was amazing how much more clarity I developed when I had to articulate, justify, evaluate, and synthesize the purpose for my choices in minutes, instructional tools, and approaches. It was incredibly invigorating to process the differences between approaches and philosophies, all to determine whether it was in my best interest to continue what I was doing or conform to the group's consensus. From that experience, I now believe that neither intentionality nor clarity can be easily found independently. I know very few teachers who ask themselves hard questions just to have the chance to articulate and process their defense. For me, it was accountability to my teammates that energized and changed my teaching forever. For them, I will be forever grateful!
>
> —Jill Yates, Kindergarten Teacher (WA)

and rewarding their teachers. Part of Dale Skinner's formula for success is that he is constantly motivating his teachers. "Whenever I could feel morale sagging a little bit, I would tell the faculty to picture the school year as a Hollywood movie and to visualize the way they wanted their characters in the movie to act. I showed clips from *Stand and Deliver, Rudy,* and *October Sky,* in which educators were portrayed as negative and ineffective. Then I would ask, 'When they make a movie out of our story, do you want your friends, family, and colleagues to see you acting like that?' I kept telling them, 'The greater the obstacles, the greater the story.' During our darkest times, and everyone who does school improvement has their darkest times, I would smile and say, 'This is going to be one of the best stories of all time.' They would usually relax and laugh, and it would lighten the moment and improve the climate. My teachers at both Loma Terrace and Villarreal had seen so many impossible things happen in our schools, some just had to think, 'Well, they just might make a movie someday about us. I better be more positive. Just in case.'"

Continuous Improvement for Students

Nothing produces continuous improvement in students like instructional tenacity (Kameenui & Darch, 1995, p. 13). This quest for success for every student—the talented, the at-risk, the needy, and the invisible students that silently fall through the cracks—is part of the accountability culture in highly effective schools. It can be seen in a variety of very specific teacher behaviors that support and build on the ten traits of highly effective schools:

- Establishing warm and encouraging relationships with students
- Treating students fairly, firmly, and with consistency
- Relying on personal authority rather than constantly sending students to the dean or principal for discipline
- Using direct, nonemotional management techniques
- Never trying to embarrass students
- Treating all students as capable and trustworthy
- Maintaining a consistent emphasis on instruction and the importance of learning
- Maintaining a consistent effort to keep students on task, interested, and aware of their individual accomplishments
- Teaching all of the students in the class, pushing them, and monitoring their work
- Maintaining a constant sense of determination not to accept the failure of students (Ashton & Webb, 1986, pp. 84–86)

THE DARK TIMES

One of the biggest challenges of school improvement comes from the "dark times," as Dale Skinner called them. We are a people-intensive endeavor, and even the strongest players on the team can go down with an injury, an illness, or even a death in the family. The reserves of eternal optimism, energy, and resiliency that are essential for being accountable may be depleted. Elmore does not include a phase in his model for the dark times, but they are an inevitable part of the human condition. However, educators who are accountable just don't give up. Michelle Gayle is one such individual.

Accountability at Griffin Middle School, Tallahassee, FL: Michelle Gayle

Nearly half of Griffin Middle School's 725 students are eligible for free and reduced-price lunch. But when she was hired, Michelle was absolutely certain that demographics would not determine the destiny of her students. The year before she came aboard as principal (2000–2001), Griffin received a grade of C on the Florida State Grading System. Michelle has never been satisfied with mediocrity and let her faculty know in no uncertain terms that a group of teachers as smart and talented as they obviously were could be getting an A. Michelle's defining attribute is *dissatisfaction*. "She always wants more," her teachers say. Michelle puts it this way, "I know we can achieve more. If you become satisfied, you slip backwards."

> It is no simple matter to reform teaching, learning, and the supporting conditions that fuel and refuel the moral purpose of teaching.
>
> —*Fullan (1997, p. 79)*

She didn't sit around waiting for things to happen. She immediately began sitting down with teachers and looking over their lesson plans and samples of their students' work. She discovered that expectations were low, many assignments were meaningless, and standards and benchmarks were virtually ignored. She communicated her expectations to teachers: Focus on what's important and throw the rest "out to the curb."

Their joint efforts paid off, and Griffin received an A for their achievements during Year 1 of Michelle's tenure. In some schools, once spring testing is over, teachers and students breathe a collective sigh and take the rest of the year off. Not at Griffin. "I had a clear idea of where we needed to sharpen our focus for Year 2," Michelle explains. "We sat down and looked at the needs of various groups of students and talked about building a rigorous program for all students that all teachers could support."

Michelle wasn't that satisfied with the A rating that Griffin received. It wasn't a solid A, and she knew that with the rising standards and increased achievement around the state, more work would be needed to maintain their standing. She signed up Griffin for the Florida Reading Initiative—60 hours of training to build the knowledge

(Continued)

(Continued)

base of teachers about reading instruction and to provide strategies they could adapt to their content instruction. Although teachers were paid a small stipend, it did not begin to cover their time commitment. But they wisely realized the need for a shared knowledge base and common language. Michelle explains, "Secondary schools really miss the boat when they try to give teachers training that doesn't pay respect to their disciplines. This training zeroed in on exactly what we needed" (Jones-Gayle, 2006).

At the end of Year 2, Griffin received a solid A—24 points above its first A grade. There was cause for celebration, but the good feelings didn't last long. During that summer, Michelle and Griffin Middle School experienced a setback. A medical emergency during the summer break put Michelle in the hospital with a serious eye condition that necessitated half a dozen surgeries over the course of the year. Her assistants kept the school running, but Michelle's instructional relentlessness and high expectations were sorely missed. When the Year 3 grade was published in the newspaper, it was a solid C. Michelle was devastated. She said, "I didn't want my teachers to be discouraged. I knew they had worked so hard. I felt as though I had let my community down. I permitted myself to feel the public humiliation that Griffin had gone from an A to a C for just one day. Then I picked myself up and determined to build our momentum back up again." Michelle is a servant leader. Even though she pushes and presses, when the news was bad, she assumed the blame. When the news is good, her faculty and students receive the credit. Michelle realized it was time for what Michael Fullan (1997) calls "refueling." Here's how she did it.

> I chose a theme for Year 3: *C-ing our way back to an A.* I thought of a list of C words to help us focus: collaboration, communication, and so on. I did shirts. I did bags. If I could have paid for skywriting, I would have. We continued with the Florida Reading Initiative and began holding strategic learning camps in reading for students. We held Saturday and afterschool academies to provide remediation in specific areas where students were deficient. I surveyed students before the academies to find out their attitudes about effort and grades, and we involved parents in our efforts to raise expectations for their children.

At the end of Year 3 (2005), our grade went up to a B—just 7 points from an A. The standards were going up around the state. We celebrated that achievement and then began to systematically look at every aspect of our school improvement plan. What allowed us to be successful? What was a total waste of time? We became action researchers, all the while remaining focused on student achievement. The teachers became more skilled at using data to determine student needs, and they became far more open to differentiated instruction. They know better than to tell me, "We can't do this."

In Year 4, the mantra at Griffin became "Aiming for Excellence" and the graphic representation was a target. The bull's-eye for Michelle was professional development. She describes what was happening: "Conversations in the faculty lounge evolved from 'That kid is driving me crazy,' to 'It's driving me crazy that I can't come up with a strategy that will work with this group of kids.' Our professional conversations have focused on higher-order thinking. We've developed a pre-AP program for a group of students identified before they enter Griffin."

Michelle is always pushing the limits, but her teachers have definitely learned to appreciate her relentless push for academic excellence at Griffin. She says, "Sometimes I've thought, 'I push 'em too hard. I ask too many questions.'" Given Michelle's continually growing expectations for what teachers and students can do, you might expect her teachers to have a degree of dissatisfaction themselves. They, however, are thrilled with their success and empowered with a renewed sense of efficacy. They nominated Michelle for the district's Outstanding Administrator Award sponsored by the teachers' union. Michelle says, "I didn't care whether I won the district award (which she did), but to have that kind of trust and respect from my faculty will keep me happy for the next 10 years" (Bryk & Schneider, 2002). Notice that Michelle said "happy," not "satisfied"! At the end of the following year, 2005–2006, Michelle and her staff were solidly back on the A team.

SUMMING UP

The kind of accountability that is evident in highly effective schools has less to do with test scores and school ratings than with the degree to which students are learning and experiencing academic success. Although the educators in highly effective schools are aware of and attentive to the accountability systems of the districts and the states in which they work, those systems are not the true driving force behind their efforts. They do what they do because of the consensus they have developed in their teams and departments around teaching the students who have been entrusted to them and being willing to be called to account for how that trust has been carried out.

WHAT'S AHEAD?

Just ahead, in the Conclusion, we'll look at the Ten Traits Audit, an instrument you can use to evaluate your school or schools in your district. Principal Cathie West describes how she used the Audit to develop her improvement goals for the school year.

Conclusion

Using the Ten Traits to Improve Your School

At present, we simply do not know whether the [school improvement] journey resembles a roller coaster ride, the long slow ascent of a high peak, or a trek consisting of slopes and plateaus.

—Duke (2006, p. 734)

Each of the ten traits of highly effective schools contributes a unique piece to the school improvement puzzle. When the traits are considered singly, as the preceding chapters have done, it is difficult to fully appreciate how they interact to get the results they do in a highly effective school. However, the picture that emerges when we put the pieces together no longer even looks like 10 assembled pieces of a puzzle. It resembles a fine oil painting on a canvas. Attempting to pinpoint where administrative leadership and teacher leadership begin and end is impossible. Strong instructional leaders recognize the power in shared decision making and collaborative work. Teachers who have opportunities to exercise their leadership talents are more effective in their classrooms as well.

Similarly, relational trust and collaboration enhance each other. In schools where teams of teachers have sufficient time to collaborate around issues of teaching and learning, relational trust develops and continues to grow. High expectations and opportunities to learn interact for a different kind of impact on student achievement. Without high expectations, educators don't have to worry about providing opportunities to learn. Without opportunities to learn, high expectations are meaningless words in a mission statement. As expectations are raised by external accountability systems, effective schools find more and better ways to meet the academic needs of all students.

There is a great deal we do not yet understand about the improvement process in schools: (1) how to detect the need for and make midcourse corrections, (2) how to anticipate unintended consequences, (3) how to deal with personnel problems that are roadblocks to improvement but are complicated by district politics and negotiated contracts, and (4) how to sustain continuous improvement (Duke, 2006). However, understanding the dynamics of the ten traits is not a prerequisite for undertaking a school improvement initiative. We cannot afford to wait until we have all the answers. We must have the courage to begin the journey with only our vision in mind.

ANYTHING CAN HAPPEN

According to the experts, when school leaders undertake a major change initiative, either to turn around a low-performing school or jump-start student achievement in a school that's stuck, anything can happen. Richard Elmore (2003) predicts that after a successful beginning that involves picking off the low-hanging fruit, educators will usually encounter obstacles through which they must persevere before they see improvement. Harvard scholar Rosabeth Moss Kanter (2004) studies change in the corporate world. She hypothesizes that when organizations achieve immediate success, leaders and managers may unconsciously relax their intensive efforts and unintentionally slow down or derail the change process. Educational change guru Michael Fullan (2001) theorizes that things happen in just the opposite way: When improvement initiatives run into difficult roadblocks before they experience at least some success, this early discouragement often derails the improvement process completely. You have encountered examples of all of these scenarios in the preceding chapters.

Although there is much that we do not know about improving schools, we have learned the following from the teachers, principals, and schools described in the book.

- School improvement, no matter where one begins, is very difficult work requiring an intense focus.
- School improvement takes commitment, courage, and vision from a strong instructional leader working collaboratively with a team of teacher-leaders. The task requires as close to 100% participation as possible. Dale Skinner requires that schools get 80% of their teachers to sign on the dotted line before he consents to work with them. The fewer the committed participants, the less likely that results will be obtained.

- School improvement is dependent on the learning and academic growth of individual students. Unless a critical mass of low-performing students gradually begin to know and do more today, or this week, or this month than they previously could, schools will not improve. Do not become distracted or seduced by activity. Focus on achievement, most especially on the achievement of individual students.

Figure C.1 defines a variety of schools on the effective-school continuum. You have seen examples of many of these throughout the book. Knowing exactly where your school stands in terms of the strength and viability of each of the traits can inform any change or improvement initiative.

Following is an example of how one principal is using the traits to create a brand-new school out of the combination of two faculties and two sets of students.

Cathie West has been an instructional leader for over 26 years in several schools in the Pacific Northwest. Her current assignment involves a somewhat different change scenario for her. The district combined her former K–3 building with a Grades 5–6 building and then split the students and teachers in half to create two new K–6 schools. Cathie's challenge is to repeat the success she enjoyed with her K–3 building in the newly constituted school—a campus with 590 students in 25 classrooms. She has been working toward that end for the past three years and decided to give her staff the Ten Traits Audit shown in Form C.1. She wanted to determine her staff's perception regarding how the newly constituted school was progressing. She planned to use the information in a goal-setting session with her School Improvement Team.

Cathie's "new" school staff is made up of about 60% new teachers and 40% of her original staff, so many of her efforts have centered on building relational trust and developing collaborative teacher teams. However, she and her teachers also faced a number of distractions that have taken attention away from the implementation of two new curricular programs: severe budget restrictions and a variety of new state mandates.

Cathie was apprehensive about giving the audit to her staff. She says, "I had confidence in the instrument—it captures the essence of highly effective schools—but I was wary of what our results would be. If the scores were low, I knew it would be a setback for my hardworking faculty."

There is always the temptation for principals to avoid asking faculty members difficult questions to which they do not already know the answers. Cathie explains, "Given all the restraining forces we had working

Figure C.1   A Typology of Schools

Type of School	*Description*
Highly Effective	An equitable and excellent school that enables all of its students to achieve academic success, regardless of their demographics or categorical labels.
Effective	An equitable and excellent school that enables at least 95% of its students to achieve academic success, regardless of their demographics or categorical labels.
Good	A school that is moving steadily toward effectiveness but is not quite there yet. Many if not all of the ten traits are present in the good school, but student achievement is not yet at 95%.
Transitional	A school that was once failing or underperforming but is now steadily improving. The transitional school is vulnerable to inalterable variables, such as the loss of a strong instructional leader or key teacher-leaders; an unexpected influx of students due to boundary changes or natural disasters, such as Hurricane Katrina; violence and death in the community or school; or the death, suicide, or serious illness of a student or faculty member.
Underperforming	A school where student achievement is acceptable to most observers, unless one considers the school's demographics. Educators in the school feel little accountability for the achievement of struggling students in their classrooms, and many of its teachers are underachieving along with their students. The achievement of high-performing students masks the low achievement of other students. The community may perceive this school to be a good school, but it is not increasing the academic capacity of all students.
Stuck	A school that is in an achievement rut. The school is not declining but neither is it improving. Test scores remain fairly stable year after year—not failing but not great, given the demographics of the student body. Leadership is not focused on building academic capacity.
Low-Performing	A school in which the principal and teachers are good people who care for their students and work very hard. The educators in this school make periodic attempts to raise achievement, but their expectations are low and their energies are largely focused on making themselves and their students feel good. School leaders are not committed to building academic capacity.
Dysfunctional	A school that has not been officially labeled as failing, but a toxic culture and absence of academic focus are contributors to extraordinarily low student achievement.
Failing	A school that has failed to make its academic targets and has been placed under sanctions by the state or federal government.

Reproduction of material from this book is authorized only for the local school site or nonprofit organization that has purchased *Ten Traits of Highly Effective Schools: Raising the Achievement Bar for All Students*, by Elaine K. McEwan. Thousand Oaks, CA: Corwin Press, www.corwinpress.com.

Form C.1   Ten Traits Audit

Directions: Circle the number that indicates the strength of each trait in your school.

1. Instructional Leadership

Our school is led by a strong instructional leader who provides unequivocal direction through consistent monitoring and supervision of program implementation while also working collaboratively with teachers to solve problems related to standards, curriculum, instruction, and assessment.

Not at All   Very Strong

| 1 | 2 | 3 | 4 | 5 |

2. Research-Based Instruction

Research-based instruction delivered by highly effective teachers is the core of our school. Instruction is the channel through which content and skills are recursively transmitted to students, and instructional strategies and lesson designs are constantly being refined through benchmarking and embedded professional development.

Not at All   Very Strong

| 1 | 2 | 3 | 4 | 5 |

3. Clear Academic Focus

Our school has a clear academic focus (the ability to concentrate on the now without becoming distracted) that encompasses a vision (a picture of what our school will become in the future), a mission (a set of statements intended to guide the near-term future of our school), and goals (the objectives the school is committed to achieving during the present school year).

Not at All   Very Strong

| 1 | 2 | 3 | 4 | 5 |

(Continued)

Form C.1 (Continued)

---

4. Relational Trust

Our school has a high level of relational trust that results in positive personal relationships between and among teachers, students, parents, and administrators. These relationships are characterized by personal regard, respect, competence, and integrity.

Not at All				Very Strong
1	2	3	4	5

5. Collaboration

Collaboration is a hallmark of our school. The collaboration of teachers and the cooperation of students provide the energy and synergy that power an ongoing increase in the instructional, academic, and leadership capacities of our school.

Not at All				Very Strong
1	2	3	4	5

6. High Expectations

The staff and administration of our school have high expectations. They believe that students can achieve, explicitly teach them how to get smart, and convey a profound and unwavering commitment to their academic success.

Not at All				Very Strong
1	2	3	4	5

7. Opportunities to Learn

Our school provides students with opportunities to learn from highly effective teachers in every classroom, along with differentiated and scaffolded opportunities to learn as needed for all students to achieve academic success.

Not at All				Very Strong
1	2	3	4	5

8. Alignment

Our school's standards, curriculum, instructional approaches, and assessments are in alignment and provide a coherent and consistent educational program for all students.

Not at All				Very Strong
1	2	3	4	5

9. Results

Our school is known for its student achievement, including but not limited to continuously improving results on measures of accountability established by the state.

Not at All				Very Strong
1	2	3	4	5

10. Accountability

Our school is characterized by high levels of internal accountability that demand continuous improvement and a results-oriented approach to teaching and learning.

Not at All				Very Strong
1	2	3	4	5

Add up the total score for the ten traits and write it in the box.

Copyright © 2008 by Corwin Press. All rights reserved. Reprinted from *Ten Traits of Highly Effective Schools: Raising the Achievement Bar for All Students*, by Elaine K. McEwan. Thousand Oaks, CA: Corwin Press, www.corwinpress.com. Reproduction authorized only for the local school site or nonprofit organization that has purchased this book.

against us, I wasn't sure the audit would reflect all of our hard work. But I was wrong. When I tallied the results, I was delighted. The faculty recognized and affirmed the trust-building efforts that we have had going on—a collaborative book study focused on effective instruction and the development of a new Code of Ethics for our reconstituted faculty. They also gave the school high marks on our alignment. We are getting there. We've combed through our assessment data and aligned the curriculum and the instruction with a focus on reading. The staff felt that overall, our expectations for students could be much higher and that our collective sense of accountability wasn't as strong as it should be. These traits were right where I expected they would be. But the results of the audit will definitely help us focus on meaningful goals for the year."

WHAT IS YOUR VISION?

If your team is about to embark on an improvement initiative, you first need to ask and answer these two questions:

1. What is your school like today?

2. What do you want your school to become in the future?

The gap between the current reality (what the school is like today) and your vision as a principal and team (what you see the school becoming) define the scope of the task ahead of you. Understanding and using the ten traits of highly effective schools can help you bridge the gap between today and the envisioned tomorrow.

I wrote this book with four goals in mind: to inform, affirm, encourage, and motivate. I hope that you have discovered in the research and the examples that the demographics of your school do not have to determine its academic destiny. I hope that readers who have been part of teams that are creating and have created effective schools feel affirmed for their accomplishments. If you are in the midst of the often long and difficult process of improving a low-performing school, I trust that the examples in the book have encouraged you. If you were hesitant about committing to a compelling mission in your own school at the outset of your reading, I hope that you now feel motivated to do so. You will never regret the adventure. Students will thank you. Parents will honor you. And you will carry the feeling of having made a difference in the lives of students and parents with you for the rest of your life.

References

Acheson, K. (1985). *The principal's role in instructional leadership.* Eugene: University of Oregon, Oregon School Study Council.

Ackerman, R. H., Donaldson, G. A., & van der Bogert, R. (1996). *Making sense as a school leader: Persisting questions, creative opportunities.* San Francisco: Jossey-Bass.

Andersen, A. (1997). *Annual report on the Jersey City and Paterson public schools* (prepared for the New Jersey Legislature Joint Committee on the Public Schools). St. Charles, IL: Author.

Andersen, B., & Fagerhaug, T. (2006). *Root cause analysis: Simplified tools and techniques* (2nd ed.). Milwaukee, WI: Quality Press.

Andrews, R. (1989). The Illinois principal as instructional leader: A concept and definition paper. *Illinois Principal, 20*(3), 4–12.

Andrews, R., & Soder, R. (1987). Principal leadership and student achievement. *Educational Leadership, 44*(6), 9–11.

Arhar, J. M., & Kromrey, J. D. (1993, April). *Interdisciplinary teaming in the middle level school: Creating a sense of belonging for at-risk middle level students.* Paper presented at the annual meeting of the American Educational Research Association, San Francisco, CA.

Ashton, P. T., & Webb, R. B. (1986). *Making a difference: Teachers' sense of efficacy and student achievement.* New York: Longman.

Bandura, A. (1997). *Self-efficacy: The exercise of control.* New York: Freeman.

Barth, R. (1976). A principal and his school. *The National Elementary School Principal, 56,* 9–21.

Black, P., Harrison, C., Lee, C., Marshall, B., & Wiliam, D. (2003). *Assessment for learning: Putting it into practice.* New York: Open University Press.

Block, J. (1971). *Mastery learning: Theory and practice.* New York: Holt, Rinehart & Winston.

Bloom, B. S. (1971). *Mastery learning.* New York: Holt, Rinehart & Winston.

Bloom, B. S. (1980). The new direction in educational research: Alterable variables. *Phi Delta Kappan, 61,* 382–385.

Borich, G. D. (2000). *Effective teaching methods* (4th ed.). Upper Saddle River, NJ: Merrill.

Bossidy, L., & Charan, R. (2002). *Execution: The discipline of getting things done.* New York: Crown.

Bottoms, G. (2003, January). *Effort, not ability* [Press release]. Atlanta, GA: Southern Regional Education Board.

Boudett, K. P., City, E. A., & Murnane, R. J. (Eds.). (2005). *Data wise: A step-by-step guide to using assessment results to improve teaching and learning.* Cambridge, MA: Harvard Education Press.

Bridgeland, J., Dilulio, J., Jr., & Morison, K. (2006). *The silent epidemic: Perspectives of high school dropouts.* Seattle, WA: Bill and Melinda Gates Foundation.

Brigham, N., & Gamse, B. (1997). Children's school days. In S. Stringfield, M. A. Millsap, & R. Herman (Eds.), *Urban and suburban/rural special strategies for educating disadvantaged children: Second year report.* Washington, DC: U.S. Department of Education, Planning and Evaluation Service.

Brookover, W. B., Beady, C., Flood, P., Schweitzer, J., & Weisenbaker, J. (1979). *School systems and student achievement: Schools make a difference.* New York: Praeger.

Brookover, W. E., & Lezotte, L. W. (1979). *Changes in school characteristics coincident with changes in student achievement.* East Lansing: Michigan State University, Institute for Research on Teaching.

Brophy, J. (Ed.). (1989). *Advances in research on teaching* (Vol. 1). Greenwich, CT: JAI.

Brophy, J. (1999). *Teaching.* Brussels: International Academy of Education.

Brophy, J. E., & Good, T. L. (1986). Teacher behavior and student achievement. In M. C. Wittrock (Ed.), *Handbook of research on teaching* (3rd ed., pp. 328–375). Upper Saddle River, NJ: Merrill/Prentice Hall.

Bryk, A., Camburn, E., & Louis, K. S. (1999, December). Professional community in Chicago elementary schools: Facilitating factors and organizational consequences. *Educational Administration Quarterly, 35,* 751–781.

Bryk, A. S., & Schneider, B. (2002). *Trust in schools: A core resource for improvement.* New York: Russell Sage Foundation.

Bryk, A. S., Sebring, P. B., Kerbow, D., Rollow, S., & Easton, J. Q. (1998). *Charting Chicago school reform: Democratic localism as a lever for change.* Boulder, CO: Westview.

Burnett, A, & Raymond Lowery, R. (2006). *Principle-centered learning.* Unpublished manuscript.

Burns, J. M. (1978). *Leadership.* New York: Harper & Row.

Bursuck, W. D., & Damer, M. (2007). *Reading instruction for students who are at risk or have disabilities.* Boston: Pearson.

California Department of Education. (2007). *Academic performance index (API) School growth report.* Retrieved August 12, 2007, from http://api.cde.ca.gov/reports/API.

Carnoy, M., & Loeb, S. (2003). Does external accountability affect student outcomes? A cross-state analysis. *Educational Evaluation and Policy Analysis, 24*(4), 305–331.

Carter, S. C. (1999). *No excuses: Seven principals of low-income schools who set the standard for high achievement.* Washington, DC: Heritage Foundation.

Charles A. Dana Center. (1999). *Hope for urban education: A study of nine high-performing high-poverty urban elementary schools.* Austin, TX: Author.

Charles A. Dana Center and the STAR Center. (2002). *Driven to succeed: High-performing, high-poverty, turnaround middle schools.* Austin, TX: Authors.

Charles A. Dana Center. (2005). *Gaining traction, gaining ground: How some high schools accelerate learning for struggling students.* Austin, TX: Author.

Chenoweth, K. (2007). *It's being done: Academic success in unexpected schools.* Cambridge, MA: Harvard University Press.

Ciofalo, J. F., & Wylie, E. C. (2006, January 10). Using diagnostic assessment: One question at a time. *Teachers College Record.* Retrieved April 4, 2008, from www.tcrecord.org. ID Number: 12285.

Coleman, J. S., Campbell, E., Hobson, C., McPartland, J., Mood, A., Weinfeld, F., & York, R. (1966). *Equality of educational opportunity.* Washington, DC: National Center for Educational Statistics.

Collins, J. (2001). *Good to great: Why some companies make the leap and others don't.* New York: HarperBusiness.

Connell, J. P., & Broom, J. (2004). *The toughest nut to crack: First Things First's (FTF) approach to improving teaching and learning.* Philadelphia: Institute for Research and Reform in Education.

Connell, J. P., Halpern-Felsher, B., Clifford, E., Crichlow, W., & Usinger, P. (1995). Hanging in there: Behavioral, psychological, and contextual factors affecting whether African-American adolescents stay in school. *Journal of Adolescent Research, 10*(1), 41–63.

Connell, J. P., & Wellborn, J. G. (1991). Competence, autonomy, and relatedness: A motivational analysis of self-system processes. In M. R. Gunnar & L. A. Sroufe (Eds.), *Self-processes in development: Minnesota Symposium on Child Psychology, Vol. 23* (pp. 43–77). Chicago: University of Chicago Press.

Corcoran, T., & Goertz, M. (1995). Instructional capacity and high performance schools. *Educational Researcher, 24*(9), 27–31.

Corno, L. (2004). Introduction to the special issue: Work habits and work styles: Volition in education. *Teachers College Record, 106*(9), 1669–1694. Retrieved April 4, 2008, from www.tcrecord.org. ID Number 11665.

Covey, S. R. (1989). *The 7 habits of highly effective people: Powerful lessons in personal change.* New York: Fireside.

Covey, S. R., Merrill, A. R., & Merrill, R. E. (1994). *First things first: To love, to learn, and to leave a legacy.* New York: Simon & Schuster.

Creemers, B. (1994). *The effective classroom.* London: Cassell.

Croninger, R. G., & Lee, V. E. (2001, August). Social capital and dropping out of school: Benefits to at-risk students of teachers' support and guidance. *Teachers College Record, 103*(4), 548–581.

Datrow, A., Park, V., & Wohlstetter, P. (2007). *Achieving with data: How high-performing school systems use data to improve instruction for elementary students.* Los Angeles: University of Southern California, Center on Educational Governance.

Dobberteen, K. (2001). *Second annual chase change award: Essay.* Unpublished document. La Mesa, CA: La Mesa Dale Elementary School.

DuFour, R. (2000). Data put a face on shared vision. *Journal of Staff Development, 21*(1), 71–72.

DuFour, R., & Eaker, R. (1998). *Professional learning communities at work: Best practices for enhancing student achievement.* Bloomington, IN: National Education Service.

DuFour, R., DuFour, R., Eaker, R., & Many, T. (2006). *Learning by doing: A handbook for professional learning communities.* Bloomington, IN: Solution Tree.

Duke, D. L. (2006). What we know and don't know about improving low-performing schools. *Phi Delta Kappan, 87*(10), 728–734.

Dunkin, M. J., & Biddle, B. J. (1974). *The study of teaching.* New York: Holt, Rinehart & Winston.

Edmonds, R. R. (1979a). Effective schools for the urban poor. *Educational Leadership, 37*(1), 15–27.

Edmonds, R. R. (1979b). Some schools work and more can. *Social Policy, 12*(2), 56–50.

Education Trust. (1999). *Dispelling the myth: High-poverty schools exceeding expectations.* Washington, DC: Author.

Education Trust. (2005). *The power to change: High schools that help all students achieve.* Washington, DC: Author.

Education Trust. (2006). *Yes we can: Telling truths and dispelling myths about race and education in America.* Washington, DC: Author.

Elmore, R. (2003). *Knowing the right thing to do: School improvement and performance-based accountability.* Washington, DC: National Governors Association Center for Best Practices.

English, F. (1992). *Deciding what to teach and test: Developing, aligning, and auditing the curriculum.* Thousand Oaks, CA: Corwin Press.

Faber, A., & Mazlish, E. (1990). *Liberated parents, liberated children: Your guide to a happier family.* New York: Avon.

Feinberg, C. (2004, July 1). The possible dream: A nation of proficient schoolchildren. *HGSEnews,* p. 1.

Fielding, L., Kerr, N., & Rosier, P. (1998). *The 90% reading goal.* Kennewick, WA: New Foundation Press.

Fielding, L., Kerr, N., & Rosier, P. (2004). *Delivering on the promise of the 95% reading and math goals.* Kennewick, WA: New Foundation Press.

Fielding, L., Kerr, N., & Rosier, P. (2007). *Annual growth for all students. Catch-up growth for those who are behind.* Kennewick, WA: New Foundation Press.

Finn, J. D. (1989). Withdrawing from school. *Review of Educational Research, 59,* 117–142.

Finn, J. D. (1993). *School engagement and students at risk.* Washington, DC: National Center for Education Statistics.

Friedman, E. H. (1991). Bowen theory and therapy. In A. S. Gurman & D. P. Kniskern (Eds.), *Handbook of family therapy* (pp. 134–170). New York: Brunner/Mazel.

Fullan, M. (1997). *What's worth fighting for in the principalship?* New York: Teachers College Press.

Fullan, M. (2001). *Leading in a culture of change.* San Francisco: Jossey-Bass.

Fullan, M. (2003). *The moral imperative of the principalship.* Thousand Oaks, CA: Corwin Press.

Fullan, M., & Stiegelbauer, S. (1991). *The new meaning of educational change* (2nd ed.). New York: Teachers College Press & Ontario Institute for Studies in Education.

Garfield, C. (1986). *Peak performers: The new heroes of American business.* New York: William Morrow.

Gentile, J. R., & Lalley, J. P. (2003). *Standards and mastery learning: Aligning teaching and assessment so all children can learn.* Thousand Oaks, CA: Corwin Press.

Glickman, C. D. (1993). *Renewing America's schools: A guide for school-based action.* San Francisco: Jossey-Bass.

Goddard, R. D., Hoy, W. K., & Hoy, A. W. (2004). Collective efficacy beliefs: Theoretical developments, empirical evidence, and future directions. *Educational Researcher, 33*(3), 3–13.

Goldsberry, L. F. (1986, April). *Colleague consultation: Another case of fools rush in.* Paper presented at the annual meeting of the American Educational Research Association, San Francisco, CA.

Goodenow, C. (1993). Classroom belonging among early adolescent students: Relationships to motivation and achievement. *Journal of Early Adolescence, 13*(1), 21–43.

Hall, S. (2008). *Implementing Response to Intervention: A principal's guide.* Thousand Oaks, CA: Corwin Press.

Hallinger, P., & Heck, R. (1996). Reassessing the principal's role in school effectiveness: A review of empirical research. *Educational Administration Quarterly, 32*(1), 5–44.

Hanushek, E. A. (2002). Teacher quality. In L. T. Izumi & W. M. Evers (Eds.), *Teacher quality* (pp. 1–12). Palo Alto, CA: Hoover.

Hanushek, E. A., & Raymond, M. E. (2004, June). *Does school accountability lead to improved student performance?* (NBER Working Paper No. 10591). Cambridge, MA: National Bureau of Economic Research.

Haycock, K. (1998). *Good teaching matters: How well-qualified teachers can close the gap.* Washington, DC: Education Trust. Retrieved April 4, 2008, from www.nesinc.com/PDFs/1999_04Haycok.pdf

Holcomb, E. L. (2004). *Getting excited about data: How to combine people, passion, and proof.* Thousand Oaks, CA: Corwin Press.

Hord, S. M. (1997). *Professional learning communities: Communities of continuous inquiry and improvement.* Austin, TX: Southwest Educational Laboratory.

Howard, J. (1995). You can't get there from here: The need for a new logic in education reform. *Daedalus, Journal of the American Academy of Arts and Sciences, 124*(4), 85–92.

Howard, J. (2003). Still at risk: The causes and costs of failure to educate poor and minority children for the twenty-first century. In D. T. Gordon (Ed.), *A nation reformed? American education twenty years after "A Nation at Risk"* (pp. 81–97). Cambridge, MA: Harvard Education Press.

Howard, J., & Howe, H. L. (1993). *Thinking about our kids.* New York: The Free Press.

Hunter, M. (1984). Knowing, teaching, and supervising. In P. Hosford (Ed.), *Using what we know about teaching* (pp. 169–192). Alexandria, VA: Association for Supervision and Curriculum Development.

Hunter, M. (1989). *Workshop on the science of teaching.* Carol Stream, IL.

International Center for Leadership in Education. (2007). *The Rigor/Relevance Framework.* Rexford, NY: Author.

Jerald, C. D. (2001). *Dispelling the myth revisited: Preliminary findings from a nationwide analysis of "high-flying" schools.* Washington, DC: Education Trust.

Johnson, D. W., & Johnson, R. T. (1989). *Leading the cooperative school.* Edina, MN: Interaction.

Johnson, D. W., Johnson, R. T., & Stanne, M. B. (2000). *Cooperative learning methods: A meta-analysis.* Retrieved April 4, 2008, from www.co-operation.org

Johnson, L. A. (1995). *The girls in the back of the class.* New York: St. Martin's.

Johnson, R. T., Johnson, D. W., & Holubec, D. J. (1994). *Cooperative learning in the classroom.* Alexandria, VA: Association for Supervision and Curriculum Development.

Jones-Gayle, M. (2006). *Professional development and school achievement through the National Staff Development Council standards.* Unpublished dissertation. Florida Agricultural and Mechanical University.

Jordan, H., Mendro, R., & Weerasinghe, D. (1997). *Teacher effects on longitudinal student achievement.* Dallas, TX: Dallas Independent School District.

Joyce, B., & Showers, B. (1995). *Student achievement through staff development.* New York: Longman.

Kameenui, E. J., & Darch. C. B. (1995). *Instructional classroom management: A proactive approach to behavior management.* White Plains, NY: Longman.

Kanter, R. M. (2004). *Confidence: How winning streaks begin and end.* New York: Crown.

Keillor, G. (1985). *Lake Wobegon days.* New York: Viking.

Kleine-Kracht, P. A. (1993, July). The principal in a community of learning. *Journal of School Leadership, 3*(4), 391–399.

Knapp, M., Copland, M. E., & Talbert, J. (2003). *Leading for learning.* Seattle, WA: Center for the Study of Teaching and Policy.

Kohl, H. (1998). *The discipline of hope: Learning from a lifetime of teaching.* New York: Harper & Row.

Kuhn, T. (1996). *The structure of scientific revolutions.* Chicago: University of Chicago Press. (Original work published 1962)

Kyriacou, C. (1991). *Essential teaching skills.* Oxford, UK: Basil Blackwell.

Leithwood, K. A. (1990). The principal's role in teacher development. In B. Joyce (Ed.), *Changing school culture through staff development* (pp. 71–90). Alexandria, VA: Association for Supervision and Curriculum Development.

Levine, D. U., & Lezotte, L. W. (1990). *Unusually effective schools: A review and analysis of research and practice.* Madison, WI: The National Center for Effective Schools Research and Development.

Lezotte, L., & McKee, K. M. (2002). *Assembly required: A continuous school improvement system.* Okemos, MI: Effective Schools Products.

Manset, G., St. John, A., Simmons, A., & Gordon, G. D. (2000). *Wisconsin's high-performing, high-poverty schools.* Naperville, IL: North Central Regional Educational Laboratory.

Marshall, K. (2003, July 9). An Orwellian view: Misconceptions on the harsh impact of standards and tests [Letter to the Editor]. *Education Week.* Retrieved April 4, 2008, from www.educationweek.org.

Marzano, R. J., Gaddy, B. B., & Dean, C. (2000). *What works in classroom instruction.* Aurora, CO: Mid-continent Research for Education and Learning.

Marzano, R. J., Kendall, J. S., & Gaddy, B. B. (1999). *Essential knowledge: The debate over what American students should know.* Aurora, CO: Mid-continent Research for Education and Learning.

Marzano, R. J., Pickering, D. J., & Pollock, J. E. (2001). *Instruction that works: Research-based strategies for increasing student achievement.* Alexandria, VA: Association for Supervision and Curriculum Development.

McEwan, E. K. (1996). *Leading your team to excellence: How to make quality decisions.* Thousand Oaks, CA: Corwin Press.

McEwan, E. K. (2001). *Ten traits of highly effective teachers: How to hire, coach, and mentor successful teachers.* Thousand Oaks, CA: Corwin Press.

McEwan, E. K. (2002). *7 steps to effective instructional leadership* (2nd ed.). Thousand Oaks, CA: Corwin Press.

McEwan, E. K. (2003). *Ten traits of highly effective principals: From good to great performance.* Thousand Oaks, CA: Corwin Press.

McEwan, E. K. (2005). *How to deal with teachers who are angry, troubled, exhausted, or just plain confused.* Thousand Oaks, CA: Corwin Press.

McEwan, E. K. (2006). *How to survive and thrive in the first three weeks of school.* Thousand Oaks, CA: Corwin Press.

McEwan, E. K. (2007). *40 ways to support struggling readers in content classrooms, grades 6–12*. Thousand Oaks, CA: Corwin Press.

McGee, G. W. (2004). Closing the achievement gap: Lessons from Illinois' Golden Spike high-poverty high performing schools. *Journal of Education for Students Placed at Risk, (9)*2, 97–125.

McLaughlin, M. W. (1993). What matters most in teachers' workplace context? In J. W. Little & M. W. McLaughlin (Eds.), *Teachers' work: Individuals, colleagues, and contexts* (pp. 79–103). New York: Teachers College Press.

Merriam-Webster's collegiate dictionary (11th ed.). (2003). Springfield, MA: Author.

Mertler, C. (2003). *Classroom assessment*. Los Angeles: Pyrczak.

Miller, K. R. (2007). *Raising DE Bar: Unlocking the power and potential in self and others*. Salt Lake City, UT: Vision Bound.

Morrissey, M. S. (2000). *Professional learning communities: An ongoing exploration*. Austin, TX: Southwest Educational Development Laboratory.

Mortimore, P., Sammons, P., Stoll, L., Lewis, D., & Ecob, R. (1988). *School matters: The junior years*. Somerset, UK: Open Books.

Mounts, N. S., & Steinberg, L. (1995). An ecological analysis of peer influence on adolescent grade point average and drug use. *Developmental Psychology, 31*(6), 915–922.

Nathan, J. (2008, January 8). How Cincinnati turned its schools around. *Education Week*, 24–25.

National Academy of Sciences. (2003). *Engaging schools: Fostering high school students' motivation to learn*. Washington, DC: Author.

National Association of Secondary School Principals. (2004). *Breaking ranks II: Strategies for leading high school reform*. Washington, DC: Author.

National Association of State Directors of Special Education. (2006). *Response to Intervention: Policy considerations and implementation*. Alexandria, VA: Author.

National Children's Reading Foundation. (2007). Retrieved June 6, 2008, from www.readingfoundation.org/programs.jsp.

Newmann, F. M., & Associates. (1996). *Authentic achievement: Restructuring schools for intellectual quality*. San Francisco: Jossey-Bass.

Newmann, F. M., King, M. B., & Youngs, P. (2000). Professional development that addresses school capacity: Lessons from urban elementary schools. *American Journal of Education, 108*(4), 259–299.

Newmann, F. M., Marks, H. M., & Gamora, A. (1996). Authentic pedagogy and student performance. *American Journal of Education, 104*, 280–312.

Newmann, F. M., & Wehlage, G. G. (1995). *Successful school restructuring: A report to the public and educators*. Madison: University of Wisconsin Education Center.

No Child Left Behind Act, Pub. L. 107–110 115, Stat. 1425H.R.1. (2002). Retrieved April 4, 2008, from www.ed.gov/nclb/landing.jhtml

Norton, J. (1999, Spring). Standards-based teaching opens up possibilities. *Changing schools in Louisville, 3*(1). Retrieved April 4, 2008, from www.middleweb.com/Lawrence.html

Oettingen, G., Honig, G., & Gollwitzer, P. M. (2000). Effective self-regulation of goal attainment. *International Journal of Educational Research, 33*, 705–732.

Office of Educational Research and Improvement. (1992). *Hard work and high expectations: Motivating students to learn*. Washington, DC: U.S. Department of Education.

Olson, L. (2006, January 5). A decade of effort. In *Quality counts: A decade of standards-based education*. Bethesda, MD: Editorial Projects in Education. Retrieved April 4, 2008, from www.edweek.org/qc06

Peske, H. G., & Haycock, K. (2006). *Teaching inequality: How poor and minority students are shortchanged on teacher quality: A report and recommendations by the Education Trust*. Washington, DC: Education Trust.

Peters, T., & Austin, N. (1985). *A passion for excellence: The leadership difference*. New York: Random House.

Pfeffer, J., & Sutton, R. I. (2000). *The knowing-doing gap*. Boston: Harvard Business School Press.

Pianta, R. C., Belsky, J., Houts, R., & Morrison, F. (2007, March 30). Opportunities to learn in America's elementary classrooms. *Science 315*(5820), 1795–1796. Retrieved online April 4, 2008, from www.sciencemag.org/cgi/content/full/315/5820/1795

Porter, A. C., & Brophy, J. (1988). Synthesis of research on good teaching: Insights from the work of the Institute for Research on Teaching. *Educational Leadership, 45*(8), 74–85.

Pritchett, P., & Pound, R. (1993). *High velocity culture change*. Dallas, TX: Author.

Purkey, S. C., & Smith, M. S. (1983). Effective schools: A review. *The Elementary School Journal, 83*(4), 426–452.

Ramsey, R. (2003). *School leadership from A to Z: Practical lessons from successful schools and businesses*. Thousand Oaks, CA: Corwin Press.

Reeves, D. (2000). *Accountability in action: A blueprint for learning organizations*. Denver, CO: Advanced Learning Centers.

Resnick, L. B. (1995). From aptitude to effort: A new foundation for our schools. *Daedalus, 124*, 55–62.

Resnick, L. B. (1999, June 16). Making America smarter. *Education Week*, 38–40.

Resnick, L. B., Nolan, K. J., & Resnick, D. P. (1995). Benchmarking education standards. *Educational Evaluation and Policy Analysis, 17*(4), 438–461.

Reynolds, D., Creemers, B., Stringfield, S., Teddlie, C., & Schaffer, G. (2002). *World class schools: International perspectives on school effectiveness*. London: RoutledgeFalmer.

Reynolds, D., Hopkins, D., & Stoll, L. (1993). Linking school effectiveness knowledge and school improvement practice: Towards a synergy. *School Effectiveness and School Improvement, 4*(1), 37–58.

Rimer, S. (2008, January 17). Urban schools aiming higher than diploma. *The New York Times*. Retrieved January 17, 2008, from www.nytimes.com

Rivkin, E. A., Hanushek, E. A., & Kain, J. F. (2001). *Teachers, schools, and academic achievement*. Washington, DC: National Bureau of Economic Research.

Rosenshine, B. (1971). *Teaching behaviors and student achievement*. London: National Foundation for Education Research in England and Wales.

Rowe, M. P. (1990). Barriers to equality: The power of subtle discrimination to maintain unequal opportunity. *Employee Responsibilities and Rights Journal, 3*(2), 153–163.

Rutter, M., Maughan, B., Mortimore, P., & Ouston, J. (1979). *Fifteen thousand hours*. London: Open Books.

Salisbury, D., & Conner, D. (1994). How to succeed as manager of an educational change project. *Educational Technology, 34*(6), 12–19.

Sammons, P., Thomas, S., & Mortimore, P. (1997). *Forging links: Effective schools and effective departments*. London: Paul Chapman.

Samuels, C. A. (2007, June 20). Texas district makes gains with spec. ed. *Education Week, 34*–37.

Sanders, W. L., & Horn, S. P. (1995). Educational assessment reassessed: The usefulness of standardized and alternative measures of student achievement as indicators for the assessment of educational outcomes. *Education Policy Analysis Archives 3.* Retrieved April 4, 2008, from olam.ed.asu.edu/epaa/v3n6.html

Saphier, J., & Gower, R. (1997). *The skillful teacher: Building your teaching skills.* Carlisle, MA: Research for Better Teaching.

Scheerens, J., & Bosker, R. (1997). *The foundations of educational effectiveness.* Oxford, UK: Pergamon.

Scheurich, J. J., & Skrla, L. (2003). *Leadership for equity and excellence.* Thousand Oaks, CA: Corwin Press.

Schlechty, P. C. (2005). *Creating the capacity to support innovations (Occasional Paper #2).* Louisville, KY: Schlechty Center for Leadership in School Reform.

Schmoker, M. (1999). *Results: The key to continuous improvement* (2nd ed.). Alexandria, VA: Association for Supervision and Curriculum Development.

Schmoker, M. (2001). *The results fieldbook: Practical strategies from dramatically improved schools.* Alexandria, VA: Association for Curriculum and Supervision.

Schmoker, M. (2004). Tipping point: From feckless reform to substantive instructional improvement. *Phi Delta Kappan, (85)*6, 424–432.

Senge, P. (1990). *The fifth discipline: The art and practice of the learning organization.* New York: Doubleday Currency.

Sergiovanni, T. (1992). *Moral leadership: Getting to the heart of school improvement.* San Francisco: Jossey-Bass.

Sergiovanni, T. J. (1994). Organizations or communities? Changing the metaphor changes the theory. *Educational Administration Quarterly, (30)*4, 214–226.

Shulman, L. (1989). Teaching alone, learning together: Needed agendas for the new reforms. In T. Sergiovanni & J. Moore (Eds.), *Schooling for tomorrow: Directing reforms to issues that count* (pp. 166–187). Boston: Allyn & Bacon.

Slavin, R. (1978). *Cooperative learning.* Baltimore: Johns Hopkins University Center for Social Organization of Schools.

Smith, S. C., & Piele, P. K. (1997). *School leadership: Handbook for excellence.* Eugene: University of Oregon, Eric Clearinghouse on Educational Management.

Snyder, C. R. (1994). *The psychology of hope: You can get there from here.* New York: The Free Press.

Spady, W. (1992, July). *Outcome-based education.* Paper presented at the Suburban Superintendents' Conference, Traverse City, MI.

Stiggins, R. J. (2001). *Student-involved classroom assessment* (3rd ed.). New York: Merrill.

Stogdill, R. M. (1990) *Stogdill's handbook of leadership: A survey of theory and research.* New York: Free Press.

Stringfield, S. (1994). A model of elementary school effects. In D. Reynolds, B. P. M. Creemers, P. S. Nesselrodt, E. C. Schaffer, S. Stringfield, & C. Teddlie (Eds.), *Advances in school effectiveness research and practice* (pp. 153–187). Oxford, UK: Pergamon.

Supovitz, J., & Taylor, B. S. (2003). *The impact of standards-based reform in Duval County, Florida, 1999–2002.* Philadelphia: Consortium for Policy Research in Education.

Teddlie, C., & Reynolds, D. (2000). *The international handbook of school effectiveness research.* New York: Falmer.

Teddlie, C., & Stringfield, S. (1993). *Schools make a difference: Lessons learned from a 10-year study of school effects.* New York: Teachers College Press.

Texas Education Agency. (2007). *Accountability system for 2006 and beyond.* Austin, TX: Author.

Togneri, W., & Anderson, S. (2003). *Beyond islands of excellence: What districts can do to improve instruction and achievement in all schools.* Washington, DC: Learning First Alliance.

Tomlinson, C.A. (2000, September). Reconcilable differences? Standards-based teaching and differentiation. *Educational Leadership, 58*(1), 6–11.

Tracy, B. (2007). Quotations retrieved from www.nonstopenglish.com.

Tschannen-Moran, M., Hoy, W. K., & Hoy, A. W. (1998). Teacher efficacy: Its meaning and measure. *Review of Educational Research, 68,* 202–248.

Waits, M. J., Campbell, H. E., Gau, R., Jacobs, E., Rex, T., & Hess, R. K. (2006, March). *Why some schools with Latino children beat the odds . . . and others don't.* Phoenix, AZ: Center for the Future of Arizona and Morrison Institute for Public Policy.

Walberg, H. J. (1986). Syntheses of research on teaching. In M. C. Wittrock (Ed.), *Handbook of research on teaching* (pp. 214–229). Upper Saddle River, NJ: Merrill/Prentice Hall.

Walberg, H. J., & Paik, S. J. (2000). *Effective educational practices.* International Bureau of Education. Retrieved February 9, 2008 from www.ibe.unesco.org/

Waters, T., Marzano, R. J., & McNulty, B. (2008). *McRELS's balanced leadership framework: Developing the science of educational leadership.* Aurora, CO: Mid-continent Research for Education and Learning.

West, C. (2005). *Code of ethics.* Unpublished document.

Willingham, W. W., Pollack, J. M., & Lewis, C. (2002). Grades and test scores: Accounting for observed differences. *Journal of Educational Measurement, 39*(1), 1–37.

Wolk, R. (1998). Strategies for fixing failing public schools. *Education Week, 18*(2). Retrieved October 8, 2007, from www.edweek.org

Wooden, J. (with Jamison, S.). (1997). *Wooden: A lifetime of observations and reflections on and off the court.* Chicago: Contemporary Books.

Yoshida, M. (1999). *Lesson study: An ethnographic investigation of school-based teacher development in Japan.* Unpublished doctoral dissertation, University of Chicago.

Zmuda, A., Kuklis, R., & Kline, E. (2004). *Transforming schools: Creating a culture of continuous improvement.* Alexandria, VA: Association for Supervision and Curriculum Development.

Index

224 Ten Traits of Highly Effective Schools

CORWIN PRESS

The Corwin Press logo—a raven striding across an open book—represents the union of courage and learning. Corwin Press is committed to improving education for all learners by publishing books and other professional development resources for those serving the field of PreK–12 education. By providing practical, hands-on materials, Corwin Press continues to carry out the promise of its motto: **"Helping Educators Do Their Work Better."**